THE KINKY RENAISSANCE

THE KINKY RENAISSANCE

Edited by Gillian Knoll and Joseph Gamble

ACMRS PRESS

Tempe, Arizona
2024

Front cover: Image used by permission

Contents

A Renaissance of Kink

Joseph Gamble and Gillian Knoll

> There will be a renaissance of sex.
> — Gayle Rubin, "The Catacombs: A Temple of the Butthole"

People like different things. What turns us on may turn someone else's stomach. What feels good to you might hurt us in a way we want to avoid. If we told you our desires, you might find them titillating, or disgusting, or boring, or simply incomprehensible. These may seem like banal truisms, but this collection argues that they can also serve as methodological guides to the study of sexuality in the distant past. For one thing, they remind us that the prevailing sexual categories of any given moment never encompass or name the totality of sexual experience at that time. The recent proliferation of (a)sexual identity categories — e.g., pansexual, demisexual, aromantic, furry, spanko — might seem, in the consistently myopic view of the normative public sphere, like a twenty-first-century phenomenon; but such inventiveness in the face of the paucity of pre-existing sexual categories actually has a much older provenance, as essays in this volume make clear. Methodologically speaking, then, "people like different things" might serve as a form of permission to acknowledge the critical value of highlighting surprising resonances between our own sexual desires, practices, and pleasures and those that we see represented in historical texts. After all, if people like different things, it's no small feat to find someone who seems to like the same things (or at least similar ones) even if that "person" is fictional, or centuries old, or both. But "people like different things" can also serve as a catchword for a critical impulse to be open to the possibility of finding and taking seriously early modern desires, practices, and pleasures that might not look like something we would want, or do, or like. One of the foundational convictions of this collection is that we must find ways to exceed the bounds of our own individual sexual imaginations in our analyses of historical sexual cultures.

In 1984, in an essay that would retrospectively be marked as one of the origin points of queer studies, the feminist anthropologist Gayle Rubin argued for a "concept of benign sexual variation" that might loosen prevailing forms of sexual normalization in both the academy and the broader public sphere.[1] In the wake of Rubin's work, and the work of other foundational LGBT and queer studies scholars, such a critical concept of benign sexual variation — a recognition that people liking different things is no cause for concern, moralizing, or legal intervention — has indeed guided much work on sexuality. In early modern studies, in particular, this concept has undergirded a robust set of scholarship on sodomy and homoeroticism.[2] But despite widespread critical con-

---

1. Gayle Rubin, "Thinking Sex: Notes for a Radical Theory of the Politics of Sexuality," chap. 5 in *Deviations: A Gayle Rubin Reader* (Durham, NC: Duke University Press, 2011), 137–181, at 148.
2. For the past several decades, early modern sexuality studies has sought to expand our understanding of the sexual possibilities of early modern England beyond the marital reproductive sex that was explicitly sanctioned by the church. Early work by Alan Bray, Joseph Pequigney, and Bruce Smith on "homosexuality" gave way to work by Gregory Bredbeck and Jonathan Goldberg on the conceptual vagaries of "sodomy," which ultimately enabled wider considerations of both "homoeroticism" — both socially sanctioned and condemned, between both men and women — by Valerie Traub, Mario DiGangi, and Jeffrey Masten. See Alan Bray, *Homosexuality in Renaissance England* (London: Gay Men's Press, 1982); Joseph Pequigney, *Such Is My Love: A Study of Shakespeare's Sonnets* (Chicago: University of Chicago Press, 1985); Bruce Smith, *Homosexual Desire in Renaissance England: A Cultural Poetics* (Chicago: University of Chicago Press, 1991); Gregory Bredbeck, *Sodomy*

sensus about the conceptual vagaries of "sodomy," the pervasiveness of early modern homoeroticism, and the anachronism of conceiving of early modern sexuality in terms of modern sexual identity categories like "straight" or "gay," early modernists have only recently, and still somewhat rarely, come to excavate, describe, and analyze representations of sexual desires, practices, and pleasures that are not primarily organized around the gender of object choice and that often lie orthogonal to the

and Interpretation: From Marlowe to Milton (Ithaca, NY: Cornell University Press, 1991); Jonathan Goldberg, *Sodometries: Renaissance Texts, Modern Sexualities* (Palo Alto, CA: Stanford University Press, 1992); Valerie Traub, *Desire and Anxiety: Circulations of Sexuality in Shakespearean Drama* (Abingdon, UK: Routledge, 1992); Mario DiGangi, *The Homoerotics of Early Modern Drama* (Cambridge, UK: Cambridge University Press, 1997); Jeffrey Masten, *Textual Intercourse: Collaboration, Authorship, and Sexualities in Renaissance Drama* (Cambridge, UK: Cambridge University Press, 1997); and Valerie Traub, *The Renaissance of Lesbianism in Early Modern England* (Cambridge, UK: Cambridge University Press, 2002). More recently, a variety of scholars have built on this foundational work, extending our understanding of the imbrication of sexuality and, among other things, religion (Rambuss; Stockton; Sanchez); law and politics (Herrup; Sanchez); English travel and colonialism, both real and imagined (Schwarz; Nocentelli); literary form (Freccero; Hammill; Saunders; Bromley; DiGangi); friendship and marriage (Shannon; Traub; Bray); and philology (Masten). See Richard Rambuss, *Closet Devotions* (Durham, NC: Duke University Press, 1998); Will Stockton, *Members of His Body: Shakespeare, Paul, and a Theology of Nonmonogamy* (New York: Fordham University Press, 2017); Melissa E. Sanchez, *Queer Faith: Reading Promiscuity and Race in the Secular Love Tradition* (New York: New York University Press, 2019); Cynthia Herrup, *A House in Gross Disorder: Sex, Law, and the 2nd Earl of Castlehaven* (Oxford: Oxford University Press, 2001); Melissa E. Sanchez, *Erotic Subjects: The Sexuality of Politics in Early Modern English Literature* (Oxford: Oxford University Press, 2011); Kathryn Schwarz, *Tough Love: Amazonian Encounters in the English Renaissance* (Durham, NC: Duke University Press, 2000); Carmen Nocentelli, *Empires of Love: Europe, Asia, and the Making of Early Modern Identity* (Philadelphia: University of Pennsylvania Press, 2013); Carla Freccero, *Queer/ Early/Modern* (Durham, NC: Duke University Press, 2006); Graham Hammill, *Sexuality and Form: Caravaggio, Marlowe, and Bacon* (Chicago: University of Chicago Press, 2000); Ben Saunders, *Desiring Donne: Poetry, Sexuality, Interpretation* (Cambridge, MA: Harvard University Press, 2006); James M. Bromley, *Intimacy and Sexuality in the Age of Shakespeare* (Cambridge, UK: Cambridge University Press, 2012); Mario DiGangi, *Sexual Types: Embodiment, Agency, and Dramatic Character from Shakespeare to Shirley* (Philadelphia: University of Pennsylvania Press, 2011); Laurie Shannon, *Sovereign Amity: Figures of Friendship in Shakespearean Contexts* (Chicago: University of Chicago Press, 2001); Traub, *The Renaissance of Lesbianism*; Alan Bray, *The Friend* (Chicago: University of Chicago Press, 2003); and Jeffrey Masten, *Queer Philologies: Sex, Language, and Affect in Shakespeare's Time* (Philadelphia: University of Pennsylvania Press, 2016).

sexual categories of early modern institutions like the church and the state.[3] "Sodomy" and "homoeroticism," in their capaciousness, point to a great many forms of sexual relation; but do they help us understand early moderns who found themselves enjoying being hit, or who played sexual roles (including the roles of animals like dogs or ponies), or who found objects like fluids to be erotically charged? By asking such questions, *The Kinky Renaissance* attempts to expand both the archive of and our concepts for understanding early modern sexuality. The essays in this volume thus seek to leverage the sexual nuances of contemporary kink cultures in order to shift the ground of early modern sexuality studies.[4]

Because many readers may not be familiar with the "sexual nuances of contemporary kink cultures," some definitions are in order. In contemporary usage, kink is both an umbrella term for sexual subcultures and a catalyst for expanding the conceptual parameters of desire and pleasure. It encompasses a wide variety of practices and identities includ-

3. See James M. Bromley, *Clothing and Queer Style in Early Modern English Drama* (Oxford: Oxford University Press, 2021); Will Fisher, "The Erotics of Chin Chucking in Seventeenth-Century England," in *Sex Before Sex: Figuring the Act in Early Modern England*, ed. James M. Bromley and Will Stockton (Minneapolis: University of Minnesota Press, 2013), 141–69; Will Fisher, "'Wantoning with the Thighs': The Socialization of Thigh Sex in England, 1590–1730," *Journal of the History of Sexuality* 24, no. 1 (2015): 1–24, https://doi.org/10.7560/JHS24101; Will Fisher, "'Stray[ing] lower where the pleasant fountains lie': Cunnilingus in *Venus and Adonis* and in English Culture, c. 1600–1700" in *The Oxford Handbook of Shakespeare and Embodiment: Gender, Sexuality, and Race*, ed. Valerie Traub (Oxford: Oxford University Press, 2016), 333–46; Gillian Knoll, *Conceiving Desire in Lyly and Shakespeare* (Edinburgh: Edinburgh University Press, 2020); Sanchez, *Queer Faith*; Melissa E. Sanchez, "'Use Me But as Your Spaniel': Feminism, Queer Theory, and Early Modern Sexualities," *PMLA* 127, no. 3 (2012): 493–511, https://doi.org/10.1632/pmla.2012.127.3.493; and Christine Varnado, *The Shapes of Fancy: Reading for Queer Desire in Early Modern Literature* (Minneapolis: University of Minnesota Press, 2020).
4. In this, we follow on the recent volume *Painful Pleasures: Sadomasochism in Medieval Cultures*, which appeared as we were making final edits to this introduction. The essays in this volume make important contributions to our understanding of medieval sexuality, and together the present volume and Vaccaro's point to a burgeoning premodern kink studies. See Christopher Vaccaro, ed., *Painful Pleasures: Sadomasochism in Medieval Cultures* (Manchester: Manchester University Press, 2022).

ing, but not limited to, various forms of bondage, domination, sadism, and masochism (BDSM); fetishism; and sexual role play. Some individuals — "kinksters" — might identify with a particular practice. One might encounter Dominants (also referred to as Doms or tops) and submissives (subs or bottoms), as well as "switches" who might play either role. Beyond these BDSM labels, some kinksters identify as fetishists (or, more specifically, as foot fetishists, or shoe fetishists, or leather fetishists, etc.); spankos (those who enjoy spanking play); or furries (those who enjoy animal-themed play), just to name a few. Crucially, such kinky identities form and are formed by sexual *communities* with their own counterpublic spheres: social networks like FetLife; subcultures of mainstream social media platforms like Reddit, Twitter, Instagram, and Tik-Tok; newsletters; group texts; clubs; and all sorts of parties and gatherings.[5] Perhaps more than any other form of sexual categorization, "kink" is largely organized around being in community with others who share similar desires, practices, and pleasures.

Though many of these sexual communities form around specific kinks, rather than the umbrella concept of "kink," the broader kink community shares an underlying concept of benign sexual variation and a conviction that everyone should have a right to sexual autonomy: people like different things, and they should get to like what they like, play how they want to play, and identify however they would like to identify. Importantly, such convictions are also premised on a community-wide commitment to consensual encounters and to care for others, in the broadest sense. Kink play, as kink communities have long avowed, should be Safe, Sane, and Consensual (SSC). More recently, kinksters have begun to speak of Risk-Aware Consensual Kink (RACK), a formulation that seeks both to avoid the potentially shaming and derogatory

---

5. For the early importance of parties, see Gayle Rubin, "The Catacombs: A Temple of the Butthole," chap. 9 in *Deviations: A Gayle Rubin Reader* (Durham, NC: Duke University Press, 2011), 224–40.

aspects of the word "sane" and to acknowledge the potential dangers of even consensual kink play. In either formulation, consent is assumed to be a primary, authorizing value.

In addition to these more readily identifiable sexual categories and communities, kink also has the capacity to point to amorphous desires that do not take categorical shapes. For instance, "kink" might point toward contingent, fleeting forms of eroticization — often but not always non-genital — that open up various, supposedly non-erotic parts of the body to pleasure. Tickling, pinching, spanking, rubbing, dressing, sniffing, licking, flicking, twisting, tying, clamping, burning, icing: any of these actions might be "kinky," insofar as they render forms of bodily contact (or the tease of contact, as in certain forms of sexual "edging") erotic. Though any of these actions might lead to sexual identities and communities — like, for example, the spanko community — they needn't necessarily. Indeed, they need not even solidify into long-standing desires and practices on the part of any individual actor. One might desire forms of kinky, inventive sexual play without desiring to recapitulate previous practices. One day playing with ice may be hot; the next it might just be cold again. Unlike sexual identity categories that are (at least in the medico-legal sphere, if not necessarily in people's actual lives) assumed to be innate and largely immutable across a lifetime — the view, for instance, that one simply "is" straight, or gay, or bi — kinks might be fleeting or perpetual, fading or enduring. As an analytic category, then, kink can encourage us to think about sexual desires, practices, and pleasures not only as historically contingent but as *individually* contingent. At both the macro scale of populations and the micro scale of individuals, sex lives vary.[6]

Two further terms bind together these multiple axes of kinky thinking and practice, and both serve as key concepts for many of the essays in

---

6. For more on the concept of the sex life, see Joseph Gamble, *Sex Lives: Intimate Infrastructures in Early Modernity* (Philadelphia: University of Pennsylvania Press, 2023).

this collection: scenes and play. Kinksters often refer to their practices as "play," emphasizing both kink's ethos of erotic creativity and its telos of pleasure — even when that playful pleasure derives from pain or humiliation. Because one consents to kink play, forms of constraint — whether physical (like ropes) or psychic (like fears) — can be transformed in the play space into new types of freedom. "Play" is also a capacious kink term, one that attaches itself promiscuously to a variety of different practices. One can often turn something kinky simply by naming it as a form of "play." For instance, those who eroticize the (carefully controlled) restriction of breathing might say that they engage in "breath play."

Many kinksters, especially those who engage in forms of BDSM or other roleplaying, organize their play into "scenes." Scenes mark the boundaries of play by offering participants mental (and sometimes physical) entrances and exits into roles, fantasies, and practices. A scene might be elaborately set, with props and toys, clothing and gear, or it might simply be a mental landscape for participants to enter together. Some scenes may be scripted, but others may simply be a set of guidelines for play. Some kinksters get off on rules; others play more loosely, though still within predetermined bounds. Both "play" and "scenes," of course, are theatrical, and many of the essays in this collection thus find surprising parallels between early modern and contemporary kink cultures of playing, playgoing, and scene-making.

As one can see from this brief overview, the contemporary use of "kink" indexes wide and vibrant lexical, conceptual, and social fields. The word itself, though, has a much longer history. According to the *Oxford English Dictionary* (OED) *Online*, "kink" began its life in English in the eleventh century as a form of breath play. To "kink (*v.1*)" is "to gasp convulsively for breath, lose the breath spasmodically, as in hooping-cough or a severe fit of laughing." Though this particular use largely fell out of fashion by the end of the nineteenth century, it persisted as one of the primary — indeed, often the only — definitions of kink in early modern dictionaries into and throughout the eighteenth century.[7] Alongside this breathless kink, "kink" also morphed in the late-seventeenth century into a kind of rope play: "A short twist or curl in a rope, thread, hair, wire, or the like" (s.v. "kink [*n.1*]," 1.a) or, more broadly, "a sudden bend in a line, course, or the like that is otherwise straight or smoothly curved" (s.v. "kink [*n.1*]," 1.b). Across the past three centuries, these material meanings have supported various figurative meanings, including "an odd or fantastic notion" (s.v. "kink [*n.1*]," 2.a) or "an odd but clever method of doing something" (s.v. "kink [*n.1*]," 2.b). Perhaps most importantly, in American slang, the noun "kink" can also name a wide variety of those who bend the course of society's "otherwise straight or smoothly curved" normative cis white heterosexual subjects: "a black person"; "a criminal"; or "a person whose sexual preferences or behaviour is regarded as abnormal or peculiar" (s.v. "kink [*n.1*]," 3.a, 3.b, 3.c).[8] Thus, as these definitions suggest, and as many of the essays in this collection will bear out, a kinky analytic entails attending to the convergences of logics of sexual shaming and denigration, racialization, and criminalization. Such convergences are built into the word itself: to "kink" a text is to "twist" it, even "to catch or get entangled" (s.v. "kink [*v.2*]," 1) in this web of logics. This collection thus approaches kink intersectionally, taking it as a critical catalyst for analyzing the knotty entanglements of various forms of embodiment, desire, practice, pleasure, and fantasy that both circumscribe and underwrite the life possibilities of early modern subjects.

---

7. See, for instance, the entries for "kink" in John Ray, *A Collection of English Words not Generally Used* (London, 1691); Benjamin Norton Defoe, *A New English Dictionary* (Westminster, 1735); and John Collier, *A View of the Lancashire Dialect* (London, 1746).

8. The *OED Online* even engages in a form of kink-shaming when it describes kink as "an instance of, practice of, or suffering resulting from sexual abnormality" (s.v. "kink [*n.1*]," 2.a). None of the examples for this entry clearly elucidate how "suffering result[s] from" kinky sexuality.

Kinky Reading

Given these definitions of kink, what does a kinky *reading practice* look like? It might begin by following the "short twists" and "sudden bends" in an otherwise smooth line of early modern verse or prose. Take for example an ordinary, even banal, exchange in William Middleton and Thomas Rowley's *The Changeling* (1622). Here is the first line of dialogue between Deflores and Beatrice-Joanna:

DEFLORES.
   Lady, your father —

BEATRICE-JOANNA.
                is in good health, I hope.
  (1.1.93)[9]

What was he going to say? Why does she interject so suddenly, and why bend his line in this direction? It is a critical commonplace to call this a shared line, but the word "shared" is a bit too harmonious; it misses the tension that splits subject from predicate, servant from mistress. "Shared" tells only part of the story — the part where Beatrice-Joanna completes Deflores's line — but it misses the part where she steals his line from him, an inchoate form of breath play that sets the tone for a stifling erotic relationship that leaves them both breathless. The power in their opening exchange lies not in its content but in its form: a stolen breath, a twist in the verse. Together, Deflores and Beatrice-Joanna make a kinky line.

To call something kinky — especially something that does not seem explicitly or clearly sexual — can enchant it, opening our ears to the

---

9. All quotations of the play are taken from William Rowley and Thomas Middleton, *The Changeling*, ed. and annotated by Douglas Bruster, in *Thomas Middleton: The Collected Works*, ed. Gary Taylor and John Lavagnino (Oxford: Oxford University Press, 2007), 1632–78. Parenthetical citations of *The Changeling* cite act, scene, and line number.

erotic currents that run beneath or beside or even against it. Taken in this way, the word "kinky" can have a performative, even incantatory quality. Applying the word where we do not expect to find it helps us notice the erotic potential in an offhand remark, a fleeting encounter, an unassuming line of verse. Was that potential always there waiting to be activated by the "abracadabra" of "kinky!", or does calling something kinky make it so? Yes to both, but also no, and certainly not all the time. As the essays in this volume make clear, kink is a plural concept, meaningful in different ways to different people in different contexts. This plurality and openness to interpretation is both exciting and terrifying, as the stakes are often so high. Kinky scenes can *look a lot like oppression,* after all, because they are so often drawn from the most serious breaches of ethics — sexual violence, nonconsent, enslavement, and abduction, to name only a few. Much of what makes something kinky is its wrongness. So: What do we do with the wrongness of Deflores and Beatrice-Joanna, especially in their early exchanges when the lady so plainly does not consent?

Annabel Patterson's introduction to *The Changeling* is attuned to this wrongness and the critical impasse it creates. Of the "protagonist's consummated sexual relationship," Patterson describes an "electric charge [that] disables or at least disrupts our evaluative reflexes."[10] This electric charge does not appear out of nowhere, and tracing its origins is perhaps the most disrupting task of all. Does the first spark ignite at the kink in Beatrice-Joanna and Deflores's opening line? Do the lady's repeated protestations of her revulsion for Deflores stymie that charge, or do they catalyze it? And how does this charged current wend its way through what is arguably the play's most tense and problematic scene, the blackmail scene? There can be no doubt in act three, scene four, that Deflores demands sex with Beatrice-Joanna in exchange for murdering her

---

10. Annabel Patterson, introduction to *The Changeling*, by William Rowley and Thomas Middleton, ed. and annotated by Douglas Bruster, in *Thomas Middleton: The Collected Works*, ed. Gary Taylor and John Lavagnino (Oxford: Oxford University Press, 2007), 1632–78, at 1632.

betrothed, no doubt that she refuses him. No scholarship exists on the erotics of this scene and with good reason: it feels, frankly, too tricky and too icky even to suggest that there is anything erotic in this encounter beyond the scope of Deflores's own myopic fantasies. But that does not stop audiences and readers from experiencing a range of layered and often conflicting responses to what they see and hear between Deflores and Beatrice-Joanna: disgust, curiosity, horror, wonder, anger, arousal. Structurally and affectively, this scene itself functions as a kink in the play; it "disables, or at least disrupts" our critical attentions to its erotic energies. If there is a charge to this scene, one thing is clear: what makes it icky also makes it hot.

A kinky analytic, then, makes available an apparatus for thinking through scenes that don't fall neatly into our feminist and queer modes of processing. It gives us a point of entry into rooms that feel locked because it starts from the premise that "someone finds this hot" — and, crucially, it affirms that person's desires. Unlocking the door to *The Changeling*'s blackmail scene is not about uncovering a hidden BDSM relationship between Deflores and Beatrice-Joanna since we know this cannot exist without her consent; it is, though, about acknowledging that someone finds this hot. (To be fair, lots of people probably do.) The formal kink in their opening line of dialogue unlocks something by tuning our ears to other kinks in the pair's linguistic rhythms that run throughout *The Changeling*'s erotics of shame and humiliation; its fascination with bondage and enclosure; its mingling of sex and violence; its scenes of object fetishism; its voyeurism; and its triangulated (sometimes quadrangulated) erotic configurations. Like a line of verse, kink is characterized by its attention to form. It is rule bound, even as it plays with rules and tests its own boundaries. The formal kink in Deflores and Beatrice-Joanna's opening line characterizes the erotic tension that builds as they steal each other's breath again and again throughout the play to tell clashing stories, all the while making new stories together, however incoherent and unbidden.

On the page, the kinky line creates a visual effect that patterns the reading practices we often apply to the play. With the two halves of the line stacked vertically but staggered horizontally, we see some of what we already know of *The Changeling*. Read vertically, it is a play about power, domination, and competing hierarchies of class and gender. But scholars like Christine Varnado and Patricia Cahill have also traced the horizontal currents that run across *The Changeling* — the homoerotic charge of Alonzo's proleptic "O, o, o" (3.2.19) when Deflores stabs him, and the queer erotics of touch, surfaces, and skin in Deflores's manipulations of Beatrice-Joanna's glove or in Beatrice-Joanna stroking his "hard face" (2.2.88).[11] The play's queer energies often run counter to its top-down power structures and exist outside the vertical economy of Middleton and Rowley's play.

A kinky reading practice follows erotic vectors that point in both directions, and it acknowledges that the play's queer desires and pleasures exist not only *within* its vertical hierarchy but also *because* of it. For example, the scene of sexual blackmail is governed by top-down (and bottom-up) power: servant blackmails mistress, man assaults woman.[12] But within the power hierarchies that structure the scene — hierarchies that should theoretically put more distance between Deflores and Beatrice-Joanna — a linguistic symmetry draws the two characters claustrophobically close. Although Deflores and Beatrice-Joanna are unable

---

11. See Christine Varnado, "'Invisible Sex!': What Looks Like the Act in Early Modern Drama?," in *Sex Before Sex: Figuring the Act in Early Modern England*, ed. James M. Bromley and Will Stockton (Minneapolis: University of Minnesota Press, 2014), 25–52; and Patricia Cahill, "The Play of Skin in *The Changeling*," *postmedieval: a journal of medieval cultural studies* 3, no. 4 (2012): 391–406, https://doi.org/10.1057/pmed.2012.26.

12. Jamie Paris writes about the racial hierarchies that structure Beatrice-Joanna's relationship with Deflores in "Bad Blood, Black Desires: On the Fragility of Whiteness in Middleton and Rowley's *The Changeling*," *Early Theatre* 24, no. 1 (2021): 113–37, https://doi.org/10.12745/et.24.1.3803.

or unwilling to hear each other, somehow they absorb and co-opt each other's language again and again. True to kinky form, these symmetries appear precisely in the moments when a character performs their power — when Deflores threatens, when Beatrice-Joanna asserts "the distance that creation / Set 'twixt thy blood and mine" (3.4.133–34). Their power struggle makes possible a linguistic intimacy that comes to characterize their erotic relationship in the remainder of the play. Here are two examples of this kinky formalism from the blackmail scene. In both pieces of dialogue, Beatrice tries to leverage her social authority and Deflores steals her words, twisting them into new meanings in a shared line that both splits them and joins them together. First,

BEATRICE-JOANNA.
   Take heed, De Flores, of **forgetfulness**;
   'Twill soon betray us.

DEFLORES.
                  Take you heed first.
   Faith, you're grown much **forgetful**.
   (3.3.97–99)

And again,

BEATRICE-JOANNA.
   Thy language is so bold and vicious
   I cannot see which way I can forgive it
   With any **modesty**.

DEFLORES.
              Push! You **forget** yourself.
   A woman dipped in blood, and talk of **modesty**?
   (3.4.126–29)

At times, Beatrice-Joanna and Deflores seem to speak two different languages. He cannot comprehend her "talk of modesty" and neither can she understand Deflores's intentions: "I understand him not" (3.4.70); "I'm in a labyrinth" (3.4.73); "I know not what will please him!" (3.4.78); "What's your meaning?" (3.4.85). But every misfire between them — every kink in their conversation — brings them closer together, until the end when Deflores zeroes them both out completely: "my life I rate at nothing" (3.4.152), while Beatrice he rates as "no more" than "what the act has made you" (3.4.138). Who is on top here? In practical terms, it must be Deflores. But his language tells another story in which both are on bottom, both submissive to some unknowable force from outside: "the act" or "the deed." When Deflores confesses earlier in the scene that "this act / hath put me into a spirit" (3.4.106–7), he plays on the indeterminacy of words like "act" and "deed" — both repeated at length in the play, and in this scene — and tethers the murder of Alonzo to any number of unnamed, imagined (or unimaginable) erotic activities. If Deflores has the power here, why does this newfound authority arouse fantasies about closing the gap that separates him from Beatrice-Joanna? It is as though the vertical makes possible the horizontal:

> DEFLORES.
>   You must forget your parentage to me.
>   You're the deed's creature; by that name you lost
>   Your first condition, and I challenge you,
>   As peace and innocency has turned you out,
>   And made you one with me.
>
> BEATRICE-JOANNA.
>   With thee, foul villain?
> (3.4.139–43)

Is this a fantasy of domination or of consummation? Or both? Deflores begins this speech by declaring himself Beatrice-Joanna's "equal" (3.4.136) in her conscience, and he concludes in a similar key: "the deed" has "made [them] one." Flattening out hierarchies, Deflores imagines sexual intimacy with Beatrice-Joanna as a likeness or merging. But the middle of his speech tells a competing story of her submission to Deflores: she "must forget [her] parentage to [him]." Now the play's hierarchies are stretched and strained rather than smoothed over, with Deflores on top as Beatrice-Joanna's new daddy, even as the two characters are "made ... one." Deflores's language is a familiar one in the context of contemporary kink culture, especially the conventions of BDSM, which can include prolonged scenes of negotiation, roles like a daddy or a princess, sexual violence, and erotic intimacies that are framed as both lateral and vertical at the same time. That the play never fully bears out these familiar scripts — Beatrice-Joanna plainly does not consent — does not cancel them out for an audience whose ears are tuned to them. Beatrice-Joanna's ears are not, and because she is either unable or unwilling to recognize these scripts, Deflores repeats them, unfolding his fantasies again and again in language Beatrice-Joanna describes as "bold and vicious" (3.4.122). The curious effect of this reiteration is that the scene begins to sound like one long kinky line. Deflores speaks, Beatrice-Joanna echoes his language with a difference (cf. Deflores: "And made you one with me," then Beatrice-Joanna: "With thee, foul villain?"), and then he rephrases, adds, and emends, twisting and bending fantasies that gain intensity and lose their coherence with each iteration. He claims to be her "partner" (3.4.158) even as she makes him her "master" (3.4.159), and somehow both end up being true by the end of the play.

In clarifying the formal intricacies of Middleton and Rowley's language, a kinky analytic also brings to light the political significance of this eroticization of power — the knotty imbrication of fantasies of domination and fantasies of mutuality, the twisting of the vertical and the horizontal. Indeed, because many forms of kink take their charge from ratcheting up, reversing, or diffusing power hierarchies, kink is a particularly fecund avenue for analyzing the intersections of gender, race, and class, especially as those categories manifest themselves in the actual lived experience of sexual practice. As Amber Jamilla Musser has argued, "Masochism [and, we might add, kink more generally] is a powerful diagnostic tool," one that "lays bare concepts of race, gender, power, and subjectivity."[13] In fact, kink — and BDSM practices in particular — served just such a diagnostic function when it became one of the primary political flashpoints of the so-called "feminist sex wars" of the late 1970s and '80s.[14] For many feminists of that era, BDSM (and pornography more generally) marked the apotheosis of the sexual subordination of women. For instance, in her reflections on the feminist sex wars, Gayle Rubin notes that groups like the San Francisco–based Women Against Violence in Pornography and Media (WAVPM), a precursor to and contemporary of the more well-known, New York–based Women Against Pornography (WAP), conflated BDSM with pornography and both with "violence against women, and female subordination."[15] These groups thus interpreted the sexual proclivities and consensual practices of kinky women as, at best, a form of false consciousness inculcated by a violent patriarchy and, at worst, simply abuse. As the feminist journalist Catherine Scott notes in her study of pop cultural representations of

13. Amber Jamilla Musser, *Sensational Flesh: Race, Power, and Masochism* (New York: New York University Press, 2014) 1, 2.

14. See Gayle Rubin, "Blood Under the Bridge: Reflections on 'Thinking Sex,'" chap. 8 in *Deviations: A Gayle Rubin Reader* (Durham, NC: Duke University Press, 2011), 194–223.

15. Rubin, "Blood Under the Bridge," 210. This conflation of BDSM and pornography, Rubin notes, "intensif[ied] a shift in the locus of legal and social concern about sexual imagery away from genital proximity and toward kinkiness," such that for porn to be considered "hard core" no longer meant simply that it included "genital exposure and contact" but that it "refers to something the viewer finds repugnant or considers 'way out there,'" which, Rubin claims, "all too often consists of depictions of kinky or S/M sexuality." Rubin, "Blood Under the Bridge," 211.

kink, "The misreading of BDSM as indistinguishable from abuse is one that dogs the mainstream public perception of kink" to this day.[16]

But, as Scott also argues, to claim that BDSM is necessarily sexual violence, one must ignore or discount the voices and testimony of a great many women who avow kinky desires and who consent to kinky sex. Such disavowals, sex-radical feminists like Rubin note, amount to a form of condescension that is surprisingly misogynist in its structure: "Those women don't know what's good for them." Scott also points out that such disavowals are surprisingly condescending toward kinky men as well:

> Ultimately, non-kinksters and anti-kink feminists can and will wring their hands over what they perceive as terrible men who've brainwashed women into thinking they want such awful things done to them. What they fail to realize is that plenty of dominant men are already practicing self-analysis and agonizing over their desires, and that what is most liberating for these men is the realization that their female partners desire and enjoy kink play — it is the perpetuation of the myth that women are passive, easily brainwashable idiots with no agency or sexual identity of their own which hinders that. And it is precisely that myth that anti-kink feminists are spreading, hardly much of a victory for women.[17]

In addition to discounting the personal desires of women who find pleasure and fulfillment in consensual scenes of submission, Scott points out, anti-kink feminists also install men as necessarily, even essentially, violent and exploitative. But, both in her interviews with other kink practitioners and in her own experience in BDSM communities, Scott notes that men who find pleasure and fulfillment in consensual scenes of domination often engage in quite a bit of self-reflection about the poten-

---

16. Catherine Scott, *Thinking Kink: The Collision of BDSM, Feminism and Popular Culture* (Jefferson, NC: McFarland & Company, 2015), 168.
17. Scott, *Thinking Kink*, 79.

tial political ramifications of their sexual desires. (One wishes the same could be said more widely for men who engage in non-kinky sexual practices.)

Kink is not merely a useful diagnostic of fault lines in feminist theorizing and activism, though. In addition to these long-standing debates about the relationship between kinky sex and gender politics, kinksters of color and, more recently, scholars of kink have also reflected explicitly and at length on the structuring capacities of racialization, race thinking, and racism in kink. As Ariane Cruz and Musser make clear in their monographs on the racialization of kink, BDSM, in particular, is a key site where sexuality and race organize and disorganize themselves. For instance, in *The Color of Kink*, Cruz deploys "BDSM as a critical aperture for elucidating the dynamics of racialized shame, humiliation, and pleasure that undergird the genre of commercial contemporary interracial pornography in the United States."[18] For Cruz, pornographic representations of interracial BDSM practices are generative for "reinvigorating debates about pleasure, domination, and perversion in the context of black female sexuality" because they dramatize the interrelation of race, sexuality, and gender not merely as abstract concepts but as visceral, embodied experiences.[19] What's more, in Cruz's analysis, racialized BDSM perverts dominant narratives of racial domination and submission, cathecting scenes of abjection and disempowerment with an erotic charge that can scramble preconceived vectors of power. It may be the case, Cruz asks us to contemplate, that bondage is exciting to some Black women not despite but precisely because of its citation of slavery. While Cruz's primary interventions lie in kink studies and Black feminism, her analysis of a wide variety of "race play" ("a BDSM practice that explicitly plays with race,"[20] in her definition) ultimately reveals that race —

---

18. Ariane Cruz, *The Color of Kink: Black Women, BDSM, and Pornography* (New York: New York University Press, 2016), 21.
19. Cruz, *The Color of Kink*, 1.
20. Cruz, *The Color of Kink*, 21.

including whiteness — structures all forms of kink, even ones that don't take their charge from the histories that suffuse the interracial play that is her monograph's focus. One of the implications of Cruz's analysis of the racialization of kink is that two white kinksters playing together will derive part of their pleasure (and pleasurable danger) precisely from their whiteness, as will two Black kinksters from their Blackness, or two Asian kinksters, etc. As Cruz argues, "Domination and submission are not just mechanisms of power but also modes of pleasure."[21] The pervasive currents of domination and submission that we call "race," then, will be central to both the power and the pleasures of kink. As Kirk Quinsland points out in his essay in this volume, this is as true in early modern England as it is in twenty-first-century America. The essays in this collection are thus driven by a critical conviction that kink's capacity to unveil and reformulate entrenched conceptions and hierarchies in one vector of power (e.g., race) cannot be disentangled from its enmeshment in other vectors of power (e.g., gender).

The Contours of Kink Studies

If you will permit a bit of armchair sociology: kinksters seem preternaturally disposed to reading. Perhaps because they are subject to such vitriol in the public sphere — even from some of those in the queer community who one might assume would be committed to a "benign theory of sexual variation" — kinksters for decades have developed a robust series of newsletters, zines, mailing lists, blogs, forums, chatrooms, YouTube channels, and even monographs. A partial list of authors of the latter would include: Patrick Califia, Catherine Scott, Margot Weiss, Mollena Williams, and Jay Wiseman.[22] Scholars have also produced historical

---

21. Cruz, *The Color of Kink*, 3.

22. See Patrick Califia, *Speaking Sex to Power: The Politics of Queer Sex* (Jersey City, NJ: Cleis Press, 2001); Scott, *Thinking Kink*; Margot Weiss, *Techniques of Pleasure: BDSM and the Circuits of Sexuality* (Durham, NC: Duke University Press, 2011); Mollena Williams, *The Toybag*

studies of particular practices like flagellation, as well as more wide-ranging studies of the philosophical underpinnings of kink concepts — particularly masochism, which has served as an anchor for a whole host of critics working across time periods.[23] *The Kinky Renaissance* thus brings recent work on actual BDSM practices and experiences into conversation with the extensive body of research on the concept of masochism in literary and cultural studies. Though the *M* comprises only one letter of the acronym, theorists of sexuality from Sigmund Freud and Jacques Lacan to Gilles Deleuze and Leo Bersani have set it apart from the *B*, *D*, and even the *S*.[24] Rita Felski classifies masochism among "the most perplexing ... of the terms bequeathed to us by the fathers of sexology," with wildly conflicting descriptions:

> Masochism has been depicted as craven submission or as willful revolt, as a form of radical self-shattering or the epitome of ironic self-consciousness. In one account, the masochistic script is an extreme instance of psychic rigidity and compulsive sexual need; from another perspective, it is the epitome of playfulness and theatricality. Some writers view masochism as an aberration; others see

Guide to Playing with Taboo (Emeryville, CA: Greenery Press, 2010); and Jay Wiseman, *SM 101* (Emeryville, CA: Greenery Press, 1996).

23. On flagellation, see Niklaus Largier, *In Praise of the Whip: A Cultural History of Arousal* (Princeton, NJ: Princeton University Press, 2007); Sarah Toulalan, *Imagining Sex: Pornography and Bodies in Seventeenth-Century England* (Oxford: Oxford University Press, 2007); and Will Fisher's forthcoming work. In addition to the work on masochism cited below, see Elizabeth Freeman's discussion in *Time Binds: Queer Temporalities, Queer Histories* (Durham, NC: Duke University Press, 2010).

24. Freud identifies primary masochism as a basic expression of the death drive, and although his accounts of masochism evolved over time, he ultimately placed the *M* before the *S*. Sadism, he would claim in his later works, is masochism projected outward. See Sigmund Freud, *Beyond the Pleasure Principle* (1920), in *The Standard Edition of the Complete Psychological Works*, trans. James Strachey, vol. 18 (London: Hogarth Press & Institute of Psychoanalysis, 1953–74), 52–64.

it as a quasi-universal condition that lies at the core of human sexuality.[25]

Common to many of these accounts is a tendency towards abstraction, in part because so many theorists (following Freud) locate masochism at the core of selfhood, ego development, and relationality. Theorizing masochism in these ways can disembody it, unkink it, and desexualize it altogether, as science journalist Leigh Cowart notes in her 2021 book *Hurts So Good: The Science and Culture of Pain on Purpose*: "While masochism can definitely be about sex, it doesn't always have to be.... Sex may be the gateway drug to getting us to talk about masochism, but masochism is so much more than kink."[26] *The Kinky Renaissance* resituates masochism in its kinky context — sex, in our view, is much more than a "gateway drug" — but our work is also indebted to studies of masochism that take a more philosophical approach, including the foundational writings of Leopold von Sacher-Masoch and the Marquis de Sade. Although Sade and Sacher-Masoch approach sexuality in different ways (Deleuze famously claims that sadism and masochism are fundamentally incompatible), their work shares a common focus on idealization. Sade's libertine thrills not to a person or a body or even a sensation but to an ideal — the prospect of total chaos, delirious destruction. The sadistic hero thus reaches for "what is not here," or "pure negation."[27] Likewise, the masochistic hero reaches toward an ideal — what Sacher-Masoch calls "supersensualism" — through the process of disavowal,

25. Rita Felski, "Redescriptions of Female Masochism," *The Minnesota Review*, nos. 63–64 (2005): 127–39, at 127.

26. Leigh Cowart, *Hurts So Good: The Science and Culture of Pain on Purpose* (New York: Public Affairs, 2021), 9. Cowart defines masochism as "the human trait of feeling bad to feel better" (10), a quality she ascribes to experiences as diverse as participating in a hot pepper eating contest, running an ultramarathon, dancing ballet on pointe, and engaging in a BDSM encounter.

27. See Gilles Deleuze's essay, *On Coldness and Cruelty*, in Gilles Deleuze and Leopold von Sacher-Masoch, *Masochism: "Coldness and Cruelty" and "Venus in Furs,"* trans. Jean McNeil (New York: Zone Books, 1989), 9–138, at 26–31.

"question[ing] the validity of the existing reality in order to create a pure ideal reality."[28] Sacher-Masoch's writings are "free from obscenity," according to Deleuze: "He has a particular way of 'desexualizing' love and at the same time sexualizing the entire history of humanity."[29] In Sade's yearning for pure negation and in Sacher-Masoch's supersensualism, sexuality is instrumentalized — sometimes subordinated altogether — by an idea.

Early modernists in particular have found in masochism an opportunity to explore the instability of the humanist subject or self. As Cynthia Marshall writes in *The Shattering of the Self: Violence, Subjectivity, and Early Modern Texts*,

> Nothing preys on the humanist model of the self-identical subject, however, like the concept of masochism. Where the existence of the unconscious introduces a structural inconsistency in the subject, masochism entails a dynamic one — a more truly paradoxical, because essentially active, movement of the self against the self, rather than the merely static existence of an elusive, internal otherness.[30]

Marshall draws from psychoanalytic theory (Freud, Lacan, Jean Laplanche, and Bersani) to foreground the role of masochism — the impulse to negate selfhood — in the formation of the early modern subject. The concept of masochism, its pleasures and its paradoxes, helps Marshall account for the proliferation of texts that enable audiences to experience the pleasures of self-shattering during a period defined by

28. Deleuze, *On Coldness and Cruelty*, 33. Severin, the narrator of Leopold von Sacher-Masoch's novella *Venus in Furs*, pens a manuscript titled *Confessions of a Supersensualist*. See Leopold von Sacher-Masoch, *Venus in Furs*, in Gilles Deleuze and Leopold von Sacher-Masoch, *Masochism: "Coldness and Cruelty" and "Venus in Furs,"* trans. Jean McNeil (New York: Zone Books, 1989), 143–293, at 151.
29. Deleuze, *On Coldness and Cruelty*, 35 and 12.
30. Cynthia Marshall, *The Shattering of the Self: Violence, Subjectivity, and Early Modern Texts* (Baltimore: Johns Hopkins University Press, 2002), 35–36.

"the so-called birth of subjectivity."[31] Other scholars of early modern sexuality have turned to masochism to analyze a broad range of early modern characters, relationships, and affects: Antonio's melancholy in *The Merchant of Venice* (Drew Daniel); Iago's theory of mind in *Othello* (Paul Cefalu); Antony and Cleopatra's longing for "the lover's pinch" (Lisa S. Starks; Gillian Knoll); and the unrequited love/lust of Shakespeare's two Helenas (Melissa E. Sanchez, Jillian Keenan, and Gillian Knoll in *A Midsummer Night's Dream*; and James Kuzner in *All's Well That Ends Well*).[32] Along with work on sexuality are early modern studies of "social masochism" (Hugh McIntosh) and "political masochism" (Amanda Bailey).[33] While the word "kink" makes few appearances in this scholarship, it is clear that the concept of kink as a set of actual practices and communities is a quiet presence. *The Kinky Renaissance* turns up the volume.

As this insistence on the value of kink's sexual practices and communities to broader literary concerns might suggest, one of the many crit-

31. Marshall, *The Shattering of the Self*, 4.
32. See Drew Daniel, "'Let me have judgment, and the Jew his will': Melancholy Epistemology and Masochistic Fantasy in *The Merchant of Venice*," *Shakespeare Quarterly* 61, no. 2 (2010): 206–34, https://doi.org/10.1353/shq.0.0144; Paul Cefalu, "The Burdens of Mind Reading in Shakespeare's *Othello*: A Cognitive and Psychoanalytic Approach to Iago's Theory of Mind," *Shakespeare Quarterly* 64, no. 3 (2013): 265–94, https://www.jstor.org/stable/24778472; Lisa S. Starks, "Immortal Longings: The Erotics of Death in *Antony and Cleopatra*," in *Antony and Cleopatra: New Critical Essays*, ed. Sara Munson Deats (Abingdon, UK: Routledge, 2005), 243–58; Gillian Knoll, "Binding the Void: The Erotics of Place in *Antony and Cleopatra*," *Criticism: A Quarterly for Literature and the Arts* 58, no. 2 (2016): 281–304, https://doi.org/10.13110/criticism.58.2.0281; Melissa E. Sanchez, "'Use Me But as Your Spaniel,'" Jillian Keenan, *Sex with Shakespeare* (New York: Harper Collins, 2016); Gillian Knoll, "*Coitus Magneticus*: Erotic Attraction in *A Midsummer Night's Dream*," *Modern Philology* 117, no. 3 (2020): 301–22, https://doi.org/10.1086/707082; and James Kuzner, "*All's Well That Ends Well* and the Art of Love," *Shakespeare Quarterly* 68, no. 3 (2017): 215–40, https://www.jstor.org/stable/48559740.
33. Hugh McIntosh, "The Social Masochism of Shakespeare's Sonnets," *SEL: Studies in English Literature, 1500–1900* 50, no. 1 (2010): 109–125, https://doi.org/10.1353/sel.0.0083; and Amanda Bailey, "Occupy Macbeth: Masculinity and Political Masochism in *Macbeth*," in *Violent Masculinities: Male Aggression in Early Modern Texts and Culture*, ed. Jennifer Feather and Catherine E. Thomas (New York: Palgrave Macmillan, 2013), 191–212.

ical desires that led to this collection was the desire to reformulate the terms of queer analysis in early modern studies. As Eve Kosofsky Sedgwick observed long ago, "queer" has both minoritizing and universalizing axes: on the one hand, some of us *are* queer, insofar as our sexual desires, practices, and lives are organized primarily outside of or against normative formations; on the other hand, because desire is slippery, anyone or anything might, in the right light or the right mood, become or be seen as queer, if only temporarily. Kink has its own analogous axes. As we discuss above, some people identify *as* kinky — or, more specifically, as Doms, subs, switches, spankos, princesses, furries, etc.; in this vein, as some of our contributors argue, kinky sexual communities, if not necessarily identities, were also operative in early modern England. But kink also has its own universalizing tendencies since it serves as an umbrella term for a wide variety of sexual practices, desires, fantasies, and communities. Most broadly, one of the promises of kink is that the possibilities of desire may not be predetermined — predetermined by anything, really: identity, the church, the state, or even the body's capacities for pleasure. What could be more universalizing than an investment in a limitless capacity to find just about anything hot?

Kink, though, is not equivalent to queer. While "queer" often positions itself *against* norms, kink also points to practices and desires that are sometimes *beside* norms and sometimes *within* them, such as BDSM practices that take some of their erotic energy from intensifying normative power hierarchies, taking them to the extreme. Indeed, while some kinksters may find pleasure in forms of resisting or subverting norms (being "naughty"), others delight in practices, fantasies, and images that are simply orthogonal to the normative membrane of sexuality altogether. "Water sports," for instance (the name for various forms of kink play involving urine), may indeed draw on the sexual energy of engaging in taboo, but "anti-normative" hardly seems to capture either the appeal or the political significance of being pissed on. Kink thus offers an opportunity to reconsider queer theory's own self-organizing impulses and to find new ways of imagining and analyzing forms of sexual pleasure and sexual politics that are not defined, in the first instance, around the conceptually straitening nexus of "normativity." *The Kinky Renaissance*, then, seeks to offer a wide variety of ways of doing "queer theory without anti-normativity," as Robyn Wiegman and Elizabeth Wilson suggest in a recent special issue of *differences*.[34]

Similarly, because kink communities explicitly center consent (recall the Safe, Sane, and Consensual or Risk-Aware Consensual Kink monikers), one of the affordances of kinky thinking is that it allows us to reconsider the concept of consent, at least provisionally, outside of the framework of adjudicating assault. To be sure, certain forms of kinky sex take their torque from their proximity to forms of bodily or emotional injury, and in this sense "consent" within kink is intimately bound up with issues of harm, violation, and the boundaries of assault. But whereas legal frameworks of consent primarily pose the question, "What constitutes an actionable violation of bodily autonomy and rights?" — that is, when is sexual activity so sufficiently harmful that the state should intervene and enact punishment? — kinky frameworks of consent primarily pose the question, "How can we mutually build an infrastructure to support our desires?"[35] As a legal category, consent purports to name the boundaries of, and thus to proleptically defend against, a sexual violation; as a kinky category, consent seeks to name the boundaries of, and thus to make possible the realization of, otherwise unnamed desires.

34. See Robyn Weigman and Elizabeth A. Wilson, "Introduction: Antinormativity's Queer Conventions," *differences* 26, no. 1 (2015): 1–25, https://doi.org/10.1215/10407391-2880582.

35. Joseph Fischel draws a slightly different distinction between legal and political consent in *Screw Consent: Sex and Harm in the Age of Consent* (Berkeley, CA: University of California Press, 2019). While he supports "affirmative consent" as "the least-bad standard available for sexual assault law," he also advocates that we "screw consent" in our politics. In place of consent, he offers "competing concepts and values — for example human flourishing, nonsuffering, nonexploitation, feminist consciousness ... autonomy and access" (23) — that work towards building "a more democratically hedonic sexual culture" (5).

Indeed, it is this recognition and elevation of the unnamed and unimagined that makes kink so powerful, both as a set of practices and as a methodological guide for queer theory and the history of sexuality. Like any good analytic, kink enlivens our capacity to notice, to pay attention. As the essays in this volume attest, and as we hope the brief reading of *The Changeling* at the beginning of this essay suggested, the pleasures of kinky thinking primarily derive from intensely close readings of texts, bodies, practices, desires, and fantasies. A common sentiment among the essays in this volume is that, as Gina Filo argues, kink "open[s] up" new vistas on a wide variety of pleasures, power relations, and even formalist concerns. Such an opening works in at least two ways: kink encourages us to think, of course, about the specificity of desire's psychic life (e.g., fantasies), but kink also encourages us to think more closely about the body's *material* capacities (e.g., how and where its sensations might become pleasures). Various essays in this volume follow one or the other — or sometimes both — of these analytic tracks as they trace the contours of kinky sexuality, and of kinky literary representation, in early modern England.

Beyond its penchant for enlivening our capacities for close reading, kink is useful to think with in all sorts of ways. Theoretically speaking, it pitches a big tent: because it libidinizes gendered and racial power hierarchies, kink needs — and poses useful questions for — feminism and critical race theory. Because it entails tracing the psychic contours of sexual fantasies, kink invites psychoanalytic methods. Because it offers ways of exploring new sensations, pleasures, and intimacies that do not include or require sexual attraction, kink aligns with studies of asexuality and aromanticism that challenge compulsory sexuality.[36] And

36. Some of the most vibrant recent conversations within early modern studies have constellated around the topic of asexualities (see the hashtag #RenAsexy), and we are grateful that scholars like Aley O'Mara, Liza Blake, Cat Clifford, and Simone Chess, among others, have made asexuality more visible as an early modern way of being and as a way of reading race, gender, disability, and aesthetic form. As for the intersections between kink and asexual-

because kinky communities are, by definition, socially marginalized (not to mention, often, ostracized), kink converges with major questions in social theory about the construction and boundaries of autonomy and the public sphere. Which is to say: if you care about how people share a world, then you can, and perhaps should, care about kink.

The methodological affordances of kink might be distilled, at least in part, into the following set of propositions:

1. Kink focuses our attention on the particularities of sexual desires beyond the gender of object choice, beyond genital stimulation, and beyond teleologies of orgasm.

2. Kink unsettles received notions of power within sexual interactions.

3. Relatedly, kink also unsettles received notions about the centrality of "norms" and "normativity" to the constitution of sexual life. That is, kink is transgressive without necessarily being non- or anti-normative.

4. Kink reconfigures our understanding of the artistic processes and concerns of even highly canonical early modern writers.

5. Kink points us to new archives of early modern sexual life.

Importantly, kink, as a critical analytic, opens up this theoretical and methodological space regardless of the kind of sexual practices and desires that are being examined. Which is to say: thinking kink makes even supposedly unkinky (sometimes called "vanilla") sex more critically interesting.

---

ity, O'Mara notes in an interview for the Ace and Aro Advocacy Project, "When I learned about asexuality, I almost immediately read that some aces are kinky, and everything made perfect sense to me. Realizing that was one of the first times that I felt like I actually knew myself" (see "Ace Week 101: Aces and Sex or Kink," October 28, 2021, https://taaap.org/2021/10/28/ace-week-21-aces-sex-kink/). See also Liza Blake et al., "A Bibliography for Early Modern Asexualities," accessed June 5, 2023, https://tinyurl.com/earlymodacebib.

What These Essays Do

The essays in this volume originated in a seminar at the 2021 annual meeting of the Shakespeare Association of America (SAA); all of our contributors thus focus primarily on English literary texts. This geographical and historical boundary is borne largely of convenience rather than a conviction that there is necessarily something uniquely kinky about early modern England. Of course, early modern English literature has kinks of its own, along with unique ways of representing and understanding broader, more familiar kinks like cuckoldry and sexual flagellation. In seventeenth-century English pornography, for example, scenes of sexual flagellation were thought to enhance fertility by producing more copious ejaculate (both male and female) and by elevating body temperature. Sarah Toulalan offers a culturally specific account of the fixation on the flagellant's reddening flesh as "a visual indicator of the body's raised heat."[37] Red marks are kinky for different reasons in other times, places, and communities — the display of bruises and reddening skin is a staple of contemporary spanko porn — and we hope the essays in this volume will contribute to a more capacious understanding of kink within and beyond the boundaries of early modern England. We hope, in fact, that readers with expertise in other national and linguistic traditions will find inspiration in these pages to produce work in their respective fields, as well as comparative work across place, language, and time. Indeed, because the concept of "kink" will vary across the different sexual configurations of different cultures, what is kinky in one context might be perfectly vanilla in another.[38]

Our contributors offer intensely close readings of early modern English literature in order to help us understand the sexual specificity of that

37. Sarah Toulalan, *Imagining Sex*, 112. See also Will Fisher's forthcoming work on flagellation as one of many early modern sexual practices.
38. See, for example, Carmen Nocentelli's work on various forms of genital modification in the early modern Pacific in *Empires of Love*.

particular time and place. James Mulder, for instance, offers a remarkably nuanced close reading of the erotics of the "rough, gauzy, pliant, slippery textures, sweet scents, and soft sounds" that are animated in Christopher Marlowe's *Hero and Leander*. Such a kinky focus on the libidinal powers of "sensory stimuli" allows him to "deprioritize both penetration and genital contact" and to think sex "radically otherwise than in the binarizing terms of power, domination, and subordination." Resisting what he calls the "gravitational pull" of penetration in early modern sexuality studies, Mulder's focus on non-penetrative and non-genital pleasures brings new insight both to the poem and to our understanding of the early modern sexual landscape.

In her contribution to this volume, Erika Carbonara emphasizes the importance of community to understanding kink in both its contemporary and early modern formations. Rather than understanding "cuckoldry" to be merely a catchword for social anxieties about women's chastity and men's sexual dupery, Carbonara looks both to early modern drama and more ephemeral cultural artifacts like pamphlets and ballads to argue that some early modern men in fact desired to be, and found pleasure in being, cuckolded, not least because it offered a socio-sexual axis along which they could form communities with other "contented" cuckolds.

Similarly revising long-standing critical narratives, Gina Filo's essay reevaluates a critical consensus about the supposedly disordered, disgusting, and misogynist sexuality of Robert Herrick's poetry. In her reading of *Hesperides*, Filo finds instead a "far wider, queerer array of nonpathological and nonpathologized pleasures and positions for the early modern sexual subject than is often assumed possible." Inviting us to reclaim Herrick's perversities as instances of benign sexual variation, Filo reframes a familiar poet whose works are frequently anthologized and taught in the undergraduate classroom. In her deft close readings, topoi from the Petrarchan pain tradition are interwoven with kinky pleasures like "switchy bondage play" to reveal "a veritable buffet of varieties of sexual expression" that have gone largely unnoticed by studies of Herrick's work.

Where these first essays critically reevaluate seemingly familiar poets and sexual identities, some essays in the collection leverage the concept of kink to reconsider thorny feminist and queer questions about power, consent, and sexual ethics. Erin Kelly, for instance, explores the role of consent in Shakespeare's *The Taming of the Shrew*, a play whose uneven reception history mostly hinges on the question of Katherine's consent to Petruchio's treatment. Kelly observes that Petruchio and Katherine are hardly ever alone onstage (arguably never alone, with Christopher Sly in the stalls) and thus extends the question of consent to sex "in the midst of the street." Drawing from research on the play's reception history and legal proceedings involving public sex, Kelly proposes that *"The Taming of the Shrew* raises questions about the ethics and legality of kink that go beyond a couple's negotiated agreements to consider what type of consent (if any) should be sought from those who witness or, through their presence, become de facto partakers in a kinky encounter."

Attuned to another ethically fraught scene in Francis Beaumont and John Fletcher's *The Maid's Tragedy* (1610), Nathaniel Leonard makes the case that the play indexes forms of kinky sexual practice and knowledge that circulated in the early modern English imagination. The centerpiece of Leonard's chapter is a scene of sexual bondage that the King instantly and enthusiastically recognizes as "a pretty new device." When his lover Evadne binds the King to his bed to enact her revenge, Leonard argues, the play stages a form of ritualized violence common to the genre of revenge tragedy. By attending to the generic features of revenge tragedy, Leonard contextualizes the long association of kinky sexual practices with (meta)theatricality and ritual.

In his essay, Kirk Quinsland looks to one of the most complex and controversial modern kinks — "race play," the consensual eroticization of racial domination — in order to reevaluate Shakespeare's representation of interracial sex in *Titus Andronicus* (1594). Quinsland argues that the concept of "race play" helps us see that the racial significations of sexual desires and practices may sometimes be more rigid and disenfranchising for those outside of a given sexual relationship than they are for those inside of it. "What Tamora and Aaron experience as a way of playing within and playing with systems of racial signification," Quinsland argues, "the Romans read as reinforcement of old stereotypes and boundaries and as a degradation of a White body tarnished by its sexual association with Blackness." "This contradiction in signification," he goes on to claim, "illustrates the need to create space for kink/sex that is pleasurable for its consenting participants, even if it violates external ethical norms." Pleasure is, in Quinsland's view, autotelic: it is not a means to an end but an end unto itself.

The final essays in the collection turn even more centrally to the relationship between kink and practices of literary representation. For instance, in her contribution to the volume, Beatrice Bradley introduces a "representational quandary" within both early modern poetry and contemporary hard-core pornography. The quandary is one of visibility — specifically of showing the climactic moment (the so-called "money shot") in bareback porn films. Bradley's essay locates a similar tension between the visual and the tactile in early modern "representations of the female body adorned with a liquid that vacillates between aestheticized droplets and amorphous muck." Tracing the path of fluids such as tears and sweat along breasts, cheeks, and clasped hands in *The Faerie Queene* and *Venus and Adonis*, Bradley lingers over those moments when fluids elide and become indeterminate. In her account, "the problems of fluidic representation function to suggest not only climax … but also a displacement of pleasure and control, eliding distinctions between characters who involuntarily produce the fluid and those who come into contact with it."

Similarly, Heather Frazier draws on the contemporary kink concept of a "golden shower" — the eroticization of being pissed on — to open up space for noticing a particular trope in early modern drama that might have otherwise flown beneath our radars: women emptying their chamber pots on men. Turning to two plays by John Fletcher, *The Tamer Tamed* (c. 1604–17) and *The Captain* (1612, co-written with Beaumont), Frazier argues that Fletcher frequently represents women "who sexually dominate men with their urine." Such water sports are not, however, unequivocally pleasure-centered kink activities. Indeed, Frazier argues that "ultimately, the conservative messages of both plays underscore a significant limitation to the expression of female sexual desire in early seventeenth-century English drama, even sexual desire coded as kinky and subversive." Frazier's reading allows us to see that certain early modern dramatists could imagine sexual practices that today might be labeled "kinks," even if such imagining is put to the service not of promoting pleasure but of shutting it down.

In the collection's final essay, Gillian Knoll locates the "eroticized experience of being controlled" in John Lyly's *The Woman in the Moon* (1595). She argues that while Lyly's Pandora — created by Nature solely for the purpose of propagating with shepherds — may seem to "begin as a heteronormative fantasy," she nevertheless comes to embody the erotic position of the submissive. The language of BDSM — of scene setting, slut training, and topping from the bottom — allows Knoll to excavate from Lyly's play a whole host of richly textured and nuanced desires within the broad, not-very-descriptive category of the "heteronormative." From a kinky perspective, Knoll shows us, actively kneeling — choosing to give up power — can in fact itself be a source of intense power and desire.

Many kinksters, especially those who engage in particularly intense scenes, also engage in rituals of exiting and processing scenes, coming down from a high, returning to the world, and resolidifying both their sense of self and their bond with their partner(s). Colloquially, such practices are known as "aftercare." In her afterword to the volume, Christine Varnado argues that such practices of aftercare are also part and parcel of academic genres: not only the monograph and the edited collection, which frequently feature codas, epilogues, and afterwords, but even the academic conference. Reflecting on both the initial event of the 2021 SAA seminar at which many of these essays were first incubated — via Zoom, due to the ongoing pandemic — and on the critical, aesthetic, and sexual-theoretical affordances of the essays' final iterations, Varnado emphasizes the *forms* of attention, thought, and imagination — as well as, ultimately, community and care — that each of our contributors enact. Excavating what she calls a "kink formalism" in these essays, Varnado suggests — and we enthusiastically agree — that the essays' attention to the formal characteristics of early modern literature in fact open up new avenues for understanding the concept of kink even outside of early modernity. The stakes of these essays, that is, reverberate beyond their most immediate objects of study, redounding onto our contemporary conceptions of kink, of sexuality, and of literary criticism.

Why Kink Now?

We sympathize with the fact that some readers may find the topic of this volume needlessly provocative (at best) or (at worst) prurient. After all, why bother studying kink when there are so many more pressing social issues in the world today — not to mention in early modernity? Such critical objections are both understandable and quite old. As Gayle Rubin writes in "Thinking Sex," "To some, sexuality may seem to be an unimportant topic, a frivolous diversion from the more critical problems of poverty, war, disease, racism, famine, or nuclear annihilation. But it is precisely at times such as these, when we live with the possibility of unthinkable destruction, that people are likely to become dangerously crazy about sexuality."[39] Rubin first published these words in 1984, but, sadly, they apply just as readily forty years later. The purpose of this volume is neither prurience nor provocation but coming to a fuller historical understanding of the possibilities of sexual life in early modern England. Because it is historical, this is an academic goal. But it is also a political goal, since this greater historical understanding is intended to redound back to the possibilities of sexual life in our own times.

Academically speaking, we hope this volume will serve as an invitation into a set of questions, reading practices, and modes of thought that might be unfamiliar to many readers, even those whose primary expertise lies in sexuality. Indeed, though some of our contributors come to early modern kink by way of expertise in sexuality studies, some have never before published on sexual topics. Ironically, the specificity of kink — over against the generality of something like "sexuality" writ large — is precisely what makes it so generative for such a wide array of scholars, since kink both opens its conceptual arms wide and also narrows our analyses down to what people want; what people do; and how, where, and with whom they do it in their daily lives. As the following essays bear out in great detail and with aplomb, this analytic-focusing also enlivens our investigations of literary representation and form. Early modern literature just looks different, in a variety of exciting ways, once you start thinking kink.

Relatedly, we also hope that this collection will offer kinky readers some historical and literary forebears. As scholars of queer and trans studies we have learned to be skeptical of the flattening effects of projects of historical recovery; at the same time, though, we understand the potential power of helping build entry points for identifications across time, what Valerie Traub once called "homo life support."[40] Building such entry points into the past can also create possibilities for connec-

39. Gayle Rubin, "Thinking Sex," 137.
40. Traub, *The Renaissance of Lesbianism,* 27.

tions in the present — both by bringing together a variety of scholars in this volume who might not otherwise have congregated and by helping future readers validate their own kinky thinking. In her account of feminist debates about lesbian BDSM in the 1970s, Rubin cogently lays out the necessity of actively creating sexual communities: "Most of us," she writes,

> are born into and raised by straight families, educated in straight schools, and socialized by straight peer groups. Our upbringing does not provide us with the social skills, information, or routes of access into unconventional sexual lifestyles. We must find our way into those social spaces where we can meet partners, find friends, get validation, and participate in a community life which does not presuppose that we are straight.[41]

Though somewhat rarefied, academic publications can often be a transformative site for providing this sort of validation and community. (Our continued citation of Rubin's work suggests as much: finding her writing early in our academic careers made it easier for us not only to *think* sex but also to be who we wanted to be.) We hope that this volume will be one such transformative site for some of our readers.

Just as importantly, understanding early modern histories and representations of kink can also provide political ballasts for our current moment. In the United States, in particular, sexual freedoms have been curtailed sharply in recent years, from the vociferous debates about the exclusion of kink from Pride events to bans on drag performances to the devastating reversal of *Roe v. Wade*, which was announced just as we were finishing the first draft of this introduction. In delivering the majority opinion in *Dobbs v. Jackson Women's Health Organization*, Justice Alito, like many conservative justices before him, insisted that in order

---

41. Gayle Rubin, "The Leather Menace," chap. 4 in *Deviations: A Gayle Rubin Reader* (Durham, NC: Duke University Press, 2011), 109–136, at 129.

to claim that a right that is not explicitly enumerated in the text of the Constitution is nevertheless protected under the Due Process clause of the Fourteenth Amendment, such a right must be "deeply rooted in this Nation's history and tradition."[42] In other cases questioning a right to sexual privacy — notably the 1986 *Bowers v. Hardwick* decision upholding a Georgia sodomy law — justices have extended such a "history and tradition" test back further beyond "this Nation," looking especially to English common law for guidance.[43] As the contributors to *Queering the Renaissance* discussed thirty years ago, judicial rulings constraining sexual behavior are often based in such broad-scale historical generalizations about past sexual behavior ("it was ever thus").[44] While in these essays our contributors focus primarily on early modern England, it has long been acknowledged that the literary, cultural, social, and political environment of colonial America and the early republic was directly influenced by early modern England. One of the goals of this collection, therefore, is to provide an academically rigorous refutation of attempts to paint kink as a modern sexual aberration and thus one that might be policed by sweeping reference to the supposed sexual practices of the past. Just as abortion — its practices but also the communities formed by such practices — long predates the Constitution of the United States of America, so too do a wide variety of sexual practices and communities long predate — and thus produce — the formation of this country. We have been here. We are here. We will be here.

---

42. Dobbs v. Jackson Women's Health Organization, 597 U.S. ____ (2022): 5.
43. Though *Bowers v. Hardwick* was overturned by *Lawrence v. Texas* (2003), Justice Thomas's concurrence in *Dobbs* explicitly suggests that the reasoning of the majority *Dobbs* opinion undermines — appropriately, in his view — the *Lawrence* decision, as well as decisions guaranteeing equal rights to marriage (*Obergefell v. Hodges*, 2015) and contraception (*Griswold v. Connecticut*, 1965).
44. Jonathan Goldberg, ed. *Queering the Renaissance* (Durham, NC: Duke University Press, 1994).

PART 1
Revising Cultural Narratives

"Mishapen Stuffe": Pleasure and Restraint in Marlowe's *Hero and Leander*

James Yukiko Mulder

Recent critical conversations in early modern sexuality studies, trans studies, and new philology offer significant methodological shifts in how we read sexual language in the literature of the period.[1] In particular, these conversations are changing how we think of the construction of the physical, material body in early modern texts and, by extension, what sexual positions are available or legible in these texts. In what follows, I extend these overlapping conversations about early modern bodies and sexualities to a close reading of Christopher Marlowe's *Hero and Leander*, a poem in which sex is at once obvious and obscured; it is both surprisingly detailed and at the same time metaphorically and narratively perplexing. Using kink as an analytic for thinking the pleasures of the poem opens up new ways to understand its numerous scenes of clinging, locked arms, and immobilizing embraces. This chapter builds

---

1. See Jeffrey Masten, *Queer Philologies: Sex, Language, and Affect in Shakespeare's Time* (Philadelphia: University of Pennsylvania Press, 2016). See also Simone Chess, Colby Gordon, and Will Fisher, eds., "Early Modern Trans Studies," special issue, *Journal for Early Modern Cultural Studies* 19, no. 4 (2019).

on developing methodologies in queer philology that are attuned to the ways that queer sexual practices and positions are encoded at the level of language. A kinky methodology can enliven critical conversations about social hierarchy and sexual normativity in the early modern period, particularly around Marlowe, an author whose work has played such a significant role in the development of queer early modern studies. Marlowe holds a prominent place in the canon of early modern queerness both as a political figure and as a poet and playwright. Famously, accusations of sodomy and atheism were leveled at Marlowe near the time of his mysterious and violent death; as a result, the fragmentary historical record of Marlowe's life offers insights into the juridical contexts in which non-reproductive pleasures were collocated with other forms of social disorder. Further, sensual and tender relationships between men in his literary work are often thought to exemplify non-heterosexual imaginaries in the early modern period.

Marlowe's *Hero and Leander* is one such queer text. The poem retells the Greek myth of the ill-fated Hero and Leander, though it ends abruptly after the sexual consummation of their relationship, prior to the lovers' tragic deaths. *Hero and Leander* was first published in 1598 with an editorial dedication identifying it as an unfinished fragment, though whether or not Marlowe intended to extend it before his own untimely death is unknown. The bulk of the poem depicts Leander's repeatedly foiled pursuit of Hero, which notably includes a detour into the arms of an amorous Neptune, who mistakes Leander for Ganymede. Because the poem so insistently displaces the (hetero)sexual narrative at its heart, it is hardly surprising that there is no small amount of critical debate about how to read Hero and Leander's bodies and, furthermore, where, when, and how they experience pleasure. In the poem, Hero and Leander's inexperience with love and sex makes their interactions stilted, often funny, and rarely straightforward. Critics have variously read their sexual encounter(s) as comic failures, genuine acts of mutual pleasure, or violent scenes of trauma. Even as Hero and Leander finally fall into bed together, determining what happens sexually between them requires some amount of decoding: as Gordon Braden puts it, the "key actions are routed through similes."[2] For Braden, however, the similes' "import is clear enough"; that is, they lead "ultimately to the physical back and forth of genital copulation."[3] In contrast, Judith Haber finds that the poem frustrates and interrupts Hero and Leander's progression toward copulation, "effectively ... making nonsense" out of the "illusion of inevitability, naturalness, and unity" created by consummation-oriented sexual narratives.[4] These critics, though they offer significantly different conclusions about erotic pleasure and frustration in the poem, do nevertheless orient their readings of the sexual encounter(s) between Hero and Leander in relation to the goal of genital penetration. Like Haber, I am interested in the ways that the poem confounds conventional expectations regarding sex, but the kinky reading I propose in this chapter deprioritizes both penetration and genital contact in order to offer new understandings of which sexual acts register as such in the poem. This chapter's first section elaborates how and why the practices of BDSM and kink enable significant re-evaluation of where erotic pleasure is located in the poem and on the body.[5] Further, as I explore later in this chapter, kinking sex in *Hero and Leander* precipitates necessary questions about how the erotics of the poem operate alongside and through the language of racial difference.

---

2. Gordon Braden, "Hero and Leander in Bed (and the Morning After)," *English Literary Renaissance* 45, no. 2 (2015): 205–230, at 210, https://doi.org/10.1111/1475-6757.12046.
3. Braden, "Hero and Leander," 210, 216.
4. Judith Haber, *Desire and Dramatic Form in Early Modern England* (Cambridge, UK: Cambridge University Press, 2009), 47, 39.
5. James Bromley offers another illuminating close analysis of the poem's bodily surfaces and non-penetrative pleasures. See James Bromley, *Intimacy and Sexuality in the Age of Shakespeare* (Cambridge, UK: Cambridge University Press, 2013), 29–48.

Negotiating A Scene

One aspect of the poem that animates critical conversations around its erotics is what Georgia Brown terms a fetishistic relation to desire.[6] For Brown, "the epyllion puts all forms of desire ... in a context that is at odds with dominant social and cultural ideologies, largely because desire, in these poems, resists categorization and remains radically polymorphic."[7] The poem, Rachel Eisendrath argues, creates an erotic tableau laden with "a confetti of buskins, baubles, trinkets, and toys" and, further, extends its fetishistic gaze to the material bodies of its protagonists.[8] Indeed, Hero and Leander variously appear as though their flesh recalls pearlescent surfaces, the play of light as it is refracted by jewels, and the gleam of silver and gold in a dimly lit room. The rich "thingliness" of the poem,[9] for some critics, seems to displace the pleasures of the body in favor of using aestheticized objects as "sexual energy conductors and go-betweens."[10] There is something delightfully kinky about the "sparrowes ... of hollow pearle and gold" that perch on Hero's knee like decorative little automata and messengers of Hero's erotic appeal (33).[11] The logic of the fetish does not, however, capture the full breadth of the kinky potentialities in *Hero and Leander*. Here, I shift my focus from the aestheticization and objectification of the bodies in this poem to the affects and sensations that cling

6. Georgia Brown, *Redefining Elizabethan Literature* (Cambridge, UK: Cambridge University Press, 2004), 106.

7. Brown, *Redefining Elizabethan Literature*, 137.

8. Rachel Eisendrath, *Poetry in a World of Things: Aesthetics and Empiricism in Renaissance Ekphrasis* (Chicago: University of Chicago Press, 2018), 82.

9. Eisendrath, *Poetry in a World*, 83.

10. Eisendrath, *Poetry in a World*, 96.

11. Christopher Marlowe, *Hero and Leander*, in *English Sixteenth-Century Verse: An Anthology*, ed. Richard S. Sylvester (New York: W. W. Norton, 1984), 498–525. All references to *Hero and Leander* are from this edition and appear parenthetically in the text by line numbers. I am also indebted to a presentation by Sophia Richardson for the characterization of the sparrows as automata. Sophia Richardson, "Marlowe's Mirrors: Mimetic Surfaces in Hero and Leander," (paper presentation, Northeast Modern Language Association, Boston, March 7, 2020).

to and circulate between bodies. Amid the overflow of rough, gauzy, pliant, slippery textures, sweet scents, and soft sounds amplified against the stillness of night, *Hero and Leander* fairly bursts with sensory stimuli that demand a more capacious theory of kinky desire and pleasure.

Kink provides a flexible analytic framework for approaching questions of sexuality in the poem. A kinky approach to thinking sex demands that we think pleasure in terms of sensations, affects, and power; furthermore, kink insists on the way in which sex acts are embedded in discourse. Among the most well-known aspects of kink and BDSM is that they enable sexual partners to "play" with power by staging scenes of dominance and submission through roleplay, physical restraints, pain play, impact play, and myriad other practices. Due in part to the common use of the terms *top/bottom* and *Dom/sub* within BDSM and kink communities, it is unsurprising that kinky sex is often thought to work through codifying or exaggerating the same active/passive power differential that organizes (hetero)normative vanilla sex. However, kink, as scholars like Ariane Cruz point out, embodies the critique of how differential relations of power are experienced in a sexual scene. Cruz argues that BDSM's "rituals of domination and subordination reveal such positions as not necessarily unstable but rather as unnatural, socially constructed, continually (re)produced, and hence possibly deconstructed and reconstructed."[12] I propose, further, that theorizing kink requires thinking sex radically otherwise than in the binarizing terms of power, domination, and subordination. My hope is that the conceptual framework of kink, broadly speaking, has the analytic potential to complicate the frameworks of active/passive and subject/object that structure the discourse of sexual positionality.

Kink provides innumerable scenes in which sexual positions do not map neatly onto binaristic conceptualizations of power. In BDSM, a fre-

---

12. Ariane Cruz, *The Color of Kink: Black Women, BDSM, and Pornography* (New York: New York University Press, 2016), 37.

quently cited dictum is that the bottom or sub is the one who "has the power," despite their position of submission to the stimuli provided by the top or Dom. In practice, this principle takes many different forms, but generally the idea is that the top or Dom's job is to pay attention to, repeatedly ask for, read carefully, and/or follow the bottom or sub's physical and vocal cues; in short, the top is responsible for understanding what the bottom needs or wants. Another related principle holds that the bottom gives control over to the top but only within the parameters determined by the bottom. Methods for determining how these scenes take shape are creative and varied. These may be linguistic (as when one uses the words *red*, *yellow*, and *green* to adjust the intensity of a given act); embodied (as when one taps a partner's body or manipulates an object to communicate); or a combination of both (as when a Dom gives a conditional command to laugh, moan, move, or remain still if one wants more of a specific sensation).

I adumbrate these practices to emphasize that kinky sexual practices are not delimited by a catalog of discrete bodily acts; rather, kinky sex relies on multiple layered practices of communication about and attunement to the shifting parameters of a sexual encounter. Two people may get off on spanking, for instance, but perhaps one enjoys it as tender foreplay, while another prefers it to be framed as an act of discipline for a transgression of some kind. The sheer volume of strategies for communicating levels of interest in specific activities beforehand as well as calibrating tonal shifts within a scene is immense. In such a context, there are multiple answers to the question of who is in the position of power and, furthermore, who directs whose behavior, pleasure, and bodily position. Indeed, though kink involves the pleasures of playing with power, imagining kink to be defined by the mere repetition or re-citation of *top* and *bottom* rather misses the point. Furthermore, a kink scene may indeed be negotiated using a list or catalog of acts that all parties agree upon, but enumerating the acts as such does not mark the end of the conversation. As scholars like Jonathan Goldberg and Valerie Traub point out, acts of sex are as determined by linguistic, social, and juridical pressures as they are by any given physical act as such.[13] Traub's *Thinking Sex with the Early Moderns* identifies a tendency among scholars to make sense of vagueness and indeterminacy in early modern literary representations of sex by "attempting to *fill in the blanks* ... to pass or paper over — or attempt to pin down — what is enigmatic or inconclusive."[14] Taxonomizing sex in this way attempts to define sex as such — to account for, as Lee Edelman puts it, "the problem of defining an encounter — of determining whether or not it takes place and of knowing precisely in what it consists."[15] Kink, I argue, gives us tools for thinking sex otherwise by placing us in what Eve Kosofsky Sedgwick describes as the "irreducibly phenomenological" register of sensation, texture, and affect.[16]

How might a kinky reading practice shift, warp, or stretch what we think is happening in *Hero and Leander*'s scenes of sex? Restraint, capture, pulling, and grasping are particular acts that seem salient to a kinky reading of the poem. John Leonard describes Leander's pursuit of Hero as "militaristic," noting that that while "conceits likening love to a siege were commonplace[,] ... Marlowe employs the conceit in an unusual way .... Leander uses real force."[17] Rather than besieging Hero with his rhetoric, Leander's approach takes the form of physical binding or holding. This is true not only of Leander but of Mercury too. In a brief digres-

---

13. See Jonathan Goldberg, *Sodometries: Renaissance Texts, Modern Sexualities* (Stanford: Stanford University Press, 1992); and Valerie Traub, *Thinking Sex with the Early Moderns* (Philadelphia: University of Pennsylvania Press, 2016).
14. Traub, *Thinking Sex*, 211–12, italics in original.
15. Lauren Berlant and Lee Edelman, *Sex, or the Unbearable* (Durham: Duke University Press, 2014), 74.
16. Eve Kosofsky Sedgwick, *Touching Feeling: Affect, Pedagogy, Performativity* (Durham: Duke University Press, 2003), 21.
17. John Leonard, "Marlowe's Doric Music: Lust and Aggression in *Hero and Leander*," *English Literary Renaissance* 30, no. 1 (2000): 55–76, at 62, https://doi.org/10.1111/j.1475-6757. 2000.tb01164.x.

sion from the central narrative of Hero and Leander, Mercury is said to have been so "enamoured" with a woman that he

> Did charme her nimble feet, and made her stay,
> The while upon a hillocke downe he lay
> And sweetly on his pipe began to play,
> And with smooth speech, her fancie to assay,
> Till in his twining armes he lockt her fast[.]
> (399–403)

Elsewhere, images of restraint recur in Hero and Leander's encounters: we see them

> like *Mars* and *Ericine* displayd
> Both in each others armes chaind as they layd.
> (789–90)

We also see Leander "cling" to Hero (798), "inclos[e] her in his armes" (776), and use "his hands … upon her like a snare" (743). In one image, Leander,

> like Thebian *Hercules*,
> Entred the orchard of *Th'esperides*,
> Whose fruit none rightly can describe, but hee
> That puls or shakes it from the golden tree.
> (769–72)

This last image is generally seen as metaphorizing the couple's much-anticipated moment of consummation, the moment in which Hero and Leander finally lose their respective virginities and experience the pleasure of penetrative sex for the first time.

Such a reading, of course, rests on the use of the verb *enter* to signify genital penetration. The other verbs in the passage are easily overshadowed by the prominence of the penetrative *enter*. For readings that treat this scene as an obvious reference to Leander's penis entering Hero's vagina, *pull* and *shake* are thought merely to extend the central metaphor and to elaborate on the act of vaginal penetration. Leonard, for example, indicates that "it matters whether Leander 'puls or shakes' Hero's fruit ... Had the narrator simply likened Leander to one who 'puls' fruit from a tree, there would be no awkward question about consent."[18] In other words, for Leonard, *enter* describes the bodily act itself, while *pull* and *shake* operate at a further remove from the literal: they offer two potentially conflicting metaphors to depict *how* Leander enters Hero. On this point, we might recall Traub's work on the "constitutive role of vagueness, imprecision, and illegibility" in early modern sexual language.[19] Traub focuses on "those moments *when words fail*. Not fail to be erotic ... but fail in their *indexical function* to denote the gender of particular bodies, the specificity of particular body parts, and the actual uses to which those parts are put."[20] At the level of language, I propose, there is no necessary reason that *pull* and *shake* should be understood as any less material to the question of what kind of sex act Leander and Hero are engaged in. Though there may be a seemingly obvious bodily referent of *enter*, I would argue that there are equally clear ways in which Leander could pull and shake Hero's body, though these acts may or may not be primarily genital. I do not mean to deny the plausibility of a penetrative reading, but I do want to register the overpowering gravitational pull that the act of penetration exerts upon our sexual vocabularies. I think it worth noting how easily and thoroughly a penetrative verb overwrites the extent

18. Leonard, "Marlowe's Doric Music," 69. Leonard elaborates to suggest that "'shakes' implies violence as well as clumsiness" (69). Though my reading pursues another line of thinking here, I do think it is worth noting that *pulling* fruit from the tree seems to read as a less violent and more consensual act of sex than *shaking*, as this may open up more conversations about how critics historically think of which sexual metaphors register normal, normative, and/or nonviolent sexual acts.
19. Traub, *Thinking Sex*, 176.
20. Traub, *Thinking Sex*, 176–77, italics in original.

to which the other verbs in the lines might register as forms of sexual contact in their own right — particularly since physical restraints play such a significant part in erotic scenes throughout the poem.

In fact, the location of the penetrative act within the scene has drawn the focus of critics and editors dating from the early nineteenth century; most modern texts actually print the lines in a different sequence than they appear in the poem's original 1598 printing. Arguments for re-ordering the scene rest on a few key actions that are thought to be unnecessarily confusing in the original sequence,[21] though, as Haber points out, the feeling of confusion arises precisely because the original sequence of lines interrupts a sense of "linear progress to consumma-tion."[22] Put differently, the emended lines resolve physical, affective, and even grammatical elements of the scene that remain illegible or non-sensical until they are reoriented toward a central act of penetration. I want to revisit the sequence of these lines, then, within the context of the affective complexity of kink.

The scene begins as Leander appears in Hero's bedroom, which star-tles her. Hero, "seeking refuge" (728), flees from him and barricades her-self in bed:

> And as her silver body downeward went,
> With both her hands she made the bed a tent,
> And in her owne mind thought her selfe secure,
> O'recast with dim and darksome coverture.
> (747–50)

She "defend[s] the fort" of bedclothes as Leander strives "in vaine, / Till gentle parlie [does] the truce obtaine" (756, 761–62). This truce is grounds for some critical uncertainty, as critics and editors struggle to

---

21. For a detailed account of the history of editorial emendations of *Hero and Leander*, see Braden, "Hero and Leander," 209–13.
22. Haber, *Desire and Dramatic Form*, 47.

make sense of its relation to what happens next. In the original printing, Hero is then said "cunningly to yeeld her selfe" (766), after which we see Leander pull and shake the fruit of the garden of the Hesperides, which I discuss above. Following this,

> Leander on her quivering brest,
> Breathlesse spoke some thing, and sigh'd out the rest;
> Which so prevail'd, as he with small ado,
> Inclos'd her in his armes and kist her to.
> And everie kisse to her was as a charme,
> And to *Leander* as a fresh alarme.
> So that the truce was broke, and she alas,
> (Poor sillie maiden) at his mercie was.
> (773–80)

In this sequence of events, Braden explains, the truce "lasts for 17 lines and astonishingly covers the triumphant penetration" described in the garden of the Hesperides.[23] Emended texts therefore restructure the scene so that the breaking of the truce leads directly to Leander's entry into the garden. This is thought to clarify its role in the scene. Yet if we decouple the truce from the question of who does or does not get to penetrate whom, the truce instead modulates the affective tone of the encounter. The lovers wrestle on opposite sides of the *tent* of bedding until *gentle parlie* gives way to *breathlesse* moments in which Leander lies whispering on Hero's breast. Kissing heightens the affect of the scene again; the truce is broken and a more forceful or combative form of contact ensues. Hero and Leander physically embody familiar rhetorical conceits that figure love as a siege; their roleplay includes a brief respite within the context of a larger scene of retreat and capture.

---

23. Braden, "Hero and Leander," 219.

To the further perplexity of critics and editors, the 1598 text concludes the scene with a half-finished simile. The poem narrates,

Love is not full of pittie (as men say)
But deaffe and cruell, where he means to pray.
Even as a bird, which in our hands we wring,
Foorth plungeth, and oft flutters with her wing.
And now she wisht this night were never done[.]
(781–85)

The grammatically unfinished comparison to a bird straining against a wringing hand implies that Hero has been overpowered, though in the line that follows, Hero expresses enjoyment; she does not want the night to end. There is both a grammatical and a temporal suspension in these lines that cannot be sutured to a single bodily act; I would argue rather that the 1598 text offers snaring, circling, pulling, shaking, wrestling, quivering, wringing, and fluttering among the multiple "pleasure[s] of this blessed night" (788).

In the spirit of BDSM, of course, we must acknowledge that Hero does not at any point depicted in the poem engage in a clear and consensual negotiation of the scene prior to being ensnared, held, tangled up, captured, and perhaps even wrung. I am reading here in the vein of speculative philology, a term I am borrowing from Marjorie Rubright,[24] to track how the text might open up alternate, kinky ways to read Hero's pleasure and the bodily sensations of restraint. Such a project aims to articulate new sexual potentialities within the text while acknowledging the ways in which, seen from another angle, Leander's use of physical force can buttress dominant and often violent gendered scripts regarding consent. I do not want to diminish the genuine discomfort we might rea-

24. See Marjorie Rubright, "Transgender Capacity in Thomas Dekker and Thomas Middleton's *The Roaring Girl* (1611)," *Journal for Early Modern Cultural Studies* 19, no. 4 (2019): 45–74, at 50, https://doi:10.1353/jem.2019.0037.

sonably feel at reading scenes of Hero's capture as pleasurable because indeed she cannot offer us a fully realized scene of negotiation regarding the specific kinds of bondage and consent play she might be interested in experiencing in a sexual scene. A kinky reading of the poem, however, makes space for the pleasure of restraint and provides apertures through which we can glimpse new sensations, inconsistencies, and illegibilities in the poem's erotic scenes. Rather than orienting us toward, to borrow a phrase from Braden, "a sequence both physically and psychologically intelligible,"[25] a kinky reading practice attunes us to the potentiality of the unintelligible.

The Pleasures of Formlessness

In this section, I consider how the poem's figurations of bodily malleability kink differential relations of power between desiring subject and desired object. The poem's figures of form and formlessness, I argue, reveal how the poem's erotic scenes complicate and confound binaristic sexual positions like active/passive, masculine/feminine, and top/bottom.[26] At the same time, I want to emphasize here that kink is an analytical framework that rewards and invites consideration of its own limitations. Even as a kinky reading unfolds a multiplicity of sensations and acts that produce the capacious pleasures of the poem, such a reading also provides important and necessary opportunities to grapple with how this poem's construction of desire is imbricated with constructions of whiteness that delimit its pleasures in specific racialized ways.

Prior to the climactic scene of sex, the bulk of the text is devoted to tracing a circuitous and comedic narrative path as Leander strives, often clumsily, to persuade Hero to abandon chastity. Meanwhile, Hero strives, also clumsily, sometimes to rebuff and sometimes to encourage

---

25. Braden, "Hero and Leander," 220.
26. Masten's philological analysis of amorous activity and passivity in the poem offers further insights; see Masten, *Queer Philologies*, 156–59.

his advances. Leander is "like to a bold sharpe Sophister" as he begins his pursuit (197), mounting an elaborate argument against virginity. He reasons,

> Base boullion for the stampes sake we allow,
> Even so for mens impression do we you.
> By which alone, our reverend fathers say,
> Women receave perfection everie way.
> This idoll which you terme *Virginitie*,
> Is neither essence subject to the eie,
> No, nor to any one exterior sence,
> Nor hath it any place of residence,
> Nor is't of earth or mold celestiall,
> Or capable of any forme at all.
> (265–74)

Virginity, Leander proposes, is formless. It lacks substance and cannot be perceived by *any one exterior sence*. Hero herself is metaphorized as *base* material in need of the *perfection* or completion that requires the *impression* of a man. Robert F. Darcy connects this passage to the poem's themes of reading: he argues that

> the metaphor also draws a relationship between the process of making something readable by means of a stamp or a printing press and the exertion of ideological influence and control over another person. Leander lets Hero know that his process of amorously reading her body has the capacity to alter her or to bind her through the "impression" that reading enacts.[27]

---

27. Robert F. Darcy, "'Under my hands ... a double duty': Printing and Pressing Marlowe's *Hero and Leander," Journal for Early Modern Cultural Studies* 2, no. 2 (2002): 26–56, at 33, https://doi.org/10.1353/jem.2002.0015.

In other words, Leander attempts to inscribe heteronormative scripts of desire onto Hero's body in order to give it a legible form. By the poem's end, as I argue above, Leander and Hero will go on to enjoy the polymorphic pleasures of playing with power, but at this early point in the narrative, Leander voices a resolutely binaristic understanding of desire, power, and sex.

Despite his stated desires for Hero to allow him to reshape her, Leander is also subject to the shaping influence of being desired. When Leander is first introduced, the poem offers the following description of his body:

Even as delicious meat is to the tast,
So was his necke in touching, and surpast
The white of *Pelops* shoulder, I could tell ye,
How smooth his brest was, & how white his bellie,
And whose immortall fingars did imprint,
That heavenly path, with many a curious dint,
That runs along his backe, but my rude pen,
Can hardly blazon foorth the loves of men.
Much lesse of powerfull gods[.]
(63–71)

The poet admits that his *rude pen* can only fail to capture Leander's beauty. Instead of visual detail, then, the poem offers a tactile account of that body. The passage equates touching Leander with tasting him; it then extends the metaphor of consuming his flesh as Leander's surpassing beauty is expressed with reference to Pelops, whose shoulder was mistakenly consumed by Demeter and replaced with a piece of ivory. This metaphor, followed by the image of *immortall fingars* molding the surface of his back, suggests that touching and taking pleasure in Leander's body have a material effect on the shape of that body.

The evident homoeroticism in this poem — first in this passage, where the poem lingers on the taste of Leander's flesh, and then in a later scene, when Neptune attempts to seduce Leander while he swims across the Hellespont — is frequently linked to a transposition of gender. For Sujata Iyengar, the description of Leander as "ready for consumption … reverses the expected association of femininity with matter and impressionability and masculinity with the imposition of firm form."[28] Abdulhamit Arvas argues that Leander is not characterized as a man but rather as "a boy whose body is in a fluid, in-between phase and space between the man and woman."[29] The role played by gender reversal and/or gender fluidity in establishing Leander's desirability is explicit: he is said to be so beautiful that

> [s]ome swore he was a maid in mans attire,
> For in his lookes were all that men desire.
> (83–84)

Being the object of desire, for Leander, is therefore firmly associated with the rumored perception of him as a *maid in mans attire*. This is evident when Neptune plies him with kisses and "gawdie toies" (671) as Leander protests, "You are deceav'd, I am no woman I" (676). For his part, Neptune seems to be fully aware that Leander is not a woman since Neptune responds with a parable about a dalliance between a shepherd and a

> boy so faire and kind,
> As for his love, both earth and heaven pyn'd.
> (679–80)

28. Sujata Iyengar, *Shades of Difference: Mythologies of Skin Color in Early Modern England* (Philadelphia: University of Pennsylvania Press, 2004), 112.

29. Abdulhamit Arvas, "Leander in the Ottoman Mediterranean: The Homoerotics of Abduction in the Global Renaissance," *English Literary Renaissance* 51, no. 1 (2020): 31–62, at 59, https://doi.org/10.1086/711601. For more on early modern eroticization of boys, see also Bruce Smith, *Homosexual Desire in Shakespeare's England: A Cultural Poetics* (Chicago: University of Chicago Press, 1991), 136.

Even so, Leander's refusal focuses on correcting what he assumes to be a misreading of his gender. The fact that Leander experiences the desire of others as imposing a gender upon him reflects his embeddedness in the discourse of receptive femininity and desiring masculinity, though it also puts him in what we might think of as a trans position with regard to that discourse: Leander, though his *attire* and self-presentation is that of a man, feels he is nevertheless interpellated as a *maid* by virtue of being desired by men.

Leander's desire to make an impression on Hero recurs when he complains:

> I would my rude words had the influence,
> To lead thy thoughts, as thy faire lookes doe mine,
> Then shouldst thou bee his prisoner who is thine.
> Be not unkind and faire, mishapen stuffe
> Are of behaviour boisterous and ruffe.
> (200–204)

In other words, though Hero's fair appearance *seems* to invite his desire, she nevertheless resists the *shaping* influence of his desire. Despite Leander's efforts to impress or influence Hero, she remains stubbornly *mishapen*. Here, again, Hero's body and her virginity frustrate Leander's desire to press them into the form he wants. At the center of this disagreement is what Leander calls the "faire jem" of Hero's virginity (247), a phrase that echoes his description of Hero's *faire lookes*. The repetition drives home an association between the desirability of fair complexion and a sort of unformed materiality, as when Leander's white back invites us to imagine the *imprint* of *immortall fingars*. The figuration of both Hero's and Leander's bodies as impressionable, malleable white material thus becomes a significant piece of the poem's erotic landscape. Recall that in the blazon, Leander's body is said to "surpas[s] / The white of *Pelops* shoulder." The figurative mutability of whiteness thus defines

Leander's desirability and his availability for consumption. At the same time, Leander's whiteness is likened to Pelops's shoulder, which is attached to Pelops's body only after it is eaten. Whiteness is at once the condition of desire in the first place and, paradoxically, a transplanted property that renders whole the body that is (mis)shaped by desire.[30]

The poem's construction of whiteness also inscribes a bodily language of blushing onto Hero and Leander's skin. Iyengar, in an attentive analysis of the poem's metaphors of color, argues that the poem constructs "red and white beauty in opposition to the mysterious, inchoate darkness of black skin or clothes,"[31] as when Hero flees "into the darke her selfe to hide" only to find that Leander is "rather drawne, / By those white limmes, which sparckled through the lawne" (723–26). In early modern English bodily discourse, the ability to blush was thought to be a capacity solely of the light-skinned and, furthermore, a bodily sign that was distinctly English.[32] For Iyengar, the poem elaborates an "erotic comedy of hermeneutics" in which Hero and Leander's blushing "reveals that the language of passion is uncalculated and corporeal" even as reading the body also produces the literary possibility of (mis)interpretation.[33] Blushing, in short, marks places where the body holds meaning, even and especially as the bodily sign produced by the blush is also a site of hermeneutic "collapse."[34] Importantly, this system of bodily signs relies on the imagined mutability of the white body, in contrast to what Patricia Akhimie describes as the "seeming immutability of meaning"

30. In an analysis of whiteness as melancholia, Arthur L. Little Jr. observes that "whiteness always already signals a failure of those who construct themselves around and through an ideology of whiteness to ever truly become ontologically so." See Arthur L. Little Jr., "Re-Historicizing Race, White Melancholia, and the Shakespearean Property," *Shakespeare Quarterly* 67, no. 1 (2016): 84–103, at 92, https://doi:10.1353/shq.2016.0018.
31. Iyengar, *Shades of Difference*, 108–9.
32. Iyengar, *Shades of Difference*, 107.
33. Iyengar, *Shades of Difference*, 112, 113.
34. Iyengar, *Shades of Difference*, 108.

attached to blackness in the period.[35] Whiteness, in other words, becomes the unmarked property of the body that means — the body that is figured as the basis of literary production. As Brown puts it, "Hero and Leander, in their total desirability, are both the motivation for discourse, the reason for writing and speaking in the poem, and the product of that discourse. They represent the desire aroused by language, and the desired object fashioned by language. As such, they are synecdoches for literature as a whole."[36] The capacity for literariness, then, is not only incidentally metaphorized by whiteness; rather, whiteness appears to be the condition of literary meaning.

As the night of Hero and Leander's climactic sexual encounter proceeds toward dawn, the poem presents another scene of restraint and foiled escape. Hero is spurred to leave the bed because

she [knows] not how to frame her looke,
Or speake to him who in a moment tooke,
That which so long so charily she kept.
(791–93)

In other words, she does not know what form to adopt in the aftermath of their first physical encounter. Hero's feeling of formlessness counterbalances Leander's previously stated desire that sex will impose a legible form onto her body. Further, as she attempts to flee, a mishap misshapes her in a rather literal way. The poem narrates,

And faine by stealth away she would have crept,
And to some corner secretly have gone,
Leaving *Leander* in the bed alone.
But as her naked feet were whipping out,

---

35. Patricia Akhimie, *Shakespeare and the Cultivation of Difference: Race and Conduct in the Early Modern World* (New York: Routledge, 2018), 32.
36. Brown, *Redefining Elizabethan Culture,* 140.

He on the suddaine cling'd her so about,
That Meremaid-like unto the floore she slid,
One halfe appear'd, the other halfe was hid.
Thus neere the bed she blushing stood upright,
And from her countenance behold ye might,
A kind of twilight breake, which through the heare,
As from an orient cloud, glymse here and there.
(794–804)

Long-standing critical consensus holds that Hero's blush suffuses the scene with shame or dread that she feels in response to the loss of her virginity.[37] This particular bodily detail draws so much critical attention, in fact, that the blush is largely treated as *the* prevailing sign of what Hero is feeling. I would argue, however, that from the perspective of a kinky reading, Hero's bodily disorganization, rather than the visual sign of the blush alone, gives a more capacious answer to the question of how the sexual encounter affects Hero's body. After Leander's sudden attempt to take hold of her, Hero is rendered *Meremaid-like*, half-exposed in the mess of bedclothes and limbs as she slides to the floor. Rather than *receav[ing] perfection* from her sexual experience with Leander, the form of Hero's body is muddled, at least temporarily impossible to discern. Her face, too, is partially hidden by her hair, which permits Leander only to see her expression *here and there*. Faced with this incomplete glimpse of Hero's body, Leander takes "more pleasure … [t]han *Dis*, on heapes of gold fixing his looke" (809–10). The literal and figurative confusion of the scene opens onto pleasure as Leander once again likens Hero to valuable gold. In this instance, however, her shape is decidedly uncertain, a marked departure from the erotic relation in which Leander once imagined impressing a legible form onto her.

37. One exception to this consensus is Braden, who suggests that the blush indicates Hero's renewed desire for Leander. See Braden, "Hero and Leander," 227–28.

The enduring critical focus on the affective meaning of Hero's blush is symptomatic of an interpretive framework in which the changeability of skin color is conflated with the capacity of the body to mean and, furthermore, in which the act of penetration defines the affective and erotic contours of a sexual encounter. If, however, we consider the capacity of Hero's body to hold erotic meaning otherwise, the scene is replete with other tactile intimations of pleasure: the exposure of her feet whipping through the air, the pressure of Leander's clinging grip, the slithering movement of her body to the floor, the slippery yet restraining tangle of fabric. It is replete, in other words, with kinky sensations, which enliven the scene with erotic potentialities beyond the violently racializing discourse that centers the blush as sign.

I have argued that a kinky reading practice enables us to appreciate more capacious erotic vocabularies in *Hero and Leander*. By focusing on sensation and affect, I aim to bring forward the ways in which a penetrative paradigm exerts a gravitational pull within scholarship on sex in the poem, orienting our readings by conferring a sense of necessary and natural directionality on Hero and Leander's roundabout erotic trajectory; but heteronormative penetration is not, of course, the only structuring force at work in the erotics of this poem. As Evelynn Hammonds points out, the *black hole* of racialized bodies and desires constitutively excluded from the scene of sex shapes the scene of sex through its visible absence.[38] The penetrative paradigm for thinking sex is inseparable from an ideological matrix in which whiteness indexes the capacity for being touched and shaped by erotic and literary desire. If Hero and Leander blur, straddle, or confound the active/passive binaries that organize desire, their mobility within those organizing paradigms is neverthe-

---

38. Evelynn Hammonds, "Black (W)holes and the Geometry of Black Female Sexuality," *differences* 6, no. 2–3 (1994): 126–45, at 139, https://doi.org/10.1215/10407391-6-2-3-126. See also Cruz, *Color of Kink*, 13.

less inextricable from the construction of their bodies as white.[39] To the extent that a kinky reading enables us to trace the contours of non-penetrative scenes of pleasure, it must also demand that we confront the ways in which the very discourse of erotic pleasure can rest upon the violent discourse of skin color, racial difference, and bodily meaning. I want to resist, therefore, along with Margot Weiss, constructing "a formal dichotomy between transgression and reification of social hierarchies."[40] Centering the pleasures of nonpenetrative sexual acts and nonnormative forms of embodiment animates complex and even politically urgent conversations, but pleasure, even kinky pleasure, is not unproblematically liberatory. As we theorize the kinky pleasures of *Hero and Leander*, it is crucial to track how race structures the discourse of sex in the poem — and, further, to track how a "semiotically charged interpretation of bodiliness,"[41] to borrow Ayanna Thompson's phrase, becomes folded into the implicitly and explicitly racialized epistemological frameworks available for thinking sex in early modern studies.

---

39. On the racializing historiography of gender nonconformity, see also C. Riley Snorton, *Black on Both Sides: A Racial History of Trans Identity* (Minneapolis: University of Minnesota Press, 2017).
40. Margot Weiss, *Techniques of Pleasure: BDSM and the Circuits of Sexuality* (Durham: Duke University Press, 2011), 24.
41. Ayanna Thompson, *Performing Race and Torture on the Early Modern Stage* (New York: Routledge, 2008), 4.

Cuckold Communities in the Kinky Early Modern

Erika Lyn Carbonara

> And if you like, you can sit in the corner of the
> room and watch. Make yourself comfortable and
> enjoy the show. After all, this is what you wanted.
> You orchestrated it, in fact.
>
> — Dennis DiClaudio, *The Deviant's Pocket Guide to Outlandish Sexual*
> *Desires Barely Contained in Your Subconscious*

What is left to say about the early modern cuckold, a figure so often discussed so as to seem commonplace?[1] As perhaps the best-known kinky figure of the Renaissance, cuckolds have typically been discussed in terms of what they might reveal about normative gender roles and heterosexuality, with scholars generally arguing that early modern cuckoldry primarily functions in literary texts as a representation of the fears of familial legitimacy and feminine duplicity. That is to say, the study

---

1. The *Oxford English Dictionary* (*OED*) *Online* defines *cuckold* as "a man whose wife or partner is sexually unfaithful, and who is typically regarded as an object of derision" (s.v. "cuckold, [*n.1*]," 1.a). A further definition suggests that the practice of cuckoldry may be pleasurable instead of demoralizing (s.v. "cuckold, [*n. 1*]," 1.b), though the *OED Online* situates this definition in the late 1900s.

of early modern cuckolds has thus far largely been the study of norms that are illuminated and more clearly defined through the exception to them.[2] But what if cuckolds are to be understood as engaging in a kink that brings them pleasure? Furthermore, what if we were to understand cuckolds not as passive onlookers to their wife's sexual wiles but as agential participants acting of their own desires? By reading cuckolds and their communities through the framework of kink, I hope not only to open up new modes of thinking about early modern cuckoldry but also to provide insight into and for contemporary kinksters.

Key to my analyses of early modern cuckoldry are repeated representations of *communities* of consenting "contented cuckolds." Although critical interrogation into the role of community in current kink circles has only just gained traction within the last decade, community has a long-standing place within contemporary kink. As the theorist Staci Newmahr has argued, community is often about much more than having similar interests; it also "represents shared histories of living on the margins."[3] To explore these shared histories as a form of community, I turn to depictions of early modern kink, in particular, the practice of cuckoldry. In this chapter, I examine depictions of cuckoldry within one early modern pamphlet and three early modern ballads to argue that many early modern cuckolds are portrayed not as unknowing or reluctant victims of infidelity but as willing participants in kinky relationships.[4]

2. See Anne Parten's 1985 article, "Falstaff's Horns: Masculine Inadequacy and Feminine Mirth in *The Merry Wives of Windsor*," in which she presents a (now) traditional argument about the function of public shame as a response to cuckoldry, as she argues that "the way in which the community treats the representative of masculine ineffectuality is prescribed by tradition" (198). Anne Parten, "Falstaff's Horns: Masculine Inadequacy and Feminine Mirth in *The Merry Wives of Windsor*," *Studies in Philology* 82, no. 2 (1985): 184–99, https://www.jstor.org/stable/4174203.

3. Staci Newmahr, *Playing on the Edge: Sadomasochism, Risk, and Intimacy* (Bloomington: Indiana University Press, 2011), 38.

4. See Sandra Clark's 2002 article, "The Economics of Marriage in the Broadside Ballad," for more on the communal nature inherent in the genre of ballads; Clark argues that audience involvement in the performance of the ballad "enhanced its potential as a medium for the

Understanding these scenarios through a kinky epistemology allows us to see the subversive pleasure found within these relationships, not only for the partners engaged in sexual activity, but also for the cuckold himself.[5] Using evidence from these four popular print ephemera about cuckolds, I argue that the key to viewing these cuckold relationships as consensual, positive relationships is the cuckold's inclusion within a wider community of cuckolds. My interrogation into these depictions of community encourages us to move beyond understanding cuckoldry solely as a shameful act committed against the cuckold by allowing us to read these acts of cuckoldry for what I argue they really are: premodern representations of the kink of cuckoldry.

Cuckoldry is such a common practice mentioned in the study of sexual history partially because we recognize it as analogous to a concept and practice that still occurs today. Furthermore, early modern representations of cuckoldry are so pervasively interrogated because of the sheer number of these representations. Early modern representations of cuckoldry, and especially of the seemingly paradoxical "contented cuckold," are reminiscent of contemporary kink relationships in which the practice of cuckoldry is negotiated and consensual, a relationship in which a woman has sex with a man other than her husband, and the husband is a willing and eager participant, who is oftentimes watching his wife's sexual antics firsthand.[6] (It is imperative to note that cuckoldry is not

expression of communal sentiment" (119). Sandra Clark, "The Economics of Marriage in the Broadside Ballad," *Journal of Popular Culture* 36, no. 1 (2002): 119–33, https://doi.org/10.1111/1540-5931.00034.

5. Although it is outside the scope of my argument, I believe there is an important distinction to be made between early modern cuckoldry and early displays of polyamory within some early modern relationships that have been previously coded as cuckoldry. However, I assert that the materials I focus on here depict true cuckoldry and are not an early form of polyamory, though these nuances warrant further critical interrogation.

6. Cuckoldry is traditionally viewed as a heterosexual experience, particularly because the complicated gender norms that are subverted through these sexual acts are deeply intertwined with the power dynamics at play. This is particularly complex in contemporary

typically a kink that is practiced by unmarried couples, particularly in the early modern period, as the subversion of the marriage vows and, more importantly, the desire for legitimate offspring necessitates marriage.) Although the male partner consents to this relationship and the subsequent humiliation and degradation that often coincide with cuckoldry, he ultimately has his desires relegated to his partner's, in that the woman's sexual pleasure is paramount. What makes this encounter kinky is the acknowledgment that, while the male partner seeks the humiliation of knowing his wife is sleeping with other men, the humiliation itself becomes essential to his own sexual and emotional gratification.

It is therefore crucial to highlight the distinction between a kinky cuckold relationship in which all partners have actively consented to participate and a relationship or sexual act that is secretive or harmful, in which the male partner is unaware of his partner's extra-sexual liaisons. Understood through a kinky framework, cuckoldry becomes an act in which the cuckold eagerly anticipates the harm or derision he might receive for his nonnormative position in the sexual hierarchy. Additionally, in contemporary kink cultures and relationships, the cuckold's humiliation is often public, and it is not a secretive venture.[7] In many ways, this humiliation is reminiscent of the very public skimmingtons of the early modern period. Skimmingtons were a form of public shame, in which a local community would gather for the procession of a cuckold (or other criticized or stigmatized figure) through the town's center while his neighbors would jeer at his nonnormative marital arrangement. What differentiates these forms of humiliation is that the humili-

---

cuckold relationships in which the cuckold is often instructed to orally stimulate his wife's partner or to clean up the ejaculate of his wife's partner.

7. It is important to note that most BDSM and kink circles consider it imperative that voyeurs consent to any sexual viewing, so this is not something that would be shared with those outside of a closed and consenting community, though typically acts that are not coded as explicitly or culturally sexual can be witnessed by those outside of the community.

ation and shaming are pre-negotiated and controlled within the context of the relationship.

As I have established, cuckoldry (whether early modern or contemporary) traditionally carries a strong negative stigma. This narrow understanding of early modern cuckoldry has caused critical stagnation regarding the early modern cuckold, as Kellye Corcoran points out: "Familiarity has bred an uncritical view of the attitudes toward cuckoldry — it is all too easy to dismiss the concept as a homogeneous cultural concept."[8] This "uncritical view" has left many potential interpretations of early modern cuckoldry unexamined, and, as I aim to demonstrate, is not an accurate portrayal of the heterogeneity of early modern cuckold depictions. For example, Thomas Middleton's city comedy *A Chaste Maid in Cheapside* (c. 1613) is a common focal point for scholars interested in portrayals of cuckoldry because of its overt display of queer and nonnormative relationships, including cuckoldry. Although the play focuses on the relationships between four couples, the relationship between the Allwits (a married couple participating in a cuckold relationship) and Sir Walter Whorehound (Mrs. Allwit's lover) is what draws early modern scholars of cuckoldry to the drama. Although this consensual relationship *does* fit the parameters of cuckoldry, Allwit's pleasure in his wife's dalliances is defined solely by the financial support that Sir Walter provides his family, and by the end of the play, the relationship between the Allwits and Sir Walter dissolves as Sir Walter's reputation degrades. Allwit is a prime example of a *wittol*, a husband who is aware of and condones his wife's extramarital partners; Jennifer Panek investigates portrayals of the wittol and argues: "By taking control of his wife's adultery and using it to his own ends, this wittol paradox-

8. Kellye Corcoran, "Cuckoldry as Performance, 1685–1715," *Studies in English Literature, 1500–1900* 52, no. 3 (2012): 543–59, at 543, https://doi.org/10.1353/sel.2012.0029.

ically evades the stigma of the cuckold."[9] Panek analyzes the relationship between wifely virtue and consumerism by articulating the ways in
which husbands effectively wield power over their wives by using these
extramarital relationships for their financial benefit.[10] Because the scope
of Panek's analysis is largely limited to the fiscal, it does not include men
who actively and eagerly seek out participation in cuckold relationships
for the sake of *sexual pleasure* — men who derive *pleasure*, not merely
financial gain, from their wife's dalliances.[11] Additionally, the scholarly
focus on premodern cuckoldry also centers primarily on the individual
character (Allwit, Master Ford in *The Merry Wives of Windsor*, etc.) as a
type on his own or within the privacy of a marriage; my primary focus in
this chapter is to understand the cuckold *outside* of any one relationship
and instead to establish that the cuckold is often situated within a larger
community of cuckolds, which is essential to the demonstration of the
cuckold's gratification.

Communal Contribution

Many of the representations of early modern cuckoldry are found within
plays and ballads; much has been said about the portrayals of cuckoldry
within early modern drama, though the distinct generic conventions
between the two allow for quite different representations of cuckolds,
necessitating further exploration into the cuckolds of ephemeral texts.
Several extant cuckold ballads focus on preparations for Horn Fair, a

9. Jennifer Panek, "'A Wittall Cannot Be a Cookold': Reading the Contented Cuckold in Early
   Modern English Drama and Culture," *Journal for Early Modern Cultural Studies* 1, no. 2
   (2001): 66–92, at 76, https://doi.org/10.1353/jem.2001.0020.
10. Panek, "'A Wittall Cannot Be a Cookold,'" 85.
11. Located on the periphery of my own analysis is Simone Chess's discussion of the contented
    cuckold as a means of interrogating disability, queerness, and extramarital desire. For
    more, see Simone Chess, "Contented Cuckolds: Infertility and Queer Reproductive Prac-
    tice in Middleton's *A Chaste Maid in Cheapside* and Machiavelli's *Mandragola*," in *Performing
    Disability in Early Modern English Drama*, ed. Leslie C. Dunn (Palgrave Macmillan, 2020),
    117–40.

celebration that occurred annually on the eighteenth of October in the parish of Charlton in Kent.[12] This festivity was "treated as little more than an excuse to engage in publicly sanctioned debauchery"[13] and was only very loosely linked to the practice of cuckoldry itself. Many of the specifics of this annual event are lost to history, but Douglas Bruster recounts two potential origin stories for this fair.[14] The more prevailing narrative is a story about a miller who discovers King John kissing his wife. King John gifts him all the surrounding land as recompense, though the miller must annually adorn himself with horns and walk to the place where his newly gifted land ends, which becomes known as "Cuckold's Point."[15] Despite the tenuous links that the fair has to the actual practice of cuckoldry, the abundance of ephemeral popular materials related to Horn Fair can help us understand the specifics and subtexts of early modern cuckoldry and allow us glimpses into these cuckold communities in ways that are not as perceptible in the drama of the period.

One such text is *Hey for Horn Fair*, which was published in 1674 and depicts a merchant who encounters nine different types of cuckolds. Each of these cuckolds is defined purely by a single adjective that describes him — *kind, contented,* and *jealous,* to name a few.[16] The pam-

---

12. According to Edward Hasted in his 1797 text, *The History and Topographical Survey of the County of Kent: Volume 1,* the Charlton made infamous for its Horn Fair was "usually called *Charlton near Greenwich,* to distinguish it from the other parish of the same name near Dover." As I subsequently mention, the origins of this fair are muddy at best, perhaps partly because of this disambiguation. Edward Hasted, *The History and Topographical Survey of the County of Kent: Volume 1* (Canterbury: W Bristow, 1797), British History Online, http://www.british-history.ac.uk/survey-kent/vol1.

13. Corcoran, "Cuckoldry as Performance," 551.

14. Douglas Bruster, "The Horn of Plenty: Cuckoldry and Capital in the Drama of the Age of Shakespeare," *Studies in English Literature, 1500–1900* 30, no. 2 (1990): 195–215, at 196, https://doi.org/10.2307/450514.

15. This is the only origin story recounted in Hasted's 1797 text, which indicates that this story very quickly became the dominant narrative.

16. T. R., *Hey for Horn Fair, the General Market of England, Or, Room for Cuckolds being a Merry Progress of Nine several Sorts of Cuckolds here Discovered ... : Full of Mirth and Merry Discourse, Newly Presented from Horn Fair to all the Merry Good Fellows in England : To which is Added, the*

phlet begins by referencing a surprising genre that annually appears at Horn Fair: the sermon.[17] Though the merchant does mention the sermon, he immediately deviates from this annual tradition: "Gentlemen, this is to let you understand, that I do not intend to make you a Sermon at this merry Fair, according to the custom … Well it is no matter, because I have not a sermon ready for you: you shall hear a Story shall be worth fiftéen."[18] Despite the merchant's assurances, he does not deliver a story; rather, the narration focuses on the merchant's attempts to engage customers or remark upon cuckoldry more broadly as exemplified by the nine specific cuckolds, who exist simply as flat character types, that pass him in the market. This sort of typological representation of cuckolds is certainly not unique to this text, but I begin with this example because it "shows us the ways in which such performances of social power can simultaneously draw on and disavow their social referents."[19] This pamphlet portrays some of the traditional anxieties surrounding early modern cuckoldry, even as it begins to gesture towards the sense of contentedness and communal fraternity I am interested in.

The frontispiece (figure 2.1) reinforces the merchant's delineation of nine different cuckold types. As evidenced by this imagery, there are many ways to be a cuckold — seven variations of horns are affixed to the staff in the middle of the image. As the merchant narrates the event, he speaks in a stream of consciousness, consistently referring back to the horns he has available for purchase, presumably displayed for sale on this pole. Although the links between Horn Fair and cuckoldry are largely titular only (as the event is more about merriment and fun), the merchant frequently links the two together: "Indeed I am afraid that Horns

---

Marriage of Jockie and Jenny [Hey for Horn Fair. Room for cuckolds. Marriage of Jockie and Jenny.], (London: Printed for F. Coles, T. Vere, and J. Wright, 1674).

17. For more on the links between cuckoldry and Christianity, specifically, see Corcoran's "Cuckoldry as Performance."

18. T. R., *Hey for Horn Fair*, n.p.

19. Margot Weiss, *Techniques of Pleasure: BDSM and the Circuits of Sexuality* (Durham, NC: Duke University Press, 2011), 17.

will be very cheap this Fair, for the Town is full of Horn-makers."[20] The term *Horn-makers* has a bifurcated meaning here. It may be a simple reference to the links between cuckoldry and the market (Bruster, 1990; Panek, 2001; Clark, 2002) that are evidenced by the merchant himself; however, it also suggests that there are plenty of wives and single men who are eager to make cuckolds out of the wives' husbands. This notion of proudly wearing horns in order to participate in the revelry of the fair is quite a transition from many of the dramatic representations of cuckoldry, such as *Arden of Faversham* (1592), *Much Ado About Nothing* (1600), *Othello* (1604), and even *A Chaste Maid in Cheapside*, that were proliferating only half a century prior to this, in which the mere mention of horns could incite a husband to rage or violence. This shift is also evidenced by the sheer number of options that this horn pole offers. Just as the merchant distinguishes nine types of cuckolds, there are also different horns for every type — diminutive horns, decorative horns, and ostentatious horns. There is also perhaps a subtle pleasure in using such a phallic object to display wares associated with and for the purpose of advertising cuckoldry. Not only does this staff act as a physical representation of the penetrative sex acts to come, it also hints at the pleasure available to those participating in the community of cuckolds who may find themselves figuratively represented by like-minded cuckolds via the merchant's staff. On the one hand, the staff serves a pragmatic function to provide the consumer with an option to find the horns that best define or suit him; on the other, it implies that there are others within the community who may use different means (or horns) to the same end.[21]

20. T. R., *Hey for Horn Fair*, n.p.
21. It is worth pausing here to mention how invested the contemporary kink community is in collecting, displaying, and owning props. Props have become central to the formation of contemporary kinky identities and to the pursuit of sex acts; the display in this pamphlet anticipates this contemporary fixation and irrevocably links kink with the emergence of capitalism that was burgeoning in early modern England.

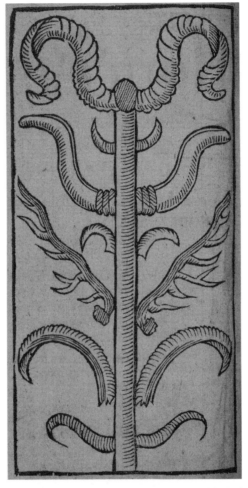

Figure 2.1. Illustration from T.R., *Hey for Horn Fair*, 1674, Call # 132227, The Huntington Library, San Marino, California. Reproduced with permission.

If *Hey for Horn Fair* represents a sort of liminal space for early modern cuckoldry, as the cuckolds appear to be in on the joke, at the very least,[22] the ballad "Cuckolds all a-Row" is a much more standard sum-

22. As Claire McEachern points out, the early modern cuckold is laughed at as a means of societal distancing; see Claire McEachern, "Why Do Cuckolds Have Horns?" *Huntington Library Quarterly* 71, no. 4 (2008): 607–31, at 610, https://doi.org/10.1525/hlq.2008.71.4.607.

mons for Horn Fair, at least on the surface. As this particular summons addresses the cuckolds as a unified group, it emphasizes the importance of the community of cuckolds. The ballad is addressed to "all Henpeckt and Hornified Tradesmen in and about the City of London" and requests "their appearance at Cuckolds-Point."[23] This ballad requests that cuckolds gather prior to the fair in order to prepare a traversable and safe path for their wives and their wives' lovers to be able to attend the annual Horn Fair, a common occurrence in many iterations of these summonses. In addition to providing a general summons for the cuckolds, this ballad also gives the men some directions about how to appear:

> For if you come not decently drest,
> they'll scoff at you all for your labour;
> The Brethren will think you some intruding Guest
> that has borrowed your Horns of your Neighbor.[24]

These lines indicate the importance of conforming to standards of dress for the events preceding and during Horn Fair. In particular, these lines demonstrate the importance of conformity for the sake of the community of cuckolds, as the narrator subtly threatens that they risk not being acknowledged by their cuckold peers if they fail to participate according to the standards laid out by the Master Cuckolds, the authors of this summons. Not only do they risk being scoffed at for their infraction, they risk being labeled an intruder and a guest — essentially, an outsider to the community. To reinforce this opposition between the cuckolds and outsiders, the summons even refers to members of the community as *brethren*, a clear indication of the communality of these cuckolds.

23. "Cuckolds all a-Row. / Or, A Summons issued out from the Master-Cuckolds and Wardens of Fumblers- / Hall; directed to all Henpeckt and Hornified Tradesmen in and about the City of London, / requiring their appearance at Cuckolds-Point. Concluding with a pleasant new Song" (Printed for R. Kell, 1685–1688), n.p.
24. "Cuckolds all a-Row," n.p.

As previously established, Horn Fair is not an event solely for cuckolds — it is a place for camaraderie and pleasurable depravity. Because many attendees may opt to don horns as a sort of caricature of cuckoldry, following the given instructions helps to cement one's status as a true cuckold and not as an impostor. For these men, wearing the "Horns of [one's] Neighbor" indicates a lack of true cuckoldry and shows to all that they do not really belong within the community. This vague threat is clearly not about the sex act at all; rather, it is about the potential for a lack of communal connection. In other words, the kinkier pleasures of being a cuckold might be as much about participating in communal fraternization as experiencing sexual infidelity. Both of these texts help to contextualize the importance of community for these early modern cuckolds, though both still present cuckoldry as a largely negative cultural phenomenon, particularly because the festivity surrounding Horn Fair occurs but once a year and can therefore be perceived as an acceptable and controlled anomaly; however, the next two ballads offer a marked distinction in that they both portray cuckoldry as something to revel in regardless of the time of year.

Communal Contentment

The undated broadside ballad "The Catologue of Contented Cuckolds," likely published in the late seventeenth century, depicts ten self-proclaimed cuckolded men, all of whom have gathered in a tavern in order to seemingly discuss their matrimonial relationships. Following traditional generic conventions, the ballad recounts the vocations of these men, which vary from a brewer to a tailor to a surgeon. Much like the cuckolds in *Hey for Horn Fair*, the cuckolds here are distinguished from one another, only to be unified by their cuckoldry. The twelve-stanza ballad devotes ten stanzas to the men: one cuckold per stanza. However, the two stanzas that frame the men's individual monologues are important in order to make clear that two things unite these men: "These

[are] good honest Tradesmen," and they are "all Cuckolds in grain."[25] The assertion that these are "good honest Tradesmen" is a subversion of the traditional perception of the cuckold who is seen as weak, effeminate, and fiscally irresponsible. The ballad depicts these cuckolds as productive and confident members of society. Furthermore, the wide range of their vocations indicates the ubiquity of cuckold relationships; cuckolds are not merely tailors (an occupation often deemed effeminate or delicate); they are also cooks and surgeons.[26] What is most noteworthy, however, is the phrase *cuckolds in grain*, a sure reference to the nature of gathering to drink. This phrase, which concludes both the first and last stanzas of the ballad, has an additional layer of meaning embedded here. The *Oxford English Dictionary (OED) Online* defines *in grain* as: "downright, by nature, pure and simple, genuine, ... indelible."[27] This layered reading makes clear that these men are not only connected through their love of drinking, but that they also share something much more intimate: an *innate*, or ingrained, sense of being a cuckold. This is a fairly progressive assertion, as it contends that cuckoldry is not merely a sexual practice for these men; it also functions as an identity, which then becomes the basis for their communal bonding.

This ballad amplifies the communality found in *Hey for Horn Fair*, in which the cuckolds are united by their individual encounters with the merchant. He, not their cuckoldry, is what unites their narratives. Here, the cuckolds appear to have established this community of their own accord. The communal atmosphere created by these men who appear

25. "The Catologue of Contented Cuckolds: Or, A Loving Society of Confessing Brethren of the Forked Order, etc. who being met together in a Tavern, declar'd each Man his Condition, resolving to be contented, and drown'd Melancholly in a Glass of Necktar. To the Tune of, Fond Boy, etc. Or, Love's a sweet Passion, etc." (Little-Britain: Printed for J.C. London, 1685), n.p.
26. For more on the relationship between vocational identity and broadside ballads, see Mark Hailwood, "Broadside Ballads and Occupational Identity in Early Modern England," *Huntington Library Quarterly* 79, no. 2 (2016): 187–200, https://doi.org/10.1353/hlq.2016.0016.
27. *OED Online*, s.v. "in grain, (n. 1)."

to have nothing more in common with each other than their cuckoldry is further exemplified by the ballad's full title: "The Catologue of Contented Cuckolds: Or, A Loving Society of Confessing Brethren of the Forked Order, etc. who being met together in a Tavern, declar'd each Man his Condition, resolving to be contented, and drown'd Melancholly in a Glass of Necktar." Considering this full title, it seems remiss to refer to these men simply as a *catologue*. Instead, though they are presented as a list of professional types, the second part of the title, which refers to them as a *loving society* and part of the *Forked Order*, gives them a kind of group legitimacy, where what legitimates them is their shared forked, or horned, status.[28] The ballad also utilizes the word *brethren*, which we have previously seen in the ballad "Cuckolds all a-Row." However, here the cuckolds are not merely brethren; they are *confessing* brethren, an important distinction. The adjectival connotation is that these are men who fully embrace and tout not *only* their cuckoldry but also their inclusion in a wider group of cuckolds. Additionally, the full title refers to these men's cuckoldry as a *condition*. Although one reading of this suggests an ailment or medical condition, this can also be interpreted as an inherent quality or state of personhood. This reading reinforces my understanding of the phrase *cuckolds in grain*, as the usage of *condition* only bolsters the sense of identity these men experience regarding their cuckoldry. The group is marked by its openness — the men in this forked community speak openly about their status as cuckolds, rather than hiding it in shame, and their gathering can be perceived as both community building and public shaming. This public shaming differs from traditional depictions of cuckold shaming, with skimmingtons being the most notorious example of this. Whereas skimmingtons are an example of a complete lack of agency,[29] the men in these depictions appear to be

28. In contemporary kink circles the man who sleeps with the cuckold's wife is often referred to as a bull. Although the horned imagery of cuckolds persists today, it is certainly less common than in the Renaissance, making this an interesting choice of terminology.
29. Corcoran, "Cuckoldry as Performance," 548.

actively participating in a cuckold relationship and defining the meanings and connotations of being identified as such.

Using one's agency to this end seems paradoxical, especially in a culture that insists on a husband's ability to control his wife and the assurance that his children are truly his own offspring. I have already established that the wittol is one type of cuckold that justifies this arrangement through financial compensation. And though the trope of the wittol applies to certain contented cuckolds, such as Allwit in Middleton's drama, the majority of the men in "The Catologue of Contented Cuckolds" do not appear merely contented, so much as pleased by the tales they share. One such account reads:

> My Wife, quoth the Brewer, is charming and fair,
> She will ramble a broad, but I never know where;
> Yet at midnight sometimes she returns with a Spark;
> Nay, I sometimes have found her at Put in the dark[.][30]

While *put* in the fourth line may simply be referring to the contemporary card game of the period, it is unlikely that this game would be played in the dark or that it would be salacious enough for the husband to remark upon it here. This innocuous reading is supplanted by a secondary meaning of *put*, which, according to the *OED Online* is "an act of thrusting or pushing,"[31] which certainly fits the sexual nature of the ballad better. This particular stanza is of special importance because it gives the wife agency much in the same way that contemporary cuckold relationships do. Eve Kosofsky Sedgwick claims that cuckoldry is "by definition a sexual act, performed on a man, by another man,"[32] largely reducing the woman to a mere participant. However, the brewer in this ballad returns the agency

---

30. "The Catologue of Contended Cuckolds," n.p.

31. *OED Online*, s.v. "put, (n. 1)."

32. Eve Kosofsky Sedgwick, *Epistemology of the Closet* (Berkeley: University of California Press, 1990), 49.

to the wife, for she is the one actively seeking out extramarital partners, and, more importantly, it is not her partner the brewer finds doing the thrusting, but the wife herself, positioning *her* as the sexual dominant. In this depiction, the male sexual partner is the one reduced to irrelevancy, and the wife and the husband become the active agents of their own sexuality, despite the fact that they are not having sex with each other. The additional partner simply becomes the conduit through which their sexual arrangement works.

In the brewer's first four lines, his tone is rather objective about his wife's extramarital encounters, reiterating them merely as fact. However, the concluding couplet of this stanza, which each cuckold repeats with minor variations throughout the ballad, seems at odds with his initial neutral tone, as the brewer hints at the emotional difficulties in navigating and maintaining a cuckold relationship:

> Yet I swear by this Glass of rich sparkling Wine,
> I will now be contented, and never repine.[33]

Moreover, the couplet indicates that the cuckolds find solace in the shared communal action of drinking together. Although their contentment may not be entirely organic and may be bolstered from the drink, this communal declaration indicates that they *actively participate* in this community.[34] The importance of community to these men is furthered by the sailor's narrative in stanza nine of the ballad, in which he addresses his fellow cuckolds as *brothers*, a common term of endearment amongst the cuckold communities we have analyzed here. Newmahr addresses the importance of communal acceptance to the contemporary kink community: "As much as community membership is derived from

---

33. "The Catologue of Contented Cuckolds," n.p.
34. In many ways, the brewer's dichotomous attitudes surrounding his cuckold relationship are reminiscent of contemporary cuckolds, who often seek out like-minded men to share both the difficulties and triumphs of navigating such kinky relationships.

identification, it is defined by drawing boundaries between people who belong in a group and those who do not …. In drawing these boundaries, the community reinforces and legitimizes group identity, and creates a safe social space for participants."[35] Although Newmahr is particularly interested in the discourses and communities surrounding sado-masochism and, more specifically, exchanges of pain, this taxonomic difference does not preclude the usefulness of applying a similar lens to cuckoldry, particularly as early modern cuckolds were certainly living on the margins of acceptable marital relationships.

Communal Celebration

The cuckold communities we have analyzed are taken to their zenith in the ballad "A General Summons for those belonging to the Hen-Peckt-Frigat, to appear at Cuckolds-Point, on the 18th of this Instant October." Despite the connotation of the title's *hen-peckt* (a common phrase applied to cuckolds), the ballad itself describes a group of men who appear quite happy to do their wives' bidding. Before the ballad itself begins, a brief argument is laid out: "Your presence is required, and are hereby lawfully Summoned (as belonging to the *Hen-Peckt-Frigat*) to appear at *Cuckolds-Point* (being the antient Place of our Randezvous)."[36] Two things are worth noting here. First, the summons for the cuckolds to appear is presented as *overly* legitimate by the phrase *lawfully summoned*. Such contractual language amplifies the legitimacy of the summons that we have already seen hinted at in "Cuckolds all a-Row." The argument concludes by once again referring to the (presumably fictitious) legality of the cuck-

---

35. Newmahr, *Playing on the Edge*, 44, 46.
36. "A General Summons for those Belonging to the Hen-Peck'd Frigate, to Appear at Cuckolds-Point, on the 18th. of this Instant October. Licensed According to Order. Your Presence is Required, and are Hereby Lawfully Summoned (as Belonging to the Hen-Peck'd-Frigate) to Appear at Cuckolds-Point (being the Antient Place of our Rendezvous) on the 18th. of this Instant October; […] Thomas Cann't-be-Quiet Beadle [Ladies of London.]" (London: Printed for J. Deacon, 1672–1702), n.p. Italics in the original.

olds' participation in the event: "whereof you are not to fail, under the *Penalty* of a Garret-Correction, and the Forfeiture of all your Goods and Chattels."[37] Secondly, the summons legitimizes cuckolds as a group by giving them historical context and a shared history by referring to "the antient place of our Randevzous," though this is not unique to this summons. Recall that the location Cuckolds Point became essential to the mythos surrounding Horn Fair; therefore labeling this location as *antient* establishes the longevity of their gathering, while the entirety of the summons solidifies their legitimacy both as individuals and as a community by giving these cuckolds historical context for their sexual and communal identities.

Figure 2.2. Illustration from "A General Summons," 1672–1702, National Library of Scotland, Crawford.EB.502. Reproduced with permission from materials on loan to the National Library of Scotland from the Balcarres Heritage Trust.

37. "A General Summons," n.p. Italics in the original.

The ballad itself echoes many of the summonses we have previously seen, by asking cuckolds to gather and prepare for the fair. However, what is most remarkable about this ballad is the woodcut preceding it, which, because of its impeccable quality and specificity, was likely created for this ballad. This woodcut, depicted in figure 2.2, has many noteworthy aspects, though I wish to focus primarily on the setting, which recalls the tavern scene in "The Catologue of Contented Cuckolds." Although both ballads do contain a woodcut, the woodcut in "The Catologue of Contented Cuckolds" merely portrays a standard tavern scene, with no cuckold paraphernalia in sight. Additionally, the woodcut used is a common one, appearing in nearly a dozen other ballads. The reusage of this woodcut does not indicate apathy on the part of the publisher; rather, it was "an incitement to engagement and debate" as "viewers had to work hard in order to locate or manufacture meaning."[38] However, the woodcut in "A General Summons" requires no work on the part of the viewer. Meaning does not need to be located or manufactured here, as the woodcut, which depicts a tavern that appears to be occupied solely by cuckolds, clearly reinforces the textual theme and tone.

It is first helpful to orient the layout of the scene. The two men in the foreground appear to be outside of the tavern, while the two men in the background are situated within the tavern itself, emphasized by the shading and the sign displayed outside the tavern. The gentleman handing out the summons carries a rather phallic staff that is adorned with horns, reminiscent of the staff utilized by the merchant in *Hey for Horn Fair*. Because of his staff, the summons, and his centrality in the image, it is possible he may be one of the Master Cuckolds depicted in many other summonses. The gentleman in the middle of the woodcut who stands at

---

38. Christopher Marsh, "A Woodcut and Its Wanderings in Seventeenth-Century England," *Huntington Library Quarterly* 79, no. 2 (2016): 245–62, at 246, https://doi.org/10.1353/hlq.2016.0010.

the threshold of the tavern noticeably has no horns, and it is likely that the ballad's admonishment to "remember your Foreheads adorning"[39] is both a literal and a figurative reminder to this man. It is possible that this gentleman's hand is extended to reach for the summons; however, the directionality of his hand indicates that he is reaching out as a form of greeting.[40] Furthermore, the two men in the background are smoking and conversing, the horns on their heads seemingly an unremarkable adornment. Additionally, the sign on the outside of the tavern depicts a pair of horns, a clear indication of the clientele they are trying to attract, though whether this is on account of the occurrence of Horn Fair or is a more permanent fixture is unclear.

The ambiguity of this woodcut adds a layer of complexity to what is otherwise a straightforward ballad about Horn Fair. Christopher Marsh notes that "the appeal of a ballad lay not only in its textual content but also in the interaction among the words, the images, the melody, and the performance."[41] This interaction amongst the constituent parts is especially important considering this particular woodcut does not appear to accompany any other ballads, and it is likely that the publisher intentionally had this image created to coincide with the text. Let us first address possible interpretations of the woodcut on its own. One potential reading suggests that Horn Fair is occurring in the immediate moment — that the tavern's sign, the gentlemen's horns, the summons and staff held by the most prominent gentleman, and their gathering are simply part of the celebration and have little to do with true cuckoldry. Another reading blurs the lines of linear temporality and suggests that the two men outside of the tavern later retreat *into* the tavern, and the men depicted inside are merely the same two gentlemen after the one has been admonished and adorned with his horns. This reading improves upon the pre-

39. "A General Summons," n.p.
40. For further reading, Christopher Marsh analyzes the posture and gesture of a man in a similar stance in a different woodcut in "A Woodcut and Its Wanderings."
41. Marsh, "A Woodcut and Its Wanderings," 246.

vious because it gives preeminence to the practices of cuckoldry and communality, as the admonishment of the summons is respected. However, both of these readings neglect to consider the confluence of the text *and* image. As I have mentioned, many of these summonses command the presence of the cuckolds to clear a path for their wives and their wives' lovers to safely traverse to Horn Fair, though many of them also remark upon cuckoldry more broadly. However, *half* of "A General Summons" is dedicated to outlining specific instructions regarding the cuckolds' gathering. These instructions include the time and place to convene, the necessary items to bring, and the intended usage of these items. Such specificities are uncommon in other summonses, and, read in conjunction with the image, suggest that the scenario depicted in the woodcut occurs *prior* to Horn Fair and that the presumed Master Cuckold is ensuring compliance before the event occurs. Read in this light, the tavern potentially takes on a sense of permanence for this cuckold community that other readings neglect. This interpretation showcases the importance of community for these cuckolds and demonstrates their willingness to display their kinky lifestyles in ways in which the previous texts we have encountered do not.

Though all of these representations of cuckold communities portray the importance of community in different ways and to different degrees, it is clear that these are depictions of kinky people coming together to form communities with like-minded people in order to participate in and celebrate their shared interests *and* to renounce (or perhaps actually to revel in) their place on the margins of normative society. In contemporary kink spaces, one is often not considered a true participant in kink if one does not have some level of community involvement, which is a testament to how necessary community is to the practice of kink. I have only begun to outline the importance of community to premodern kink through these glimpses into early modern cuckold communities, which allow us to draw parallels between kink in the early modern period and the twenty-first century. These depictions help legitimize contemporary kinky practices by providing historical evidence of these shared identities — the same objective that "A General Summons" has for its cuckolds.

Kinky Herrick

Gina Filo

Despite the pervasive eroticism of his work, Robert Herrick has enjoyed relative anonymity in recent gender- and sexuality-oriented literary scholarship, his sexual politics occasioning little critical debate or even interest. I say *enjoyed* not because I expect Herrick would like being passed over — his work certainly provides evidence to the contrary — but rather because when his poetry does gain critical attention, its erotic content is frequently taken to indicate either a psychosexually stunted or a misogynistic psyche (or, often, both). Lillian Schanfield, for example, notices that Herrick

> lurks, leers, glides, spies, melts, yearns, swoons, heaves, pants, and dreams ... perseverates about women's physical parts, body movements, and clothing ... mentally disrobes his idealized mistresses ... in raptures about their lips, breasts and nipples, hair, teeth, legs, bellies, buttocks, waists, calves, thighs, skin, feet and sundry "parts" ... praises their shoes, fabrics, petticoats and other articles of feminine clothing ... sniffs sweat, perfumes and other odors ... [and] fantasizes about kissing.[1]

1. Lillian Schanfield, "'Tickled with Desire': A View of Eroticism in Herrick's Poetry," *Literature and Psychology* 39, no. 1 (1993): 63–83, at 63.

As Schanfield's list indicates, Herrick's collection *Hesperides* (1648) indexes an extraordinary variety of sexual activity, the speaker an unrepentant fantasist, fetishist, and connoisseur of female bodies and accoutrement. For Schanfield, however, these erotic investments are not forms of benign sexual variation but rather indicate a pathology, conveying a "furtive air of unhealthy sexuality" that indicates the poet's own "sexual problems related to immaturity, passivity and possibly impotence."[2] Schanfield is admittedly singular in the transparency of her diagnostic reading, yet in a similar vein, feminist critics of Herrick have often uncritically applied Nancy Vickers's account of Petrarchism's ostensibly inherent misogyny to accuse Herrick of the "impulse ... to dominate, control, and display [women] to delight the male reader and to perpetuate the cultural repression of women," in Moira Baker's phrase.[3] Similarly, Bronwen Price asserts that, for Herrick, the woman's "dissected form" is placed in "subjection to classification, identification, definition and ultimate mastery of the male gaze."[4] While part of the persistence of these accusations of misogyny can be explained by the relative neglect of Herrick's work in the twenty-first century — accounts of the sexual politics of early modern love poetry have been greatly nuanced in the past thirty years — as recently as 2010, Pamela Hammons assessed that women in Herrick are "rendered passive, still, silent, and empty

2. Schanfield, "Tickled," 64, 65.
3. See Nancy Vickers, "Diana Described: Scattered Woman and Scattered Rhyme," *Critical Inquiry* 8, no. 2 (1981): 265–79, https://doi.org/10.1086/448154; Moira P. Baker, "'The Uncanny Stranger on Display': The Female Body in Sixteenth- and Seventeenth-Century Love Poetry," *South Atlantic Review* 56, no. 2 (1991): 7–25, at 22, https://doi.org/10.2307/3199956.
4. Bronwen Price, "The Fractured Body — Censorship and Desire in Herrick's Poetry," *Literature and History* 2, no. 1 (1993): 23–41, at 32, https://doi.org/10.1177/030619739300200102. Cf. Michael Schoenfeldt's remark that "piecemeal misogyny ... often infiltrates Herrick's attitude to the female body" ("The Art of Disgust: Civility and the Social Body in *Hesperides*," *George Herbert Journal* 14, nos. 1–2 (1990/1991): 127–54, at 143, https://doi.org/10.1353/ghj.1990.0011.

of agency."[5] Even as Hammons acknowledges "the limits to Herrick's ability to imagine consistently a heteronormative male subject who is absolutely independent of and master over object," she identifies a persistent "fear of a male subject trans-shifting into a passive, static object controlled by others" in his verse.[6] Similarly, in 2021 Katie Kadue asserted that women are literal "garbage" for Herrick: "They already are and always were refuse, masquerading as human women. Specific human body parts — legs, thighs, breast, teeth, hair, eyes, head — are disposed of as false figures for what a woman really is: a vague 'something,' made of 'stuffe.'"[7] For Kadue, Herrick's fetishism is naked evidence of his perception of women as so much trash. As Michael Schoenfeldt both summarizes and assesses, "Commingling fear, disgust, and desire in its confrontation with the female body, *Hesperides* seems intent on forestalling the eroticism it stirs."[8]

Despite this tone of critical disgust, the general observation subtending their assessments — that Herrick's eroticism is idiosyncratic, fetishistic, and voyeuristic — is, in fact, a good one. Herrick's erotic poetry is one of fragmented bodies, of kissing, panting, and stroking, of voyeurism and scopic pleasures, and of whipping and binding; it also rejects male penetration, ejaculation, and orgasm as particularly desirable teloi of sexual encounters. Given the overwhelming normativity of critical accounts of his erotic imaginary, then, it seems to me that Herrick is due for a queer — indeed, a kinky — reassessment, one that embraces rather than pathologizes these very perversities for which he has been castigated. The recuperative impulse in my reading, that is, is not to interpolate Herrick's eroticism into a normative paradigm, as

---

5. Pamela S. Hammons, *Gender, Sexuality, and Material Objects in English Renaissance Verse* (New York: Routledge, 2010), 35.

6. Hammons, *Gender, Sexuality, and Material Objects*, 41.

7. Katie Kadue, "Flower Girls and Garbage Women: Misogyny and Cliché in Ronsard and Herrick," *Modern Philology* 118, no. 3 (2021): 319–39, at 334, https://doi.org/10.1086/712403.

8. Schoenfeldt, "Disgust," 148.

does David Landrum when he argues that Herrick is not the "voyeuristic effeminate pervert" his reputation makes him out to be.[9] Rather, in this chapter I trouble negative critical accounts of Herrick's opinion of women and "perverted" sexual acts more generally through exploring his kinky fantasies of being beaten, bound, penetrated, and dominated. In so doing, I will problematize not his fantasies but rather the critical impulse to reflexively diagnose pathology or misogyny when confronted with such modalities of desire. Disputing Schoenfeldt's claim that *Hesperides* "represent[s] sexual desire in ways that necessarily preclude satisfaction," a formulation that forecloses the possibility that nongenital eroticism — and thus nonteleological sex acts — can be satisfactory,[10] I will argue that Herrick's nongenital erotics, his kinky and masochistic fantasies, are nonpathological examples of benign sexual variation with significant implications for our understanding of both his work and early modern sexual formations more generally. Informed by Catherine Bates's account of early modern poetic speakers who adopt postures of masochistic impotence, as well as Karmen MacKendrick's concept of counterpleasures, I demonstrate both Herrick's kinkiness and its queer, antimisogynistic ethos.[11] Furthermore, I will briefly adumbrate how Herrick's erotic ethic not only fails to entail a pathological fear of and desire to control women but also demonstrates a broader, queerer array of early modern sexual formations and pleasures than is often allowed by modern scholarship.

While not all of the pleasures I will here discuss fit within the paradigm of masochism — falling under the more general rubric we often call BDSM — masochism's critical allure has generated an array of theories

9. David Landrum, "Robert Herrick and the Ambiguities of Gender," *Texas Studies in Literature and Language* 49, no. 2 (2007): 181–297, at 188, https://doi.org/10.1353/tsl.2007.0012.
10. Schoenfeldt, "Disgust," 146.
11. Catherine Bates, *Masculinity, Gender, and Identity in the English Renaissance Lyric* (Cambridge, UK: Cambridge University Press, 2007), 1; Karmen MacKendrick, *Counterpleasures* (New York: New York University Press, 1999), e.g., 12.

for understanding nonpathological forms of pleasure-in-pain. One such paradigm can be found in MacKendrick's concept of counterpleasures. To begin, MacKendrick examines Freud's discussion of forepleasures, or pleasures that "are essential as preliminaries to 'normal' sexual pleasure but which, if lingered over, become 'perverse.'" These pleasures, she continues, "may be so strong that instead of being promptly and properly rushed through, these preliminaries become themselves the 'aim' of sexual activity." This is a problem for Freud, not least because, being part of normative sexual activity themselves, forepleasures reveal "the inherent perversity of the 'normal'" — if forepleasures are part of normative intercourse, the line between normal and perverse becomes difficult to assess.[12] For MacKendrick, however, dwelling in forepleasure is not pathological, but rather allows one access to counterpleasures, or "pleasures that tend away from all sorts of teleologies," of which masochism is only one of many examples.[13] These counterpleasures resist the circuits of linear, heteronormative sexuality and are indeed particularly pronounced in masochistic or BDSM contexts, as Brandy Simula's social science research has shown. As Simula demonstrates, "Despite the longstanding use of orgasm as an indicator of 'good sex,' recent research … has suggested that for many individuals, orgasm is not a required and, in some cases, not even an important or desired component of sex."[14] Participants in her BDSM research in particular "resisted the importance of orgasm as an indicator of a sexual experience or sexual fulfillment."[15] In a similar way, Herrick's resistance to being the agent of penetration and experiencing orgasm, his insistence on "perverse," nongenital pleasures suggests a means of resistance to dominant, (proto-)heteropatriar-

---

12. MacKendrick, *Counterpleasures*, 7
13. MacKendrick, *Counterpleasures*, 12. For masochism, see e.g., 14–15 and 51–64.
14. Brandy L. Simula, "'A Different Economy of Bodies and Pleasures'?: Differentiating and Evaluating Sex and Sexual BDSM Experiences," *Journal of Homosexuality* 66, no. 2 (2019): 209–37, at 210, https://doi.org/10.1080/00918369.2017.1398017.
15. Simula, "Different Economy," 219.

chal penetration-and-ejaculation narratives that prioritize male orgasm as the sine qua non of sexual experience. That is to say, Herrick's kinky embrace of perverse pleasures offers speakers and readers alike a means of resistance to normative paradigms of heteropatriarchal, (re)productive forms of sexual experience.

As Catherine Bates has shown, Renaissance Petrarchism is shot through with the topoi of masochism, the lover's abjection problematizing ideals of male social and sexual sovereignty. Bates notes that

> Renaissance lyric is populated by ... figures who appear by choice to defy the period's model of a phallic, masterly masculinity — these adopted positions of impotence, failure, and gendered discontent seeming willfully to pervert what might otherwise have been seen (indeed, might thereby be defined) as the patriarchal norm.[16]

Many of Herrick's fantasies draw on the tropological matrixes familiar from this Petrarchan pain tradition; in the fifth of his five poems titled "To Dianeme," for example, the speaker finds himself in abject servitude to the "unkind" (14) and "cruell" (16) Dianeme, the uncompromising sadist to his helplessly devoted masochist.[17] When Dianeme is "Stung by a fretfull Bee" (2), the speaker immediately places himself in erotic and physical service to relieve her pain:

> I the Javelin suckt away,
> And heal'd the wound in thee.
> (3–4)

That is, Dianeme has been violently penetrated by a third party's "Javelin," which the speaker seeks to heal through an act of oral devotion. Dianeme is not the only sufferer, however; carrying a "thousand thorns,

16. Bates, *Masculinity*, 1.
17. All quotations from Herrick are from *The Poetical Works of Robert Herrick*, ed. L. C. Martin (Oxford: Clarendon Press, 1956).

and Bryars & Stings" (5) in his "poore Brest" (6), the speaker's interior
state is a veritable honeycomb, little more than a series of holes and
wounds. Where the speaker is eager to alleviate the pain of penetration
for his Dianeme, though, she is uninterested in returning the favor.
Dianeme is not indifferent to his suffering but sadistically revels in it; she
"sit[s] and smile[s] / To see [him] bleed" (10–11), requiring him to endure
the violence of penetration while offering her his oral ministrations.

Herrick's speakers are, indeed, repeatedly penetrated in ways they
seem to find both nominally objectionable and secretly thrilling; in "The
Cheat of Cupid," "Upon Cupid," and "Love's Play at Push-pin," for example, they recount being painfully yet excitingly shot through with Cupid's
arrow, or, in the case of "Push-pin," a pin:

I put, he pusht, and heedless of my skin,
Love prickt my finger with a golden pin.
(3–4)

The speaker eagerly initiates a sexual encounter — *put* has a range of
contemporary meanings including to "thrust, poke, or push at"; to "urge,
incite; to instigate"; to "drive or plunge (a weapon or sharp object) *home*,
or *in* or *into* something or someone"; and to "attempt to mate" — but
finds himself quickly outmatched by a sadistic Love.[18] Explicitly "heedless" of the boundaries of the speaker's body, Love "prickt" the hapless
speaker, causing a wound that "festers" (5) with "poyson" (6) and thus
creates a lasting malaise with his "childish," playful, and sadistic tricks.
While the image of Love shooting a helpless speaker with his cruel
arrows is common in Petrarchan poetry, Herrick stages this scene time
and time again; dwelling on the physical mechanics of penetration, his
speakers find themselves compulsively repeating the moment in which
they first experience the irresistible torments of desire — that is, they

---

18. *Oxford English Dictionary Online*, s.v. "put (*v.*)." Emphasis in original.

continually return to the inception of their painful, pleasurable, and unmistakably kinky relationship with L/love.

The Petrarchan pain tradition is not restricted to violent penetration but entails a variety of physically unpleasant sensations, including the ubiquitous dialectic of heat and cold, of burning and freezing; that is, the central literary matrix through which early modern desire was expressed encompasses a variety of nongenital erotic counterpleasures whose kinky implications are not yet recognized in the extensive criticism on this literary mode. Herrick's speakers, however, are well aware of and alive to these pleasures in poems like "The Frozen Heart." In this lyric, the speaker coyly embraces his suffering, complaining

> I freeze, I freeze, and nothing dwels
> In me but Snow and *ysicles*.
> (1–2)

This highly conventional imagery of freezing soon shifts to burning, and, though the speaker initially begs for release — "For pitties sake give your advice / To melt this snow, and thaw this ice" (3–4) — he soon realizes that he does not, in fact, desire relief:

> I'le rather keepe this frost, and snow,
> Then to be thaw'd, or heated so.
> (7–8)

The burning-freezing motif recurs in "The Frozen Zone: or, Julia disdainfull" and "To Dewes"; in the latter, Herrick again underscores the masochistic element of unrequited love, the poem beginning,

> I burn, I burn; and beg of you
> To quench, or coole me with your Dew.
> (1–2)

Emphasizing the pleasures of this pain, the speaker continues,

> I frie in fire, and so consume,
> Although the Pile be all perfume.
> (3–4)

He may be burning and begging for mercy but that does not stop him from noting the sensually pleasant aspects of his experience, the *perfume* released upon his burning. The nine poems called "Upon Love" in *Hesperides* similarly register the pains of love on the one hand and express a desire to remain in that painful space on the other. The second "Upon Love" is a particularly good example of this; the speaker characterizes love as "full of pensive fear" (2), "terrour" (7), and "Flames" (10) that provoke "horrour" (9) in an embodied way, his "haire then stand an end" (6). While the speaker initially laments the pains of love, however, as the poem progresses he moves to an outright embrace of its tortures:

> But if horrour cannot slake
> Flames, which wo'd an entrance make;
> Then the next thing I desire,
> Is to love, and live i'th fire.
> (9–12)

In this short lyric, we see Herrick beginning in Petrarchan conventionality — lamenting the pains of love — but ending in radical acceptance of his situation as a permanently tortured subject. He concludes, that is, by expressing desire to live in the space of infinite pain and infinite delay that characterizes the masochistic subject position — thus demonstrating the centrality of such a kinky subjectivity to Petrarchism and Renaissance discourses of desire more generally.

Indeed, the first of two poems called "The Dreame" does not simply dabble in kink but stages a functionally complete BDSM scene from start to finish:

Me thought, (last night) love in an anger came,
And brought a rod, so whipt me with the same:
Mirtle the twigs were, meerly to imply
Love strikes, but 'tis with gentle crueltie.
Patient I was: Love pitifull grew then,
And stroak'd the stripes, and I was whole agen.
Thus like a Bee, *Love-gentle* stil doth bring
Hony to salve, where he before did sting.
(1–8)

The speaker first endures the *gentle crueltie* of love, *whipt* with a *Mirtle* rod; then, he luxuriates in what we might think of as aftercare, a personified Love tending to both the physical and psychological distress he has inflicted, growing *pitifull* and *stroak*[ing] *the stripes* he left on the speaker. Fascinatingly, through this encounter, the speaker becomes *whole agen* — that is, he is disarticulated through Love's erotic violence and yet reintegrated by Love's loving ministrations. In this overtly homoerotic encounter, then, the speaker adopts a passive, receptive position (one normatively associated with femininity then and now); both loses and regains the self through a kinky erotic experience; and takes pleasure in so doing. We see another rehearsal of a masochistic scene in "To the little Spinners," in which the speaker pleads with "pretty Huswives" (1) to "spin / A Lawn ... so fine and thin" (3–4) that it could repair the damage caused by "cruell Love" (5). Love has, the speaker reveals, beaten him mercilessly, leaving him

so whipt,
That of my skin, I am all stript.
(6–7)

The speaker, that is, has been stripped not only of his clothing, his outer lendings, but also his skin; Love's violence to the speaker's physical body obliterates the protective membrane between speaker and world. The speaker's use of *stript* doubles down on both the pathos and the prurient interest of the lyric, allowing him to remind the *pretty Huswives* of the nakedness of "each part" (10) of his body. His further plea that the housewives "skin again each part" (10) invites these women to contemplate and repair a variety of locations on his naked body. The use of *skin* here is a fascinating choice; the verb is far more often used to signify the *removal*, not the repair, of flesh. In his use of this autoantonymic verb, then, the speaker asks the women to cover his body with a prosthetic skin woven out of fine lawn, redoubling the emphasis on his nakedness; on the dismemberment of the physical body (which will here be repaired only through the addition of prosthetic skin); and on the lyric's kinky impulses, the repair itself framed in the language of violence.

"The Wounded Heart" similarly conjoins female textile arts with a radically passive male masochism, but here, the beloved's artistic abilities are framed as indicative of *her* sadistic attitude. The poem begins

Come bring your *sampler*, and with Art,
Draw in't a wounded Heart[.]
(1–2)

While the speaker uses the imperative case, he is a desperate suppliant rather than a commanding poet-speaker. Instead, the mistress takes the artist's role, begged to *Draw* a *wounded Heart* in her artful *sampler*. Not only does the speaker cede his aesthetic control, but he thus also proposes that the normatively feminine act of sewing a sampler is a means of artistic creation. The speaker contrasts the beloved's ability to pierce the embroidered heart with the impenetrability of her own body:

> Not that I thinke, that any Dart,
>   Can make your's bleed a teare:
>   Or peirce it any where;
>   Yet doe it to this end: that I,
>   May by
>   This secret see,
>   Though you can make
>   That *Heart* to bleed, your's ne'r
>   will ake
>   For me.
> (4–12)

Objectifying himself, the speaker embraces his status as suffering objet d'art created by the mistress who will never herself *ake* for the speaker. However, while her impassivity and control are rendered on the page, the speaker does not castigate her cruelty or indifference, as would the traditional Petrarchan lover; rather, he seems to revel in her artistic prowess, marveling at her ability to construct something she does not herself feel and taking pleasure in the aestheticization of his suffering.

Similarly, as suggested by the title of "To Anthea, who may command him any thing," the speaker engages in a total power exchange with another dominating female figure. The poem begins with the speaker begging Anthea to command him to live, love, and remain faithful:

> Bid me to live, and I will live
> Thy Protestant to be:
> Or bid me love, and I will give
> A loving heart to thee.
> (1–4)

Cheekily blasphemous, the speaker's Protestantism lies not in a rejection of idols — indeed, he promises to return her commands with idolatrous worship and the devotion of *A loving heart* — but rather in his protestations of love for the godlike Anthea. As the speaker elaborates on this image of the heart in the following stanza, he strikingly frames it as *A*, rather than *my* heart — "A heart as soft, a heart as kind / A heart as sound and free" (5–6) — dissociating from his own body in the pledge of his heart to Anthea. Indeed, the speaker never once claims his heart for his own, displacing it as *a*, *that*, or *it*. The speaker seems unbothered by this division, regarding it not as a troubling self-estrangement but rather as a pleasurable ceding of control to Anthea. As the poem progresses, he asks her to make increasingly negative commands, such as to "bid it [the heart] to languish quite away" (11) and to "Bid me to weep" (13), "despaire" (17), or "die" (20). These pleas to be tortured by a powerful, threatening female figure align the speaker with the Deleuzean masochist, the "victim in search of a torturer ... who needs to educate, persuade, and conclude an alliance with the torturer" via a specifically contractual relationship.[19] Anthea may have "command of every part" (23), yet this control is in accordance with the speaker's own desires. We can, then, see in this poem an example of a mutual masochistic scene; the speaker leaves the ball in Anthea's court, her agency in the situation coming not from arbitrary, tyrannical control of his body and heart but rather her choice of whether or not to fulfill the speaker's fantasies. That is, rather than a pathology or reflex of misogyny, here we see a speaker respectfully asking a woman to join him in a kinky, counterpleasurable encounter.

Ceding control of the body to threateningly alluring female figures is also central to "Disswasions from Idlenesse," which takes several familiar tropes — advice against love and the figuration of female bodies as

---

19. Gilles Deleuze, *Coldness and Cruelty*, in Gilles Deleuze and Leopold von Sacher-Masoch, *Masochism: "Coldness and Cruelty" and "Venus in Furs,"* trans. Jean McNeil (New York: Zone Books, 1989), 20.

traps for unwary men — and inverts them, suggesting that male passivity and ensnarement by women is a desirable state. The speaker begins conventionally, providing his interlocutor, young Cynthius, with "good doctrine" (2) to "Play not with the maiden-haire" (3), before proceeding to enumerate more perils to be found on female bodies; each curl on a woman's head is a "snare" (4) and her face is full of "traps to take fooles in" (6). Continuing to describe the "fetters" (12) of women's bodies, as the speaker proceeds lower, the dangers of female flesh become increasingly acute:

> Armes, and hands, and all parts else,
> Are but Toiles, or Manicles
> Set on purpose to enthrall
> Men, but Slothfulls most of all.
> (7–10)

Men are manacled, enthralled, and made prisoners and slaves by these female figures — at this point, we appear to be in the realm of a fairly orthodox misogyny, and it would seem that the solution is to "Live employ'd" (11) rather than slothfully, in order to "live free" (11). However, the speaker then shifts to admit not only that he has been captured, but also that he *likes* it: rather than taking his own advice, he has instead

> found, and still can prove,
> *The lazie man the most doth love.*
> (13–14)

This unexpected sententia retroactively ironizes the poem's title; the idle speaker is a lazy lover, fettered, manacled, and enthralled by women and their bodies — and is perfectly happy to be so. Herrick returns to this theme in "The silken Snake," in which his frequent beloved Julia

For sport ... threw a Lace
of silke and silver at [his] face.
(1–2)

Though the speaker has a moment of "affright" (5), the putative snake
is harmless; it "scar'd" but "did not bite" (6), startling but not harming
the speaker. Julia's aggressive but ultimately benign gesture suggests a
space of fantasy, one in which a garment typically used to contain female
flesh transforms into a phallic snake as it is thrown at a hapless male.
(It also points to a recurring cross-dressing motif in Herrick that war-
rants further consideration than I will be able to offer here.) Engaging the speaker in harmless play, the encounter evokes the beginning
of a striptease whose titillation comes not from the woman's removal
of clothing but rather the possibility of engaging in bondage play, the
pleasurable threat posed by the garment itself as it makes its way to the
speaker.

"Upon a black Twist, rounding the Arme of the Countesse of Carlile"
similarly draws erotic inspiration from the restrictive possibilities of
female adornment. The Countess wears a "curious twist" of "blackest
silk" (2) on her arm that the speaker quickly eroticizes; the bracelet,

Which, circumvolving gently, there
Enthrall'd her Arme, as Prisoner.
Dark was the Jayle; but as if light
Had met t'engender with the night[.]
(3–6)

The Countess's arm is *enthrall'd*, rendered a *Prisoner* in a *Dark ... Jayle*, language of confinement that emphasizes the physical restriction incurred
by the wearing of the band. This language of imprisonment is combined,
however, with that of sexual generativity; the Countess's "spotlesse
wrist" (1), or *light, Had met t'engender with the night* of the *Dark ... Jayle*.

Beyond the simple fact of sexualization, there are a number of interesting features of this characterization. First, the grammar of the line gives agency to the prisoner, not the jailer; the light meets the night rather than the other way around. In other words, the power lies with the person in bondage in ways that mirror the logic of the masochistic contract. Second, like the overwhelming majority of Herrick's verse, this erotic encounter is neither penetrative nor ejaculative but emerges through the pleasurable mingling of surfaces, here the wrist and the black twist.[20] And third, despite this lack of penetration, the encounter is nevertheless reproductive, an act of *engender*[ing]. While the politics of discursively foisting such reproduction onto a woman are certainly questionable, what is most notable for my purposes is the confluence of these three factors — the expression of masochistic agency; a highly erotic yet non-penetrative encounter; and the implication of reproduction resulting from this assignation. The poem's erotic tenor becomes even more interesting in its back half, in which the speaker both identifies with the imprisoned Countess and desires to take her place:

> … if there be
> Such Freedome in Captivity;
> I beg of Love, that ever I
> May in like Chains of Darknesse lie.
> (9–12)

Not merely asking but *beg*[ging] Love to imprison him in *Chains of Darknesse* perpetually, the speaker's fantasy both aligns him with a female figure, problematizing any assumed distinction between male and female, and places him in a passive, pleasurable, and masochistic position for perpetuity.

20. See James Bromley, *Intimacy and Sexuality in the Age of Shakespeare* (Cambridge, UK: Cambridge University Press, 2012), which tracks the early modern consolidation of "the body's pleasures based on a hierarchized opposition between depths and surfaces" (1).

The enthralling possibilities of manaclesque bracelets are similarly explored in "The Bracelet to Julia" in which the speaker and Julia engage in switchy bondage play. The speaker ties a "silken twist" (2) around Julia's wrist to demonstrate that she is his "pretty Captive" (5). While he initially represents himself as the dominant figure in the relationship, he quickly moves to more metaphorical bondage in which he is the subordinate partner. Julia is subject to mere physical captivity; as he tells her, "Tis but the silke that bindeth thee, / Knap the thread, and thou art free" (7–8), insisting that her bondage is easily broken. The speaker, conversely, is her "Bondslave" (6), "bound, and fast bound" (10) to her in ways that exceed the physical. While Julia's bonds are easily broken through the cutting of a thread, when the speaker characterizes his own imprisonment, he doubles down, insisting that he is not merely *bound* but *fast bound*, emphasizing the permanency of this position of bondage. *Bondslave* also suggests a stronger degree of subjection and longer duration than *Captive* and naturalizes the unequal relationship dynamics, suggesting an element of class subordination on the part of the speaker, and emphasizes the *bond*, or the promise or obligation that connects — indeed, binds — them. Conversely, Julia's characterization as a *Captive* suggests an illegitimate, rather than naturalized, imprisonment. While it is conventional to suggest that love makes one into a slave, there is no recrimination, no regret, and no anger; rather, the speaker closes the poem by saying "from thee I cannot go; / If I co'd, I wo'd not so" (11–12) — even granted his freedom, he would choose to remain eternally bound to Julia.

As one final instance of Herrick's kinky fantasies, I would like to consider "Upon Julia's haire, bundled up in a golden net," a short lyric toward the end of *Hesperides* that again is fascinated with the restrictive potential of women's clothing. Fixated on both Julia's hair and the net that binds it, the speaker urges Julia to shed the "rich deceits" (1), "goldene Toyles, and Trammel-nets" (2) that restrain her locks:

Set free thy Tresses, let them flow
As airs do breathe, or winds doe blow.
(7–8)

His argument hinges on Julia's self-possession; "thine hairs" (3), he states,
are "Already tame, and all thine owne" (4); that is, she is already wholly
in control of her self and her entire body. While one could perhaps question the racialized implications of such positive valuation of *Already tame*
hair, more immediate for my purposes here is the speaker's lack of pos-
sessiveness; he pleads that she let her hair down but recognizes his lack
of right to make dictates about her body, which is *all thine owne*. While
Julia is self-possessed, needing no restraint, the speaker requires confinement:

Tis I am wild, and more then haires
Deserve these Mashes and those snares.
(5–6)

Abjecting himself with his argument that he *deserve*[s] to be *mash*[ed],
snare[d], and confined, the speaker closes with a plea to

let such curious Net-works be
Lesse set for them [her hair], then spred for me.
(9–10)

Unlike Julia, the speaker both needs and desires physical restriction.
Prostrating himself before a self-sovereign female figure, the speaker
fantasizes a scene of cross-dressed bondage in which women's clothes
are used to confine and control his body — and one in which he takes
unmitigated, unproblematic pleasure.

In this chapter, I have tracked only one of many patterns of erotic
deviance in Herrick's poetry, his kinky interest in being penetrated and
beaten, and bound and confined; as these examples have hopefully sug-

gested, however, *Hesperides* is full of fetishistic interest in body parts and accoutrement, non-genital erotic contact, erotic entanglements with flowers and insects, kissing, and voyeurism, to name only a few — a veritable buffet of varieties of sexual expression. To borrow a quote from Melissa E. Sanchez, *Hesperides*, in short, "make[s] visible early modern images of pleasures and intimacies that challenge heteronormative ideals of companionate marriage and 'homonormative' ideals of egalitarian friendship — both of which tend to define sex that is tender and monogamous as the optimal sex."[21] Is Herrick a pervert? According to conventional definitions of perversion — the refusal of teleological sexuality, the lingering over process rather than ends, fetishistic pleasures in accoutrement, a desire for erotic bondage — clearly yes. The point is not to recuperate Herrick from such a designation, to reslot him into normative paradigms of sexual expression. Rather, it is to show how *Hesperides* engages perversion to open up new and different forms of power relationships, of sexual politics, of identification, and of pleasure, for speaker and reader alike; despite their ostensible heteroeroticism, its poems offer a far wider, queerer array of nonpathological and nonpathologized pleasures and positions for the early modern sexual subject than is often assumed possible.

21. Melissa E. Sanchez, "'Use Me but as Your Spaniel': Feminism, Queer Theory, and Early Modern Sexualities," *PMLA* 127, no. 3 (2012): 493–511, at 494, https://doi.org/10.1632/pmla.2012.127.3.493. Sanchez is speaking most immediately in the context of violent female homoeroticism in early modern literature, but the point carries to forms of sexual expression that lie outside of an ostensibly healthy, egalitarian-companionate dyad more generally.

PART 2
Sexual Ethics

The Taming of the Shrew and Sex "in the midst of the street"

Erin E. Kelly

George Bernard Shaw called Shakespeare's *The Taming of the Shrew* disgusting. To be precise, he described Shakespeare's shrew play as "altogether disgusting to modern sentiments" to the extent that "no man with any decency of feeling can sit it out in the company of a woman without being extremely ashamed of the lord-of-creation moral implied in the wager and the speech put into the woman's own mouth."[1] But the same play that Shaw condemned as "one vile insult to womanhood and manhood from the first word to the last" has been described by oth-

---

1. George Bernard Shaw, *Shaw on Shakespeare*, ed. Edwin Wilson (London: Cassell, 1962), 178. Shaw responds here to the main plot of Shakespeare's play, which centers around a Paduan woman named Katherine whose unruliness makes her undesirable to local men and thus blocks her younger sister, Bianca, from being permitted to wed any of her numerous suitors. Petruchio arrives in town seeking a wealthy wife and determines to marry Katherine if her dowry is sufficient; through a series of power moves, he manages to marry Katherine and to "tame" her. The play's final scene demonstrates that Petruchio has transformed her into the most obedient of the play's wives — or, at least, the one most willing to perform obedience — by having her come at his command, throw her hat on the ground, and deliver a long speech advocating for female subservience. A subplot in which Bianca elopes with an unauthorized suitor who disguises himself as a Latin tutor and an opening frame that sets up the Katherine and Bianca scenes as a play-within-a-play round out the action.

ers as showcasing a loving partnership and a good marriage.[2] Declarations that this play is disgusting, misogynistic, or even admirable usually focus on its display of a wife submitting to her husband, and such judgments implicitly evaluate Katherine's obedience speech (and the "taming" encounters that lead up to it) in relation to the concept of consent. It is possible to judge that Katherine and Petruchio have achieved a felicitous union in which the woman's yielding to a dominant man is an expression of love so long as we believe that Katherine meaningfully consents to the way she is treated. One can then debate whether female submission of the sort Katherine describes as what wives owe their husbands is particular to this couple or a necessary condition for any successful heterosexual marriage.[3]

But if we acknowledge that submission and dominance can generate erotic energy, *The Taming of the Shrew* is a play whose central couple ought to be seen as kinky. Ample evidence exists of a long tradition of individuals finding within Katherine and Petruchio's courtship and marriage a model — bolstered by the authority of Shakespeare — that helps to make both legible and acceptable what Gayle Rubin would term their *benign sexual variation*.[4] In her memoir *Sex with Shakespeare*, for example,

2. Examples of scholarly arguments that describe Katherine and Petruchio as winding up with a satisfying, functional marriage include Jeanne Addison Roberts, "Horses and Hermaphrodites: Metamorphoses in *The Taming of the Shrew*," *Shakespeare Quarterly* 34, no. 2 (1983): 159–71; and David Daniell, "The Good Marriage of Katherine and Petruchio," *Shakespeare Survey* 37 (1984): 23–32; additional examples are mentioned below. There is a long history of theatrical productions that present the play as a rollicking romantic comedy with a happy ending; see Elizabeth Schafer, "Introduction," in *The Taming of the Shrew: Shakespeare in Production* (Cambridge, UK: Cambridge University Press, 2002), 1–76, esp. 49–52.

3. For thoughtful exploration of how heterosexual marriage from the early modern period to the present day is figured as dependent upon the wife's negotiated subservience to her husband, see Frances E. Dolan, *Marriage and Violence: The Early Modern Legacy* (Philadelphia: University of Pennsylvania Press, 2008); my reading of *The Taming of the Shrew* differs from Dolan's (see esp. 120–27), but her sense that servants are part of the marital relationship has helpfully shaped my thinking.

4. Gayle Rubin, "Thinking Sex: Notes for a Radical Theory of the Politics of Sexuality," chap. 5 in *Deviations* (Durham NC: Duke UP, 2011), 137–81, 148.

Jillian Keenan turns to *The Taming of the Shrew* to explain how the spank-ings she enjoys differ from physical abuse. For Keenan and her readers, an association with Shakespeare's cultural cache frames kinky desire as not disgusting.[5] If "kink is useful to think with," *The Taming of the Shrew* seems an especially useful play with which to think about kink.[6]

And there are complex issues about kink we can explore by expanding our focus beyond the erotics of the play's central couple. Katherine and Petruchio are alone onstage for only one or two scenes, and the opening frame suggests they are always being watched; at times, they make other characters who observe their encounters into participants. As such, *The Taming of the Shrew* raises questions about the ethics and legality of kink that go beyond a couple's negotiated agreements to consider what type of consent (if any) should be sought from those who witness or, through their presence, become de facto partakers in a kinky encounter. Consent matters in these situations not only because of ethical concerns but also because legal protections in Western countries for a wide range of sex-ual practices are often predicated on a presumed right to privacy. Can kink be benign (and not criminalized) only if it is private? Are there lim-its on the number of people in a sexual encounter and where that activ-ity occurs if it is to be deemed *private?*[7] What types of intimacy might be construed as wholly private given that, as Lauren Berlant and Michael Warner have suggested, even what is construed as vanilla, heteronorma-tive sex is "mediated by publics"?[8] These are the ethical and legal matters

---

5. Jillian Keenan, *Sex with Shakespeare* (New York: Harper Collins, 2016).
6. See the introduction to this volume, "A Renaissance of Kink," by editors Joseph Gamble and Gillian Knoll.
7. See Pat Califia, "Public Sex," 1982, reprint in *Public Sex: The Culture of Radical Sex* (Pitts-burgh PA: Cleis Press, 1994), 71–82, for a helpful historical perspective on how both spaces (e.g., bathhouses) and numbers of people (e.g., more than two people) can and have been used to identify sex as not-private and thus to criminalize behavior of sexual minorities.
8. This analysis of how sexual cultures rely upon behaviors in public — and how a limited range of heterosexuality becomes normative, invisible, and thus seemingly "private" through law, custom, and other publicly acknowledged infrastructure — can be found in Lauren Berlant and Michael Warner, "Sex in Public," *Critical Inquiry* 24 (1998): 547–66.

we can explore by moving beyond questions of consent within Katherine and Petruchio's marriage to consider the positionality of the play's other characters. Paying attention to the individuals in *The Taming of the Shrew* who start as bystanders and get drawn into erotic play as spectators and sometimes props or accomplices can help us think about the myriad ways that sex can be public.

Marriage Models

Indisputably, Shakespeare's play features Petruchio taunting Katherine in their first encounter (2.1.180–93) and then humiliating her with his behavior and appearance on their wedding day (3.2.183–240).[9] He at moments figures Katherine as an animal, most memorably comparing his plan to tame her, by withholding food and preventing sleep, to the way he would treat a hawk (4.1.177–200). He exerts control over her clothing, movement, and speech. And the outcome of Petruchio's domineering is Katherine's offer to put her hand under her husband's foot and her declaration that she is perfectly content to "serve, love, and obey" (5.2.170). Katherine explains that her changed attitude results from the realization that women's bodies are "soft, weak, and smooth" and that their "lances are but straws" (5.2.171, 179). If we see Petruchio as a stand-in for all husbands and Katherine in her final speech as an exemplar for all wives, then these lines, and the play in which they feature, support patriarchal values.

Critical and theatrical interpretations of *The Taming of the Shrew* inevitably come into conversation with this moral lesson when determining whether the play's ending is happy. Shaw's critique assumes that Katherine's expression of obedience to Petruchio would be received positively by those who understood women's submission to men (or at least

---

9. Parenthetical references to the play cite act, scene, and line numbers in William Shakespeare, *The Taming of the Shrew*, ed. Barbara Hodgdon (London: Arden Shakespeare/ Methuen, 2010).

wives' submission to their husbands) as natural. Some clearly received such a lesson from this play; a notable example appears in Mary Cowden Clarke's nineteenth-century prequel in *The Girlhood of Shakespeare's Heroines.*[10] For Clarke, Katherine's shrewishness is a manifestation of high spirits that became unruly because of parental neglect and inadequate education. Katherine has a flash of contentment, though, when a young man named Giulio responds to her acting out at a party by tying her to a tree. The result is that "as her woman's frame involuntarily yields to his masculine strength ... there is an inexplicable acquiescence, an absence of resentment and resistance, altogether unwanted, and surprising to herself."[11] Alas, Giulio departs for a naval assignment the next day, and news soon arrives that he has drowned. Within this story for young female readers, Clarke suggests that Katherine has already had an encounter with the pleasurable feeling of "finding herself completely overcome — *mastered*" that accounts for her final acceptance of Petruchio's regime.[12] Long after Clarke's book was published, even critics and directors who might not describe women as innately dependent on men have posited that Petruchio's "taming" makes Katherine happy by enabling her to become a functional member of society and a beloved wife.[13]

10. Mary Cowden Clarke, "Katherine and Bianca: The Shrew, and the Demure," *The Girlhood of Shakespeare's Heroines in a Series of Tales* (New York: A. C. Armstrong, 1881), 95–184.

11. Clarke, "Katherine and Bianca," 169.

12. Clarke, "Katherine and Bianca," 169. Clarke's text does not intentionally present this instance of bondage as kinky, although we might now interpret it as such. Nineteenth-century assumptions that women were naturally submissive to the point of masochism rendered Victorian male-Dom/female-sub relationships largely *invisible* according to Peter Tupper, *A Lover's Pinch: A Cultural History of Sadomasochism* (Lanham: Rowman and Littlefield, 2018), 146–47.

13. For scholarly examples, in addition to articles referenced above, see Margaret Mikesell, "'Love Wrought These Miracles': Marriage and Genre in *The Taming of the Shrew*," *Renaissance Drama* 20 (1989): 141–67. Schafer's "Introduction" describes director Jonathan Miller's productions as presenting Petruchio as a "therapist" who cures Katherine's disfunction (49).

Condemnations of the play then need only reject the idea that women are naturally submissive to men to argue that Katherine is a victim and Petruchio is abusive. Charles Marowitz's 1970s *The Shrew* seems to literalize Shaw's characterization of *The Taming of the Shrew* as *disgusting* by interspersing contemporary episodes of a heterosexual couple's dating experiences among renditions of scenes from Shakespeare's play in which Katherine is tortured and raped; Katherine presents her final "obedience" speech in a monotone, appearing as an abuse victim whose will has been broken.[14] It seems inevitable that numerous other twentieth-century readings and adaptations of *The Taming of the Shrew* see the play as problematically misogynistic given that the seventeenth-century sequel suggests that even early modern audiences might have thought Petruchio a bully. John Fletcher's *The Woman's Prize, or The Tamer Tamed* focuses its happy ending on Petruchio's capitulation to his second wife, Maria, who refuses to tolerate his shrew-taming ways.[15]

To be clear, tying a woman one has just met to a tree and raping one's partner are forms of assault. But the play text of *The Taming of the Shrew* does not demand explicit physical violence against Katherine. While at her most shrewish moments Katherine strikes her sister (2.1.22sd) and Petruchio (2.1.221sd), there is no stage direction in Shakespeare's play indicating Petruchio hits his wife (although he does beat his servants) — yet physical discipline of Katherine is repeatedly imagined in productions and adaptations. In the late seventeenth-century *Sauny the Scot*, Petruchio threatens to pull out the teeth of his shrewish wife.[16] In the

---

14. Charles Marowitz, *The Shrew (Freely Adapted from William Shakespeare's "The Taming of the Shrew")* (London: Calder and Boyars, 1975), esp. 77–79.

15. John Fletcher's play likely dates to 1609/10 but didn't appear in print until 1647 in Francis Beaumont and John Fletcher, *Comedies and Tragedies* (London, 1647; Wing B1581). For examples of critical arguments that call out Shakespeare's play for misogyny, see Coppélia Kahn, "The Taming of the Shrew: Shakespeare's Mirror of Marriage," *Modern Language Studies* 5, no. 1 (1975): 88–102, https://doi.org/10.2307/3194204; and Lynda Boose, "Scolding Bridles and Bridling Scolds: Taming the Woman's Unruly Member," *Shakespeare Quarterly* 42, no. 2 (1991): 179–213, https://doi.org/10.2307/2870547.

16. See Schafer, "Introduction," 6–7.

eighteenth century, John P. Kemble's performance in David Garrick's *Catherine and Petruchio*, a condensed version of *The Taming of the Shrew*, popularized the convention of Petruchio carrying a whip.[17] By the twentieth century, the potential for a husband to physically discipline his wife manifested in productions that featured spanking. Most memorably, carrying on a bit of stage business featured in Lynne Fontanne and Alfred Lunt's 1930s production of Shakespeare's play, both the 1949 stage musical *Kiss Me, Kate!* and its 1953 film version have lead actor Fred Graham (who happens to be playing Petruchio in a musical version of *The Taming of the Shrew*) put his former wife Lilli Vanessi (in the role of Katherine) over his knee for an extended onstage spanking.[18] The 1963 western film adaptation *McLintock!* concludes with John Wayne, in the title role, reconciling with his estranged wife Katherine, played by Maureen O'Hara, after the entire town helps him chase her down and then watches as he beats her bottom with a shovel.[19]

The popular sense of Katherine and Petruchio's interactions, especially the cultural memory of whips and spankings, makes the play available to inspire kinky and BDSM fantasies.[20] *The Taming of the Shrew* has been referenced in both suggestive and hardcore erotic texts. A Google search of *Taming of the Shrew* and *porn* yields 359,000 results, including a video in which a woman recites the obedience speech while masturbating, a short film in which the feuding actors trying to rehearse a produc-

---

17. Schafer, "Introduction," 9–12.
18. Schafer, "Introduction," 30–33.
19. Clips of *McClintock!*, *Kiss Me Kate*, and other films that feature husbands spanking their wives, a number of which include references to *The Taming of the Shrew*, can be found in Andrew Heisel, "'I Don't Know Whether to Kiss You or Spank You': A Half Century of Fear of an Unspanked Woman," *Jezebel*, April 12, 2016, https://jezebel.com/i-dont-know-whether-to-kiss-you-or-spank-you-a-half-ce-1769140132.
20. There have been productions that associated *The Taming of the Shrew*'s central couple with the trappings of BDSM, but most seem to have done so to signal the play is misogynistic or violent; see Schafer, "Introduction," 41–44, esp. 44.

tion of the play wind up having sex, and a number of spanking scenes.[21] Whether or not Katherine and Petruchio are a model married couple, for those seeking a script to guide their erotic play — or perhaps just to locate in Shakespeare's works evidence that their proclivities have a long history — *The Taming of the Shrew* is a useful resource.

Questions of Consent

We can believe that Katherine finds her marriage to Petruchio satisfying because it relies upon dominant/submissive power plays and that the so-called taming process involves two people happily discovering their kinks are compatible. But even for those who find this dynamic worth imitating, if only in the context of fantasy, it is worth reflecting on how it gets established. Within the context of contemporary discussions of BDSM, the ethics of an action hinge on consent, and *The Taming of the Shrew* includes no clear statement from Katherine consenting to marriage,[22] much less to domination. Early modern wives were arguably so legally disempowered as to preclude meaningful consent; some the-

---

21. Number derived from a Google search performed August 2022. amina_okeefe, "Taming of the Shrew," *T'nA Flix: Just Tits and Ass*, https://www.tnaflix.com/fetish-videos/Taming-of-the-Shrew/video4394825, accessed August 10, 2023, presents a spanking scene in the context of a theatre company rehearsing *Shrew*; Caitlyn8787, "Hysterical Literature: Taming of the Shrew," *PornHub*, 2020, https://www.pornhub.com/view_video.php?viewkey=ph5e5be84f07bf4, features a woman masturbating to Katherine's obedience speech.

22. The omission becomes obvious when one compares Shakespeare's play to the roughly contemporary *Taming of a Shrew*, in which Katherine has an aside in which she declares,

> But yet I will consent and marry him,
> for I methinks have lived too long a maid,
> And match him too, or else his manhood's good.
> (3.sd168, 169–71)

The Taming of a Shrew, ed. Stephen Roy Miller (Cambridge, UK: Cambridge University Press, 1998). (Subsequent references to *A Shrew* cite this edition parenthetically.) While much ink has been spilt trying to determine the relationship between Shakespeare's play and this anonymous text first published in 1594, as *A Pleasnt Conceited Historie Called The Taming of a Shrew* (London, 1594; STC 23667), for the purposes of this argument it doesn't matter which came first.

orists have questioned whether women's consent to be submissive to men is possible within the context of societies that have not achieved gender equality.[23] Even now, eliding the language of love and mutuality with consent is problematic. Recognizing that power imbalances might exist within what appears to be an encounter between two mutually attracted people, current standards for ethical kink assume that all parties involved must explicitly consent to participate.

Adding to the possibility of understanding Katherine as coerced, Petruchio's plan relies on what we would now describe as gaslighting. In a soliloquy he promises,

> If she deny to wed, I'll crave the day
> When I shall ask the banns, and when be married.
> (2.1.178–79)

He then tells Katherine, "[W]ill you, nill you, I will marry you" (2.1.273); and he declares to the men who have just witnessed Katherine saying to him she would rather see him hanged than marry him (2.1.302),

> Tis bargained 'twixt us twain, being alone,
> That she shall still be curst in company.
> (2.1.308–9)

Petruchio denies Katherine's reality, making it impossible for her to say no. The closest the play comes to allowing her agency is Katherine's outburst when Petruchio is late for the scheduled wedding as she describes herself as being in an impossible position:

---

23. For an overview of the constrained legal status of early modern English wives, see Dolan, *Marriage and Violence*. Cheryl Hanna, "Sex is Not a Sport: Consent and Violence in Criminal Law," *Boston College Law Review* 42, no. 2 (2001): 239–90, summarizes legal, ethical, and historical understandings of consent, including an overview of arguments by "regulatory feminists" Andrea Dworkin and Catharine MacKinnon that question the possibility of women's consent within a patriarchal system (282–83).

> I must forsooth be forced
> To give my hand opposed against my heart
> Unto a mad-brain rudesby.
> . . . .
> Now must the world point at poor Katherine
> And say, "Lo, there is mad Petruchio's wife,
> If it would please him come and marry her."
> (3.2.8–10, 18–20)

At best, we can say that Katherine makes a choice in not actively refusing to marry Petruchio.

If there is a moment of positive consent in *The Taming of the Shrew*, it comes in Katherine's final speech, especially if we perceive her as crafting a performance that puts obedience in quotation marks.[24] Katherine justifies female submission on the grounds that a husband is

> one that cares for thee
> And for thy maintenance; commits his body
> To painful labour both by sea and land,
> To watch the night in storms, the day in cold,
> Whilst thou liest warm at home secure and safe.
> (5.2.153–57)

Her vision does not fit with what the play shows us of her own marriage; that is, Petruchio's only labor takes the form of seeking a wife and bossing servants, and her experience consists of not being secure and safe while trying to sleep in his house. But the speech proposes a contract: if the husband will "[commit] his body / To painful labour," the wife will return "love, fair looks, and true obedience" (5.2.154–55, 159). Some

---

24. There is a long performance history of actors signaling through action or intonation that their declaration of obedience is insincere or ironic; see Schafer, "Introduction," 34–36, 43–44, and 66–68, for examples, especially for a discussion of Mary Pickford's famous wink.

rules around power dynamics are negotiated here through self-con-sciously counterfactual language that resembles Petruchio's when he calls the sun the moon before insisting that Katherine do the same.[25]

Particularly if one sees Petruchio as accepting that Katherine is role-playing at servility — and that is a plausible interpretation of his verbal response to her speech: "Why, there's a wench" (5.2.186) — this wife and husband might be understood to have collaboratively created a script for consensual dominant/submissive encounters. People who now look to *The Taming of the Shrew* for erotic inspiration ought to negotiate their own boundaries more explicitly before breaking out a riding crop. But if they assume the play's central relationship is consensual, then they can find in it a model of how a couple might develop something mutually sat-isfying; this ideal is beautifully captured in Gillian Knoll's analysis: "Love and marriage are creative acts for Petruchio and Kate — they *make* mar-riage just as we make love. Their lies are inseminating; from them germi-nates an intimate, erotic, shared and ever so private imaginary in which 'men and women are alone.'"[26]

In Company

Yet Katherine and Petruchio are almost never alone. Key moments, like the final obedience speech, when they could be seen to create a *shared and ever so private imaginary*, mostly take place in a range of public settings — and this raises even more complex questions about consent. Except for a hundred lines of dialogue when they first meet (2.1.180–276), Kather-ine and Petruchio have no sustained private moments onstage — and even that encounter is bookended by Baptista leaving to send Kather-

---

25. Shakespeare's obedience speech offers more room for female agency than the equivalent moment in *Taming of a Shrew*, which has Katherine describe hierarchical husband/wife dynamics as an eternal state of affairs put in place by "The King of kings, the glorious God of heaven" (*A Shrew*, 14.127).

26. Gillian Knoll, *Conceiving Desire in Lyly and Shakespeare: Metaphor, Cognition, and Eros* (Edin-burgh: Edinburgh University Press, 2020), 221.

ine in and then returning to see how the wooing progresses. Considering how much time Katherine and Petruchio spend in the presence of family members, friends, neighbors, and servants, it's fair to say their erotic encounters are always on public display. Relatedly, I believe, we can understand a key element of their erotic play lies in the experience of performing dominance and submission in the company of other people.

As he undertakes the project of taming his wife, Petruchio engages his servants as both audience for and participants in his acts of domination. They at times apparently revel in the chance to demonstrate their submission to the head of household by functioning as instruments that extend their master's power over others. Even though he has chastised them (as "you rogue" [4.1.133] and "whoreson villain" [4.1.141]), Petruchio's men are not just aware of but actively support his plan for managing Katherine, with one accurately noting, "He kills her in her own humour" (4.1.169). Even though Petruchio's only marital and primary romantic relationship is with Katherine, he acts out his dominance over her with the help of a number of willing submissives; his servants function as members of a leather household.

Individuals in this household seem to learn from their master and from one another the range of experiences and actions available to submissives. Grumio gets his opportunity to dominate by following Petruchio's orders. This servant keeps food from Katherine and teases her while imitating his master by insisting he is only concerned with her health — fretting that "too choleric a meat" (4.3.19) will make her ill when he denies her a variety of dishes before finally offering, as though being generous, "mustard without the beef" (4.3.30). Grumio is the servant sent to Katherine with Petruchio's order "I command her come to me" (5.2.100).[27] Katherine's obedience speech then parallels, with its

27. Grumio might be read here as a minor version of the kind of eroticized go-between exemplified by Moll Cutpurse in *The Roaring Girl* or Bellario/Euphrasia in *Philaster* as discussed by Christine Varnado in "Getting Used and Liking It: Erotic Instrumentality and the Go-Between," chap. 1 in *The Shapes of Fancy: Reading for Queer Desire in Early Modern Literature*

hyperbolic expression of submission, Grumio's earlier insistence that he will not follow Petruchio's request to "knock me here soundly" (1.2.8) because, as he queries while being beaten for his refusal to knock on Hortensio's door, "was it fit for a servant to use a master so?" (1.2.31–32). Both Grumio, by embracing the role of protective servant, and Katherine, by over-identifying as a perfect wife, justify what amounts to disobedience, topping from the bottom.

Petruchio brings Hortensio into his household, making him a party to the taming campaign. While visiting the newly married couple, this friend withholds food from Katherine by following Petruchio's instruction "Eat it all up, Hortensio, if thou lovest me" (4.3.52). As Petruchio dismisses the tailor's man and denies his wife clothing, Hortensio aids in the smooth expression of the husband's dominance by acceding to the command "Hortensio, say thou wilt see the tailor paid" (4.3.163). Not only Petruchio declaring, "It shall be the moon or star or what I list / Or e'er I journey to your father's house" (4.5.7–8), but also Hortensio advising, "Say as he says, or we shall never go" (4.5.11) motivates Katherine to yield. Her proclamation offers obedience while acknowledging a set of rules:

[S]un it is not, when you say it is not,
And the moon changes even as your mind,
What you will have it named, even that it is
And so it shall be for Katherine.
(4.5.20–23)

Hortensio here becomes both participant in and witness to the couple's play of dominance and submission. Although he does not seem aroused by following Petruchio's orders, he gets what he wants by helping Katherine understand the rewards of acquiescence — they are all able to

(Minneapolis: University of Minnesota Press, 2020), https://manifold.umn.edu/read/the-shapes-of-fancy/section/5bd47c92-ddc2-40c6-844d-02b6f10e0d86#ch01.

travel to her sister's wedding only if Katherine gives in. Hortensio clearly sees his male friend as a model to emulate, declaring,

> Well Petruchio, this has put me in heart.
> Have to my widow, and if she be forward,
> Then hast thou taught Hortensio to be untoward.
> (4.5.78–80)

The play's final scene shows Hortensio to be less successful as a wife-tamer, but Petruchio's public domination of Katherine presents a script for what Hortensio desires, and he consistently seems a willing participant in the couple's scenes.

But it is more difficult to describe Katherine and Petruchio's engagement with others as equally consensual. Vincentio, who enters immediately after Katherine calls the sun the moon, gets treated as an occasion for play, even as a prop. After Lucentio's father Vincentio comes upon them on the road, Petruchio describes the older man as a "Fair lovely maid" (4.5.35), thus motivating Katherine to greet him as "Young budding virgin, fair, and fresh, and sweet" (4.5.38). While amusing for knowing spectators, the person being misidentified might reasonably be upset; Hortensio seems correct to surmise "A will make the man mad, to make a woman of him" (4.5.36-37) since Vincentio reveals he has experienced discomfort (at least from confusion and possibly from fear of insanity) by admitting "your strange encounter much amazed me" (4.5.55). Albeit fleeting, this moment of dragging into their role-playing scene a stranger who happens to occupy the same public space is arguably the first instance in which Katherine and Petruchio mutually negotiate their engagement with one another — and it notably deviates from what many would see as basic ethical standards for kink by failing to obtain consent from all participants.

Having his wife perform obedience in front of others seems to excite Petruchio given his repetition and heightening of orders to perform such

actions. He wins the wager not just because Katherine comes at his command, throws down her hat, and publicly declares her submission but
as a result of this behavior taking place in front of a house full of wedding guests. And even if Katherine and Petruchio both fully consent to
playing out this Dom/sub encounter, they make at least some of their
witnesses function as less than willing participants. After Petruchio tells
her to "fetch" (5.2.109) Bianca and the Widow to their husbands, Katherine chooses to obey, but the other women are forced, having previously
refused to come and then being led onstage in a manner that causes
Petruchio to describe them "as prisoners" (5.2.126). Katherine follows
Petruchio's command when she launches into her speech, but both members of the couple ignore the Widow's clear refusal to participate as she
states, "[W]e will have no telling" (5.2.138) and "She shall not" (5.2.140).
Petruchio seems to enjoy Katherine's public declaration of the duty that
wives owe to husbands, and other men present laud her as "a wonder" (5.2.195). But the women who are demeaned by being compared
to "a fountain troubled, / Muddy, ill-seeming, thick, bereft of beauty"
(5.2.147-49) are coerced, if only momentarily, into unwanted submissive roles.[28] If Katherine and Petruchio were alone, their mutual consent
would be sufficient — by making their erotic play public, however, they
engage in actions that touch upon complex issues of both ethics and law.

---

28. *Taming of a Shrew* holds open other possibilities, suggesting that even if Katherine takes
pleasure from submission, other married women need not do so. After that play's version
of the obedience speech, Katherine's sister Emilia seems to negotiate a different dynamic
with her new husband, responding to him calling her a shrew by pointing out, "That's better than a sheep" (14.60). Polidor might not have a tamed wife, but Emilia's wit promises
the excitement of a woman with some spirit; for more on the powerful and erotic implications of women's wit, see Pamela Allen Brown, *Better a Shrew Than a Sheep: Women, Drama,
and the Culture of Jest in Early Modern England* (Ithaca, NY: Cornell University Press, 2003).

Doing It in Public

While all agree that consent remains central to questions about when any erotic act becomes ethically problematic (or even amounts to criminal assault), what is recognized as legal in terms of kinky sex has often been determined to rely not just on consent but also privacy. When behaviors take place in public — spaces where others might witness them — legal discussions normally assume that the rights of those who would find an act disgusting, distasteful, upsetting, or unwanted must be protected. Stuart P. Green's work on legal aspects of sex describes public acts as potentially problematic because of what he identifies as negative sexual autonomy, "the right *not* to engage in, or be subject to, one or another form of sexual conduct."[29]

Exhibitionism, which Green discusses under the more general heading *indecent exposure*, can be ethically and legally tricky because there are situations in which public nudity or even public sexual behavior might inadvertently subject others to something they don't want to see — for example, a couple having sex in a park because they have no other place in which to be intimate would not intentionally be exhibitionistic. Intent matters when it comes to determining whether nudity is indecent or even criminal, and deliberate sexual exhibitionism is even more fraught.[30]

The ethics of exhibitionism raise particularly complicated questions within communities that identify as kinky. For instance, in the Reddit forum r/BDSMAdvice a person wrote,

> My bf [boyfriend] is really into exhibitionism but I'm not. I won't do anything too public bc [because] of the consent issue (bystanders). I tried suggesting bdsm clubs (or zoom calls lol) but he wasn't inter-

29. Stuart P. Green, *Criminalizing Sex: A Unified Liberal Theory* (Oxford: Oxford University Press, 2020), 22.
30. Green, *Criminalizing Sex*, chap. 13.

ested. He says the risk of getting caught is what does it for him, not the flashing(?). Do [*sic*] anyone have any ideas?[31]

All sixteen replies to this posting argue that it is unethical (as well as legally risky) to have sex where just anyone could stumble on their encounter. Making a similar point, sexuality educator Charlie Glickman has criticized the Kink.com site Public Disgrace because "the [video] shoots [of sexual activity] that take place in public settings are forcing observers to participate in the experience."[32] It is in part for this reason that Greta Christina at the end of a blog post pondering "The Ethics of Public Sex" writes, "I'm coming up blank on this one."[33]

While those who enjoy exhibitionism discuss how best to practice this kink ethically, legal rulings have made the situation more complex by broadly construing what counts as public sex. The 2003 US Supreme Court case *Lawrence v. Texas* ruled unconstitutional laws that prohibit sexual acts — including sodomy and oral sex — between any consenting adults regardless of their gender. That ruling relied on precedents positing a constitutional right to privacy to insist a couple's behavior within their own home would normally be protected. But what conditions make a space public rather than private? A dissenting justice in the *Lawrence v. Texas* case went so far as to query whether situations involving more than two people merit protection; legal scholar Lior Jacob Strahilevitz records that "[Antonin] Scalia wondered aloud how 'privacy' could possi-

31. Supersecretspecialac, "Ethical Exhibitionism?" r/BDSMAdvice, Reddit, August 26, 2020, https://www.reddit.com/r/BDSMAdvice/comments/ihcz40/ethical_exhibitionism/.
32. Charlie Glickman, "Consent and Public Disgrace," *Charlie Glickman PhD* (blog), March 20, 2011, https://charlieglickman.com/consent-and-public-disgrace/; see also Glickman, "The Nuances of Consent: More Thoughts about Public Disgrace," *Charlie Glickman PhD* (blog), March 29, 2011, http://new.charlieglickman.com/the-nuances-of-consent-more-thoughts-about-public-disgrace/.
33. Greta Christina, "The Ethics of Public Sex," *Greta Christina's Blog*, October 9, 2009, https://gretachristina.typepad.com/greta_christinas_weblog/2009/10/ethics-of-public-sex-1.html.

bly cover five people, let alone some larger number, such as 'the number of people required to fill the Coliseum.'"[34]

In raising this objection, Scalia echoes past instances when people's actions were determined not to merit the protections afforded to private behavior. For example, in 1976 the United States Fourth Circuit Court ruled that a married heterosexual couple was not allowed to claim that their sexual acts were private because they had invited another man to join them for a threesome. The case came about after one of their children brought to school polaroid photos these adults had taken of their consensual encounters; the couple was then charged with sodomy. The court specifically ruled that "once a married couple admits strangers as onlookers, federal protection of privacy dissolves."[35] Both the British and European legal systems invoked similar reasoning in the so-called Spanner case, a 1993 legal judgment in England against a group of men who engaged in sadomasochistic acts as members of a private sex club. Although consensual homosexual activity was legal in England at the time, the charge brought under the Offenses Against Persons Act classified the behaviors in the club as assault. The European Court of Human Rights then upheld the men's conviction in part on the grounds that their encounters were not private. While Article 8 of the European Convention for Human Rights and Fundamental Freedoms declares, "Everyone shall have the right to respect for his private and family life," because what took place in the club was videotaped, the court determined the sexual encounters could not be considered private and therefore were not legally protected.[36]

---

34. Lior Strahilevitz, "Consent, Aesthetics, and the Boundaries of Sexual Privacy after Lawrence v. Texas," *DePaul Law Review* 54 (2005): 671–700, at 671.

35. Strahilevitz, "Consent," 672–73.

36. Hanna, "Sex Is Not a Sport," 263–67. See also "History of the Spanner Case," *The Spanner Trust*, accessed August 10, 2023, http://www.spannertrust.org/documents/spannerhistory.asp.

These and other cases that have come to the attention of law enforcement suggest how shaky it is to build legal protections on the foundation of privacy. The 2022 United States Supreme Court case overturning *Roe v. Wade* further calls into question whether Americans have a constitutional right to privacy. And making sexual content visible to an observer — whether as a participant in a threesome or as part of an audience as large as the one Scalia imagined would fill the Coliseum — complicates the ethics of consent beyond what those following Safe, Sane, and Consensual practices might be able to negotiate in advance of any encounter.[37] But just as *The Taming of the Shrew* offers test cases for the ethics of doing it in public in scenes that feature Katherine and Petruchio's exhibitionistic Dom/sub play, it also hints at some different ways of negotiating consent in the context of public erotic behavior.

Playgoing with Christopher Sly

Shakespeare arguably smooths over what would be a tangle of ethical and legal questions by signaling that Katherine and Petruchio exist in the context of a play — specifically the "kind of history" being staged by a group of traveling players for Christopher Sly.[38] Indeed, it is because of the opening frame that Jillian Keenan asserts — even after she describes Petruchio's process for taming Katherine as "uncomfortable and alarming" — that "their relationship is a literal fantasy. It's play." She then

37. For useful definitions of Safe, Sane, and Consensual; Risk-Aware Consensual Kink; and other guidelines, as well as discussions of the implications of each set of parameters, see D. J. Williams et al., "From 'SSC' and 'RACK' to the '4Cs': Introducing a New Framework for Negotiating BDSM Participation," *Electronic Journal of Human Sexuality* 17 (2014), http://www.ejhs.org/volume17/BDSM.html.
38. For an example of how attending to the opening Christopher Sly frame shapes reception of the Katherine-Petruchio plot, see Michael Shapiro, "Framing the Taming: Metatheatrical Awareness of Female Impersonation in *The Taming of the Shrew*," *Yearbook of English Studies* 23 (1993): 143–66, https://doi.org/10.2307/3507978. This sort of argument is troubled by the fact that so many productions of the play omit the Sly scenes; see Schafer, "Introduction," 51–64, for an overview of the ways Sly material has been treated.

queries, "Should we hold play to the same standards as reality?"[39] We could find pornography that skips discussions of safewords and limits acceptable because we understand the video we are watching to be a staged fantasy rather than a document of a spontaneous reality.[40] Katherine and Petruchio's interactions might seem similarly unproblematic as long as they are situated within a theatrical entertainment "[w]hich bars a thousand harms and lengthens life" (Ind.2.132). More interesting, I believe, is how the opening frame of *The Taming of the Shrew* explores the complex pleasures that are made possible when an audience member consents to allow a particular amount of risk.

The varying levels of consent the opening frame of *The Taming of the Shrew* sets up are readily apparent when one compares it to the roughly contemporary, anonymous *Taming of a Shrew.* In neither play does the Lord seek or obtain consent from the inebriated, unconscious tinker who awakes to find himself dressed as a nobleman and surrounded by people telling him that he has a fine house, servants, and a wife. *The Taming of the Shrew* highlights the power dynamics of the deception when one of the Lord's huntsmen comments on the Lord's scheme: "Believe me, lord, I think he cannot choose" (Ind.1.41). But others are given more or less mediated access to plans regarding the scenarios in which they will perform. In *A Shrew,* the boy ordered to play the role of the tinker's wife receives both explicit instructions about what to do as well as an opportunity to offer enthusiastic consent — he declares,

---

39. Keenan, *Sex with Shakespeare*, 97, 98.

40. Highlighting the difference between reality and fantasy seems to me exactly the point made in the closing frame of the anonymous *Taming of a Shrew.* After being once again dressed in his own clothes and deposited on the ground outside the tavern, Sly awakens to tell the Tapster he does not worry that his wife will be angry at him for being out (and drunk) all night — after all, "I know now how to tame a shrew. / I dreamt upon it all this night till now" (15.16–17). Part of the joke here is that Sly conflates a play world with his real life.

Fear not, my lord, I'll dandle him well enough,
And make him think I love him mightily.
(1.77–78)

In *The Taming of the Shrew*, the parallel boy character only receives indirect orders to dress and behave as a lady would (Ind.1.104–34). The boy in *A Shrew* is a member of the Lord's playing company, whereas in *The Taming of the Shrew* the page Bartholomew is a member of the Lord's household; based on their official positions, only one of these individuals has agreed that his work includes playacting. And the players receive different briefings about the Lord's intentions; those in *A Shrew* get told that the Lord will pretend to be a servant as part of a prank (1.64–68) while those in *The Taming of the Shrew* are informed only that they will be performing for a nobleman who "never heard a play" and thus might behave strangely (Ind.90–98, 95).[41]

The fact that the Lord in Shakespeare's play does not offer everyone complete information about his plans is notable given that he clearly intends the scene featuring Sly-as-lord will be erotically charged. The Lord anticipates the pleasure he will take from watching the tinker and his page interact: "I long to hear him call the drunkard 'husband'" (Ind.1.123). He orders servants to carry Sly into "my fairest chamber," which they should "hang ... round with all my wanton pictures" (Ind.1.45–46). It is later revealed that the images in these *wanton* pictures link sex to power imbalance (in the case of Venus and Adonis), deception (Jove and Io), and force (Apollo and Daphne). The Lord's encounter with Sly extends these mythological coercive encounters into the present and clarifies why the duping of Sly is so exciting for him. The Lord, in sum, offers a problematic case study of an individual's "fantasy" authorizing a lack of consent from all participants.

---

41. For arguments about the implications of differences between the induction of *A Shrew* and *The Shrew*, see Leah Marcus, "The Shakespearean Editor as Shrew-Tamer," *ELR* 22, no. 2 (1992): 177–200.

But even in the absence of explicit agreements spelled out before the start of their erotically charged performances, the characters in the opening frame of *The Taming of the Shrew* offer numerous examples of on-the-fly negotiations of consent. After being introduced to his "wife," Sly wants to address this person respectfully, possibly as an equal, and asks,

> Are you my wife and will not call me "husband"?
> My men should call me "lord";
> I am your goodman.
> (Ind.2.101–02)

Despite getting a response to his request for her given name — "'Al'ce madam'? or 'Joan madam'" (Ind.2.107) — that directs him to use a generic form of address — "'Madam', and nothing else. So lords call ladies" (Ind.2.108) — Sly attempts something more personal, addressing the person before him as "Madam wife" (Ind.2.109). This attempt to connect with the wife as an individual with some agency explains his reaction to her lament that she has been "all this time abandoned from your bed" (Ind.2.112). His response, "Madam, undress you and come now to bed" (Ind.2.114), inevitably gets a laugh from audiences who know he is speaking to a boy dressed as a woman, but, fundamentally, this is an attempt to meet his wife's needs. And it is easy to overlook how quickly Sly backs off when she refuses his advances. The page improvises a boundary by saying,

> [L]et me entreat of you
> To pardon me yet for a night or two ...
> For your physicians have expressly charged ...
> That I should yet absent me from your bed.
> (Ind. 2.115–20)

Sly then respects this limit. Their exchange amounts to a couple cooperatively establishing the parameters of how they will engage with one another. In this moment, Sly and his "wife" present the clearest example of openly negotiated power dynamics within a marital relationship we find in *The Taming of the Shrew*.

Because the entire opening frame relies on levels of coercion and deception, it cannot be said to offer a straightforward model for ethical kink — but it does invite us to consider the complexity of shifting but sometimes acceptable levels of risk and consent. Who in this scene is consenting and when? Who has not explicitly consented but seems to be willingly participating and deriving pleasure from ongoing play? Most importantly, who is harmed? What goes right in the scenario the Lord has created for his own enjoyment, and what could go wrong? Such questions not only allow for nuanced discussions of ethical kink but also point to a different legal foundation for protecting sexual expression, including acts that are not entirely private: a reasonable expectation of a right to bodily autonomy.

This principle underpins a Canadian ruling that extended legal protections to those who engage in group sex. In 2005, the Supreme Court of Canada overturned laws that had criminalized bawdy houses as a threat to public morality and thus made people who engaged in consensual sexual activity in group settings (such as a club or dungeon) subject to prosecution. The cases that led to this decision had been brought against a man named Labaye for running a members-only sex club and another named Kouri for encouraging indecency by managing a sex club that allowed entry to couples who paid an admission fee. The Supreme Court determined that sex need not be completely private — or approved of by the majority of the population — to be legal. Rather, as long as such activity took place in what could be defined as a semi-public space, it was protected by an individual's right to autonomy rather than their right to privacy. Both consent and morality could be delimited by an individual's decision to enter a group sex club or other *semi-public* space and their autonomous understanding of themselves as deriving benefit from their participation.[42] In such a situation, meaningful consent resides in the individual's choice to avoid a space, to enter and remain in it, or to enter and then leave.

This concept of bodily autonomy makes possible individual determination of what is and is not more pleasurable than it is harmful within a negotiated set of limits. It therefore suggests a legal parallel to the ethical principles laid out by those who advocate for Risk-Aware Consensual Kink. And it offers possible guidelines for those inclined to exhibitionism. We see a version of this idea in the responses to the Reddit post requesting advice about how the writer and their boyfriend might ethically have sex in public that suggest creating a scene in which potential witnesses consent to being surprised — for instance, in a recommendation that they arrange for willing friends to "catch" them in the act.[43] This scenario doesn't necessarily rely on explicitly negotiated consent for all that might happen; the exhibitionistic couple and their potential witnesses need not discuss in advance every act that someone might witness in what they establish to be a semi-public erotic space. But advanced planning takes seriously the bodily autonomy of the people who will walk in on the couple and see them having sex; potential observers offer consent regarding whether or not to enter a room in which they know a sexual scenario might take place but then can negotiate on the fly how they wish to watch, participate, or depart.

In other words, exhibitionists and others who enjoy sex in public can ethically create scenes that work like improvisational rather than scripted and meticulously rehearsed theatre. For those planning such

---

42. Detailed summaries and discussion of these two Canadian cases, which were brought to the Supreme Court together, can be found in Elaine Craig, "Laws of Desire: The Political Morality of Public Sex," *McGill Law Journal* 54, no. 2 (2009): 355–85, https://doi.org/10.7202/038658ar.
43. supersecretspecialac, "Ethical Exhibitionism?"

improvisations, *The Taming of the Shrew* provides both scripts for Dom-sub encounters and a case study for working through questions about consent, harm, and pleasure. And, as a play, it offers fodder for the thoughtful exploration of how we might reasonably seek and obtain consent from those who are potential witnesses to erotic acts. Anyone participating in semi-public or public sex can draw from the model of how theatres — for instance by providing a content warning about nudity and adult content on the ticket sale website — presume consent to watch without seeking approval from each audience member for exactly what will be presented onstage. Perhaps live theatre, and especially *The Taming of the Shrew,* can help mediate heated debates about sexual ethics, including recent disputes about whether sex scenes on television are problematic because not all viewers consent to see such material and annual arguments about whether to allow kink at Pride given that not all people want to see fetish gear, nudity, or suggestive behavior.

Taking Kink to the Street

Most importantly, *The Taming of the Shrew* suggests why those who do not think of themselves as kinky — even those who consider kink at Pride inappropriate or disgusting — would benefit from some reflection on the ethical and legal complexities of public eroticism. The title of this essay quotes the one moment in *The Taming of the Shrew* that speaks directly to such an action. Katherine's response to Petruchio's order "kiss me, Kate" (5.1.134) is "What, in the midst of the street?" (5.1.135). She clarifies that she is not shy about kissing her husband but "ashamed to kiss" (5.1.137) where almost anyone could see them. Ultimately, she yields to her husband's request and thus meets the condition Petruchio has set to join her sister's wedding party rather than to return to his house. While some might perceive Katherine and Petruchio, the only two characters onstage at this moment, to be in private, Katherine's line suggests the street is a public space where different rules for behavior operate. Her objection further reminds us that the standards of what is public or private, as well as what is disgusting or acceptable (what counts as benign or upsetting, kinky or vanilla), change over time.

A kiss between spouses, even in a public setting, seems innocuous to modern audiences but might have been understood among early modern people as improper outside the context of a wedding or a greeting. Understandings of privacy in sixteenth- and seventeenth-century England differed from our own. In households comprised of multi-generational family members and servants, sex would necessarily occur not only in places where someone might come upon a couple but also in shared rooms and even beds. Both in the street and in what we would consider public indoor spaces, some actions we typically characterize as private might be acceptable since, as Laura Gowing puts it, "the distinction between public and private was still ... in the making; the private family was hard to conceptualise when so much of domestic life had a public context."[44]

Community standards as well as definitions of community change, and debates about what is and is not ethical (or legal) need to take seriously that privacy is a shaky foundation on which to build a case for the right to consensual sexual expression. Berlant and Warner note that heterosexual relationships benefit from *a notion of privacy* that is not extended to queer encounters while also showing through vivid examples that a particular act between consenting heterosexual partners might be denigrated as problematic, kinky, or disgusting as soon as it is made public.[45] Even George Bernard Shaw's evaluation of *The Taming of the Shrew* as *disgusting* calls attention to the complexities of social contexts; Shaw objects not just to the *lord-of-creation moral* but to the expe-

---

44. Laura Gowing, *Common Bodies: Women, Touch, and Power in Seventeenth-Century England* (New Haven: Yale University Press, 2003), 29. For further discussion of changing ideas of privacy, see Lena Cowen Orlin, *Private Matters and Public Culture in Post-Reformation England* (Ithaca: Cornell University Press, 1994).
45. Berlant and Warner, "Sex in Public," 547.

rience of being a man in a theatre seated next to a woman and therefore possibly perceived by his companion and others present as approving of patriarchal principles.

But both *The Taming of the Shrew* and a contemporary of George Bernard Shaw's with whom he might have seen a production of this play point to other ways of delimiting individual rights and public morality, private consent and semi-public bodily autonomy. Actress Mrs. Patrick Campbell, who originated the role of Eliza in Shaw's *Pygmalion,* when asked for her opinion of two men's intimate relationship reportedly replied, "Does it matter what these affectionate people do — so long as they don't do it in the streets and frighten the horses!"[46] This quotation invites us to reflect on whether public sex (and the display of behavior related to sex, such as kink at Pride) is problematic because it takes place in a space where others who have not explicitly consented might witness it — that is, because someone is doing it in the street — or only if it causes distress or harm — that is, if it frightens the horses. Even if the latter, how might those assumed to have a right to bodily autonomy be reasonably expected to encounter and manage risk? (Is the problem that the horses are frightened? Or might anyone on a crowded Edwardian street need to keep in mind that a frightened horse might trample a person?) For exhibitionists as well as others whose proclivities might require or attract spectators, whether they pursue their pleasures in public or semi-public spaces, legal and ethical debates are not yet fully settled. Rather than continuing to focus on the lessons it offers about the presumed insularity of heteronormative married relations, *The Taming of the Shrew* seems more useful as a play through which we can safely explore kink, even the ethics of public sex *in the midst of the street.*

---

46. A biography of Mrs. Campbell can be found in Elaine Aston, "Campbell [nee Tanner], Beatrice Stella [performing name Mrs. Patrick Campbell]," *Oxford Dictionary of National Biography,* (Oxford: Oxford UP, 2021), https://doi.org/10.1093/ref:odnb/32261. The quote presented here is widely attributed to her; see "Mrs. Patrick Campbell," *Wikiquote,* last modified October 6, 2021, at 19:34, https://en.wikiquote.org/wiki/Mrs_Patrick_Campbell.

"What pretty new device": Bondage and Liminality in Beaumont and Fletcher's *The Maid's Tragedy*

Nathaniel C. Leonard

It is easy to overlook the potential for kink in revenge tragedy. This should come as no surprise given the importance of norms, particularly regarding gender and violence, to most readings of the genre. In fact, the celebration and stabilization of heteronormative, cis-gendered masculine violence is so fundamental to a great deal of discourse on revenge tragedy in Renaissance England that it has become a critical commonplace. As Roxanne Grimmett astutely observes, "Revenge tragedy is a dramatic sub-genre that conventionally develops an unsettling level of audience sympathy for male characters who are, essentially, murderers."[1] The figure of the revenger has in fact become so closely aligned with masculinity in the discourses on the genre that twentieth-century critics have largely ignored the unique qualities that differentiate autonomous female revengers from their male counterparts. This is completely

---

1. Roxanne Grimmett, "'By Heaven *and* Hell': Re-evaluating Representations of Women and the Angel/Whore Dichotomy in Renaissance Revenge Tragedy," *Journal of International Women's Studies* 6, no. 3 (2005): 31–39, at 31.

understandable given that so many of the great female roles in revenge tragedy participate in the revenge plot by acting as agents for the primary male protagonist or rely on male characters to act as intermediaries who carry out violence on behalf of a female character. Bel-Imperia (*The Spanish Tragedy*), Lavinia (*Titus Andronicus*), and Castiza (*The Revenger's Tragedy*) all inhabit this role by acting as the primary male revenger's "girl Friday"; Maria (*Antonio's Revenge*) and Domitia (*The Roman Actor*) similarly participate in their respective revenge plots but only as co-conspirators in a plan that the reader is meant to associate with the male protagonist. In the case of characters like Beatrice-Joanna (*The Changeling*) and the Duchess of Malfi (*The Duchess of Malfi*), male characters act in their name to enact the violence of the narrative. In other words, the English early modern tradition of revenge tragedy has very few characters like Medea, the autonomous female revenger of antiquity that John Kerrigan uses to organize his chapter focused on feminism in *Revenge Tragedy: Aeschylus to Armageddon.*[2]

That is not to say that autonomous female revengers are absent from the period; in fact, when they do appear, they have a profound ability to highlight the systemic misogyny of early modern culture. One of the primary examples, Evadne in Francis Beaumont and John Fletcher's *The Maid's Tragedy*, is a particularly nontraditional revenger who utilizes her liminal position as the King's paramour to invert traditional erotic power dynamics through the overt use of sexual bondage. And, interestingly, it is her relationship to this early modern expression of kink

---

2. This chapter effectively ignores English Renaissance revenge tragedies. It should be noted that Kerrigan's move should not be read as an absence of influence. See John Kerrigan, "Medea Studies: Euripides to Pasolini," chap. 4 in *Revenge Tragedy: Aeschylus to Armageddon* (Oxford: Clarendon Press, 2001), 88–110. Tanya Pollard has very persuasively argued the influence of female characters from the ancient Greek tragedy on the English early modern revenge tradition, but that influence is limited to the manner in which those ancient plays use female characters to generate "powerful solicitations of audience sympathies." See Tanya Pollard, *Greek Tragic Women on Shakespearean Stages* (Oxford: Clarendon Press, 2017), 110.

that serves as the foundation of her resistance to immoral patriarchal authority in the climactic moments of the play. Beaumont and Fletcher's portrayal of Evadne clearly demonstrates that kink, rather than being anachronistic, is an important lens for discussing early modern culture due to how explicitly *The Maid's Tragedy* engages with BDSM practice. The play's utilization of the logic of bondage indicates not only that kink existed in the period but also that it was recognizable enough to the London theatre-going public to be referenced by popular writers without need for explanation.

The challenge for modern readers when discussing any female autonomous revenger in early modern drama, like Evadne, is that it is difficult to divorce ourselves from the expectation that revenge tragedy revels in inherently masculinized fantasies of violence. This is part of the reason that the lens of kink, and more specifically in this case BDSM, is so valuable as a critical tool when reading texts like *The Maid's Tragedy*; these frameworks, because of their investment in inverting power dynamics and nontraditional sexual identities, offer a uniquely effective means for discussing cultural resistance to the overreach of normative patriarchal power structures. The limitations of viewing revenge tragedy as inherently masculine are particularly apparent in the work of a number of recent critics who have discussed the manner in which Evadne's role as female revenger allows her to transcend and critique traditional gender roles. They understandably tend to read her violent actions in terms of this same traditional gender model and also tend to pass over the importance of her sexual practice. For example, Alison Findlay goes so far as to posit that "Evadne becomes a monstrous parody of phallic power" and sees her violent behavior as inherently driven by the manner in which the text masculinizes her.[3] While others don't necessarily go as far as Findlay, they do often describe Evadne's behavior in terms of

---

3. Alison Findlay, *A Feminist Perspective on Renaissance Drama* (Oxford: Blackwell Publishers, 1999), 73, 72–76.

standard masculine narratives or as an absolute rejection of traditional femininity. For example, Janet Clare's position that *The Maid's Tragedy* is "the only play of the period in which a woman avenges her own honour" shows this inclination to inscribe Evadne within traditional gender models.[4] Instead we should build on readings like Cristina Leon Alfar's, which invites us to see Evadne's struggle with identity in masochistic terms, when she points out that Evadne's desperate attempts to salvage her marriage with Amintor are based on a need to reclaim a patriarchally sanctioned feminine role within the marriage economy "because otherwise she is nothing."[5] The text of the play invites an alternative interpretation of Evadne's navigation of gender that destabilizes a standard gender binary. Evadne certainly describes the loss of her chastity, her preparation for revenge, and her act of regicide as separating her from her femininity, but instead of replacing her femininity with masculine discourse, she utilizes her mastery of kinky sexual practice to leverage her suspended gender position in a futile attempt to repair her relationship to her femininity. This embracing of what twenty-first-century readers might recognize as a genderqueer construction of identity in which her gender position is inherently protean, even if the play characterizes it as dehumanizing, points to the text's investment in a more nuanced interrogation of early modern gender models.

English forays into revenge narratives in the early modern period are often preoccupied with inherent social critiques housed in the genre's basic assumptions, which they see outlined in the precedent set by Seneca. Both metatheatrical devices and alternative inset cultural performances act in these plays to reduce the immediacy of the seditious

---

4. Janet Clare, "'She's Turned Fury': Women Transmogrified in Revenge Plays," in *Revenge and Gender in Classical, Medieval and Renaissance Literature*, ed. Lesel Dawson and Fiona McHardy (Edinburgh: Edinburgh University Press, 2018), 221–36, at 231. This is a position that is at the very least arguable. See Isabella in Thomas Middleton's *Women Beware Women*.

5. Cristina Leon Alfar, "Staging the Feminine Performance of Desire: Masochism in 'The Maid's Tragedy.'" *Papers on Language and Literature* 31, no. 3 (Summer 1995): par. 16.

potential latent in the staging of regicide, cannibalism, and private revenge.[6] *The Maid's Tragedy* uses kink, in particular BDSM, as one such cultural performance, which in this particular case generates the same stabilizing aesthetic distance that a play like *The Spanish Tragedy* creates through the use of the-play-within-the-play. This use of kink in Beaumont and Fletcher's play also serves to justify and stabilize the violence perpetrated by an autonomous female revenger against the man who benefits from exerting patriarchal authority over her and demonstrates the lack of recourse that women in the period had when it came to the problematic ways that they were trafficked.[7] The limited authority that female characters like Evadne are able to generate in these moments is largely due to the revenge tragedy genre's investment in the restaging of cultural performance as a medium for exploring how individuals negotiate cultural competence.[8] Beaumont and Fletcher negotiate the relationship between feminine authority and cultural competence in the play through language that elides violence, sexuality, and ritual, which in turn blurs the boundaries between them and contextualizes all three practices as forms of performance. And it is through the play's investment in the performative and ritualized nature of sexuality, as well as the importance of Evadne's skill as a sexual practitioner, that the centrality of kink to the text and its strategies for generating aesthetic distance become all the more apparent.

6. *Cultural performance* was coined by Milton Singer and describes "particular instances of cultural organization, e.g., weddings, temple festivals, recitations, plays, dances, musical concerts, etc." See Singer, Milton, *Traditional India: Structure and Change* (Philadelphia: The American Folklore Society, 1959), xiii.

7. See Gayle Rubin, "The Traffic in Women," in *Literary Theory: An Anthology*, 2nd ed., ed. Julie Rivkin and Michael Ryan (Malden: Blackwell Publishing, 2004), 770–94.

8. I'm using *cultural competence* in Pierre Bourdieu's sense of the term, which references the relative knowledge of the structures and rules of a given artistic or cultural system that allow one to fully engage with it. To use Bourdieu's words, "A work of art has meaning and interest only for someone who possesses the cultural competence, that is, the code, into which it is encoded." See Pierre Bourdieu, *Distinction: A Social Critique of the Judgement of Taste*, trans. Richard Nice (Cambridge, MA: Harvard University Press, 1984), 2.

For Evadne in *The Maid's Tragedy*, the kinky performances she uses to manipulate the plot and the cultural competence necessary to do so are byproducts of her atypical position within the early modern marriage economy. Much like another autonomous female revenger, Bianca in Thomas Middleton's *Women Beware Women*, Evadne is removed from the traditional patriarchal hierarchy because of the sexual desire of a patriarchal authority figure, all of which leads her to become functionally independent of masculine oversight. Evadne's apparently consensual involvement in state-sanctioned cuckoldry and extramarital sexuality are foundational to her occupying a sexual identity outside the norm of early modern conceptions of sexuality. Evadne is alienated from the traditional gender position of *woman* by her unchaste past, not her mastery of kink, but kink does complicate her relationship to gender as she tries in vain to recover an unproblematic feminine identity. While her practice of kink marks her as aberrant, it also allows Evadne to generate a uniquely subversive authority, which empowers her to resist tyranny and certain patriarchal power structures.

Kink as Cultural Performance

Evadne's sexual practice is not only central to her character but also foundational to the manner in which she perpetrates her revenge. In order to expand on these ideas and given the relative obscurity of *The Maid's Tragedy*, summarizing the details of Evadne's portion of the plot is particularly important. The play begins with a marriage between Evadne and Amintor, who had until very recently been engaged to Aspatia, who is still in love with him. Amintor's marriage to Evadne has been arranged by the King, and Amintor discovers on his wedding night that the marriage is intended as a means of concealing a long-standing extramarital affair between Evadne and the King. Evadne goes so far as to rebuff Amintor's sexual advances and to tell him that she intends to have sexual relations exclusively with the King. Amintor plays along with the charade, in fact feigning an active sexual relationship with his new wife well enough that it elicits jealousy from the King, who briefly believes that Evadne has slept with Amintor. While Amintor's loyalty to the King keeps him silent about the farcical nature of his marriage at first, the dejection brought on by it catches the attention of Melantius, Amintor's close friend and Evadne's brother. When Melantius presses Amintor on the cause of his ill humor, Amintor eventually explains the situation, which, understandably, angers Melantius, who later confronts Evadne and urges her to kill the King. Once devoted to the King, Evadne vows to kill the King to avenge her honor. She enters the King's bedchamber while he is asleep, ties him to the bed, and, once he is awake, stabs him to death. She then escapes the bedchamber and seeks out Amintor in an attempt to salvage their marriage. Amintor, who is increasingly remorseful for his treatment of Aspatia (though he has just, unbeknownst to him, mortally wounded her in a duel while she was disguised), rejects Evadne's offer of reconciliation and she, in turn, kills herself. Soon after, the dying Aspatia reveals her true identity and dies, which leads Amintor to commit suicide.[9] As the play's plot makes plain, the practical details of Evadne's sex life are not only central to her narrative, but they serve as the catalyst for the play's justification of her ability to take on the role of revenger. In fact, it is her sexuality that aestheticizes and ritualizes the violence that she perpetrates in the play and creates the representational distance that mediates the taboo and destabilizing nature of those acts.

Unlike the bulk of the female revengers in the period, Evadne's act of revenge is framed by intimacy and directly embedded in sexual practice. Most female revengers, and in fact the bulk of male revengers, take their revenge publicly in scenes that are often stabilized by inset cultural performances. Revenge tragedy, at its heart, is a genre engaged

---

9. Francis Beaumont and John Fletcher, *The Maid's Tragedy*, ed. T. W. Craik (Manchester: Manchester University Press, 1988). All subsequent references are to this edition and refer to act, scene, and line number.

in social critique, though not always related to gender, which in the genre's early modern form relies on stock strategies to mediate the taboo potential of each play's plot. The core of the revenge formula is that the revenger takes action to right a wrong that existing power structures are unable or unwilling to punish. The seditious potential of this foundational plot led playwrights in the period, following Thomas Kyd's example, to use restaged moments of cultural ritual as *screens* that generated representational distance between the act of revenge and the real world of the actual audience. This results in English Renaissance revenge tragedy's inherent investment in inset logics with codified protocols that revengers can manipulate. Whether we look at Hamlet's fencing match, Titus and Lavinia's feast in *Titus Andronicus*, Hieronimo and Bel-Imperia's play-within-the-play in *The Spanish Tragedy*, or the masque that ends *Women Beware Women*, this tendency to use ritualized moments with discreet social rules and expectations creates a space within the play's narrative where a revenger's mastery of those rules, or that character's cultural competence more generally, allows them to invert the traditional power structures that protect and empower those who have wronged the play's protagonist. Evadne's murder of the King is equally *screened*, but the social ritual that provides the necessary framework is sex, specifically extramarital sex infused by the ritualized rules of one type of kink play, the power dynamics of bondage. *The Maid's Tragedy* encourages the spectator to view the sexual subject matter of the play as inherently ritualized and performative from its opening act. Beaumont and Fletcher's play consistently displays the ritual importance of sexuality in early modern English culture in order to prepare the viewer to see Evadne's binding of the King in the bedroom as analogous to *screening* strategies used by other revengers in the period. *The Maid's Tragedy*'s primary strategy for conditioning the audience to view the kink space of the King's bedchamber as a ritualized performance space is to consistently collapse the language used to describe sexuality, violence, ritual, and performance throughout the text. This in turn invites the viewer to see Evadne's use of bondage and her general sexual skill as evidence of her cultural competence within the kinky sexual performance space of the bedchamber.

From the first act of the play, *The Maid's Tragedy* invites the viewer to see sexuality, and in particular Evadne's sexuality, as inherently connected to performance and ritual. The inset masque in act one, scene two, which is a play-within-the-play and constitutes the kind of metatheatre that is so common in revenge tragedies, invites us to view the sexual consummation of the marriage between Amintor and Evadne as an extension of the marriage ceremony that the play-within-the-play effectively replaces. Specifically, the three songs that are performed within the masque each center the sexual act of the wedding night as the marriage rite's literal and figurative climax. The first song bids the day not come "Till the rites of love are ended" (1.2.218), while the second bids the Night, a character in the inset masque, to

confound her [the bride's] tears and her shrill cryings,
Her weak denials, vows, and often-dyings;
  Stay, and hide all,
  But help not though she call.
(1.2.237–40)

Here the masque sets the linguistic tone that will follow by actively asking the audience to see the act of consummation as a *rite* and to associate that ritual logic with its evocative descriptions of coitus. The second song goes so far in its discussion of the sounds that unwilling brides make, with a coerciveness that for modern readers almost certainly evokes rape, to invite both the staged audience and the actual viewer to imagine the sound of the bride's orgasms, or "often-dyings." The third song completes the process by inviting Hymen, the classical god of marriage, to escort the bride to the marriage bed and highlights

the liminal nature of the wedding night as a space that acts as the threshold between maidenhood and the bride's new role as wife,

> That they may kiss while they may say a maid;
> Tomorrow 'twill be other kissed and said.
> (1.2.251–52)

Here the play makes plain the manner in which the wedding night acts as
a coming-of-age ceremony for the bride, whose social transformation is
largely a byproduct of sex.[10] This emphasis on the social transformation
of maid to wife through the culturally sanctioned sexual act embedded in
the marriage ceremony also highlights how Evadne's unchaste relationship with the King prevents her from accessing traditional womanhood
through the nuptial ritual.

Just two lines after the completion of the masque, the play transitions
this ritual logic out of the inset masque and into the main action of the
play. The King approaches Evadne and Amintor and tells them,

> [To Evadne] We will not see you laid. [To Amintor] Good night,
> Amintor;
> We'll ease you of that tedious ceremony[.]
> (1.2.285–86)[11]

Here the King indicates that they will not observe the tradition of the
bedding ceremony, which involved wedding guests escorting the bride
and groom to their bed and in some European cultures observing or
overhearing the couple's intercourse. The King's line has an immediately
apparent double meaning within the context of the plot, which points

10. For more on liminality, its relationship to coming-of-age ceremonies, and how that relates
to theatrical performance, see Victor Turner, *From Ritual Theatre: The Human Seriousness of
Play* (New York: PAJ Publications, 1982).
11. While I have included Craik's bracketed stage directions here for the sake of accurate quot-
ing, I must admit that I am not persuaded by them.

to him literally calling off the bedding ceremony and also reminding Evadne of her vow not to sleep with Amintor. That said, it also reminds the audience of the possibility of sex as a literal performance as well as consummation as a component of a ritualized cultural performance. And it is this blended emphasis on the sexual act as performance, with its inherent voyeuristic implications, that permeates the explanation of the social implications of sex in much of the rest of the play.

This discussion at the outset of the plot regarding the performance of the sexual act is further developed throughout the text by its focus on female sexual competence. Dula's humorous comments on Evadne's wedding night are of particular interest. Dula is one of the ladies who helps Evadne prepare and during that process mocks her relentlessly. When she banters with Evadne about sex, Dula says, it is a "trick" (2.1.17, 19), and that

A dozen wanton words put in your head
Will make you livelier in your husband's bed.
(2.1.20–21)

Here we get the play's first reference to sex as a performance for one's sexual partner. This is an idea that Evadne echoes later as part of a rather mercenary exchange with the King:

Why, it is in me, then,
Not to love you, which will more afflict
Your body than your punishment can mine.
(3.1.180–83)

While much is made throughout the play of Evadne's beauty, this scene invites the viewer to see her as a character whose allure to the King goes beyond her physical appearance and begins to hint at the importance of kink to their relationship. Evadne explains the power she holds over the

King in terms of the pain her absence would cause him, but importantly she does so not by talking about longing, loneliness, or sadness; instead, she focuses on the language of physical "punishment." In particular, she observes that the retribution of the state would be less torturous to her than the suspension of her affections would be to the King. Her use of these words to counter the King's assertion of political authority demonstrates that she possesses a performed sexual authority that is rooted in skill; to put it simply, Evadne knows she's good in bed and that proficiency generates an authority that we will see is related to kink practice and the ritual space it generates. And it this ability to *afflict* his *body* with the absence of her performed sexual competence that is made all the more transparent in the lead-up to the King's murder.

In the fifth act, *The Maid's Tragedy* gives us a glimpse into the sexualized performance space of the King's bedchamber and the kink logic that permeates that space. The unique rules that govern this part of the palace are first suggested by Evadne's discussion with the Gentleman who appears to be guarding the King as he sleeps. As Evadne approaches, he recognizes her and happily allows her access to the King. Before she enters, they have the following exchange:

EVADNE.
                    Give me the key then, and let none be near;
  'Tis the King's pleasure.
GENTLEMAN.
  I understand you, madam: would 'twere mine!
  I must not wish good rest unto your ladyship.
(5.1.2–5)

The Gentleman's wordplay, with its lewd interpretation of Evadne's reference to "the King's pleasure," as well as the assumption that Evadne and the King's activities will preclude sleeping, indicate just how much the social conventions in and around the King's bedchamber have been shaped by kink practice. Evadne's past sexual encounters with the King have created alternative codes of behavior that give her degrees of access and license that allow her the opportunity to murder the King. The violence that Evadne perpetrates against the King is not itself kinky; instead past kink practice and the alternate power dynamics that come with it have created a space where Evadne's cultural competence allows her to generate control and authority.

The unique authority that Evadne leverages in the bedchamber is highlighted by the King's misinterpretation of her preparation for revenge as kink practice. Later in the act, after Evadne has entered the bedchamber and tied up the King, he wakes up and says,

> What pretty new device is this, Evadne?
> What, do you tie me to you? By my love,
> This is a quaint one. Come, my dear, and kiss me.
> I'll be thy Mars; to bed, my Queen of Love,
> Let us be caught together, that the gods may see
> And envy our embraces.
> (5.1.47–52)

The King's initial response to being bound by Evadne is not one of suspicion; in fact, he immediately interprets it as a practice meant to increase sexual pleasure. It should be noted that his interpretation of being tied up as a "pretty new device" demonstrates that kink as a methodological lens is far from anachronistic. Here we see not only clear textual evidence of kink practice embedded in the dialogue but also an indication that this specific kink, sexual bondage, was recognizable to the play's early modern audience without detailed explanation. While kink may be a modern term, Beaumont and Fletcher's language demonstrates its practice was not just present in early modern England but was widespread enough for a play to reference sexual bondage offhandedly with the expectation that the audience was familiar with the concept. Additionally, as the dialogue around "affliction" in act three, scene one, and directly leading up to this moment indicates, this performed kink practice in the period carried with it the potential for inverting traditional power dynamics by creating a space where the participants were "upon even terms no more" (5.1.37). In other words, kink practice then bears a more than passing resemblance to kink now.

The King not only misreads his bonds in this scene as a practice associated with kink but goes on to compare his bondage to the snaring of Mars and Venus in a net, a story mentioned in both Homer's *Odyssey* and Ovid's *Ars Amatoria*. Unlike the myth, in which the snaring of the two deities is the means by which their extramarital affair is made public, ridiculed, and eventually ended, the King sees his binding as "quaint" and, as editor T. W. Craik notes in his footnote, any discovery of their relationship would result in "envy" not derision.[12] The King's reading of the situation points to two important elements of his relationship with Evadne: that this type of kink was not alien to their existing relationship (his description of it as a "new device" implies the existence of at least one old device) and that similar practices must be common enough that being surprised with a new one produces excitement rather than anxiety. Both of these ideas indicate that this staged sexual practice shares important common ground with the ritualized consummation of marriage and the restaging of other cultural performances, like the masque that appears earlier in the play. This shared logic points to the play framing kinky sexual practice as its own type of performance that carries its own set of culturally encoded rules and expectations. The choice to place this type of ritual logic on stage effectively generates layers of dramatic representation, in much the same way as a metatheatrical inset, which allow for the performance of kink to generate the same type of *screening* effect that is prevalent in other revenge tragedies of the period. In other words, the performance of kink practice, much like a play-within-the-play, creates

12. Beaumont and Fletcher, *The Maid's Tragedy*, 173.

a representational distance, which helps to mitigate the taboo nature of Evadne's act of regicide. The appearance of bondage, and by extension kink more generally, in the play acknowledges the potential power, particularly for women, embedded in sexual practice as something more than reproductive. It points to the skill of making sexual activity more pleasurable as a form of *cultural competence* that allows women a type of authority within the liminal, ritualized space of sex as a cultural performance that inverts traditional power dynamics. And it points to kink practice as a particularly potent means to access this potentially subversive type of control.

It should also be noted that the King's comparison of Evadne to Venus and his use of the word "quaint," with its pun on *cunt*, is part of a larger rhetorical strategy to mark Evadne as inherently feminine. While at first this language is part of the sexual banter in which he incorrectly thinks he is participating, later in the scene the choice to describe her as "sweet and gentle" (5.1.74), "not meant thus rugged" (5.1.84), and as "the soul of sweetness" (5.1.97) is functionally a form of self-defense. The King's refusal to accept that Evadne plans to kill him is wrapped up in his view that a woman would be incapable of such an act. What the King does not realize is that from Evadne's perspective her gender position has been wildly destabilized by her inability to progress from *maid* to *wife* by their extramarital sexual relationship. She points specifically in the scene to the fact that he has stolen her "fair name" (5.1.63) and a few lines later to the fact that she was once chaste until he poisoned her character (5.1.77–79). Evadne's emphasis on the loss of her fairness and chastity demonstrates that she sees the King's attempts to mark her as feminine as inaccurate. The King's whoring of her has placed her outside of the standard models of gender against her will. She wants to return to the traditional feminine role she has lost, but the only method she can devise to do so requires her to embrace her suspended gender position and to misappropriate kink by weaponizing it — a choice that not only misfires but that the play clearly sees as inherently unethical.

The suspension of Evadne's gender position plays into one of the hallmarks of revenge tragedy: the disruption of social systems. As Katherine Graham astutely observes, the generic conventions of revenge tragedy often divorce the revenger from standard codified expectations of behavior, so it should come as no surprise that these plays also have the potential to complicate the protagonist's gender expression.[13] But while Evadne's role as the primary revenger certainly works to destabilize her femininity, it is her connection to nontraditional sexual practice, specifically her extramarital relationship with the King, that causes her to transcend the gender binary. For Evadne, this suspension of her feminine gender position is rooted in her belief that her sexuality has made her *monstrous*, which though caused by her extramarital sex is intensified by her relationship with kink. In an attempt to repair her disrupted womanhood, she chooses to lean into her now-suspended gender position to rid herself of the King, whom she sees as the root cause of this disruption. Her success in accessing and murdering him is built on her competency with kink, which allows her to create a space with alternative codes of behavior that she is able to use to disrupt social and sexual hierarchies.

Nowhere in the play is Evadne's nontraditional gender position and the manner in which it is complicated by kink practice more apparent than when she is confronted by Melantius. While he describes her with words like "whore" (4.1.51, 69, and 95), "sickness" (4.1.57), and "canker" (4.1.85), inviting the audience to see her actions as aberrant by nature of their connection to gendered sexual transaction or the taint of disease, Evadne initially rejects those models. Finally admitting her relationship with the King, she swears to avenge her honor,

---

13. Katherine M. Graham, "'[Nor] Bear I in this Breast / So Much Cold Spirit to be Called a Woman': The Queerness of Female Revenge in *The Maid's Tragedy*," *Early Theatre* 21, no.1 (2018): 107–126, at 121.

There is not in the compass of the light
A more unhappy creature; sure, I am monstrous,
For I have done those follies, those mad mischiefs,
Would dare a woman. O, my loaden soul,
Be not so cruel to me, choke not up
The way to my repentance.
(4.1.181–86)

Instead of describing her actions in feminine terms, she functionally rejects such a straightforward gender position. Not only does she admit to doing things that women would not do, she describes herself as "monstrous" — a word that carries very distinct sexual connotations in the period. As Graham points out in her own reading of the text,

While the play itself does not posit that Evadne is a sodomite or tribade, when Evadne uses, or is referred to by, the term 'monster,' the play brings into view the bodies of the sodomite and the tribade, bodies which are resonant through their links to excessive sexual desire, patriarchy (and their threat to it), beasts, and, most importantly, their monstrosity.[14]

What Graham's reading does not address is that only a few scenes after self-labeling herself as "monstrous," Evadne will functionally identify with the exact type of monstrousness that Graham describes — the King's sexual interpretation of being tied up by Evadne as one of her "tricks" indicates that their past sexual behavior could be seen as sodomy from a Renaissance perspective. As the *Oxford English Dictionary* reminds us, sodomy was regularly used in the period to describe "any form of sexual intercourse characterized as unnatural or immoral, or otherwise cul-

---

14. Graham, "[Nor] Bear I in this Breast," 120.

turally stigmatized."[15] In other words, Evadne collapses her extramarital sexuality with kink, both of which she understands as taboo and views them as the catalyst for her monstrosity and, as she will explain to the King, the reason she no longer meets her own idealized definition of femininity.

By the time Evadne enters into the bedchamber and begins to utilize the cultural performance of sexual practice to enact her vengeance, she has moved to a gender position that transcends a simple masculine and feminine binary. Instead, she has transitioned into a non-defined, neuter gender space with all the dehumanizing effects that that language communicates in English grammar. In response to Evadne drawing the knife she will soon use to murder him, the King asks her a question that prompts her to clarify how her gender position has shifted in the liminal space of the diverted erotic encounter,

> KING.
> How's this Evadne?
> EVADNE.
> I am not she, nor bear I in this breast
> So much cold spirit to be called a woman:
> I am a tiger; I am any thing
> That knows not pity.
> (5.1.64–72)

Evadne views her role as revenger as inherently separate from any gendered identity she may have possessed earlier in the play. Instead, within the liminal ritual she has fully embraced the monstrous and become an unfeeling instrument of vengeance. She begins by denying that she is Evadne by rejecting the identifying pronoun "she" and stating she is not accurately described as a woman. But, it should be noted, that does not

---

15. *Compact Oxford English Dictionary*, 2nd ed. (Oxford: Oxford University Press, 1999), s.v. "Sodomy, *n*."

mean that Evadne embraces the masculine. In its place she embraces the neuter position of "thing," going so far as to describe herself as "a tiger" whose sole identifying characteristic in her description is its lack of "pity." It is striking just how similar Evadne's sentiment in these lines is to Lady Macbeth's spell-like request,

> unsex me here,
> And fill me from the crown to the toe top-full
> Of direst cruelty.
> $(1.5.39-41)$[16]

In many ways Evadne is embodying the genderless position that Lady Macbeth aspires to — an identity where femininity is erased without need for a masculine identity to replace it. That said, this role as genderless revenger is short-lived.

Just a few lines later, Evadne returns to the language of taint and corruption that Melantius used to describe her in act four. She tells the King,

> I was once fair,
> Once I was lovely, not a blowing rose
> More chastely sweet, till thou, thou, thou foul canker,
> (Stir not!) didst poison me.
> $(5.1.76-79)$

It is in many ways her uncomplicated feminine gender position that Evadne has come to avenge as well as reclaim. The King is the "canker" that must be removed to enable her to uncomplicate her gender expression. This is the logic that underpins her assertion to Amintor a few scenes later that she has come to him transformed and without "her mischiefs" (5.3.111). She makes the case, unsuccessfully, that by embracing

---

16. William Shakespeare, *Macbeth*, in *The Norton Shakespeare*, ed. Stephen Greenblatt et. al. (New York: W. W. Norton & Company, 1997): 2564–2618, at 2572.

her monstrous gender position she is able to enact a rite that has a social force on par with a coming-of-age ceremony or a marriage. This self-fashioned ritual has, in her eyes, allowed her to purge her feminine identity of the "canker" that poisons it.

Needless to say, Amintor rejects the efficacy of Evadne's rite and in so doing the possibility of salvaging their marriage, which leads to her eventual suicide. Once she has died the play quickly shifts away from Evadne as Amintor's attention is drawn to Aspatia, who still has not died despite having been stabbed over seventy lines earlier. Unlike Ophelia in *Hamlet*, Anne Frankford in *A Woman Killed with Kindness*, and a number of other female characters in the drama of the period, Evadne is not mourned by the male characters in the play once her sexuality is stabilized in death. Her position as an autonomous female revenger puts her beyond the pale of early modern dramatic logic. Beaumont and Fletcher's tragedy pushes the logic of revenge tragedy in a different direction from their Jacobean peers — instead of reveling in the over-the-top violence that we associate with the genre at the time, *The Maid's Tragedy* aestheticizes gender, sexual practice, and the taboo of kink itself.

Evadne's repeated and misguided references in act five to the taint of her unchaste self being removed by her act of murder of the King further develop her understanding of the link between vengeance and cultural performance. Her statement that she "was not free till now" (5.3.121) is prefaced by the line she speaks to Amintor as she enters, which ends with

It is Evadne still that follows thee,
But not her mischiefs.
(5.3.110–11)

In her admission of guilt, Evadne frames the act of violence as inherently transformative. Unlike the majority of revengers from the period who die rather immediately after they have achieved their revenge, Evadne not only lives long enough to communicate the news to Amintor but in this moment attempts to frame the act of killing as a new beginning. Revenge itself is only one motivator; the other, potentially more important reason is the personal metamorphosis she erroneously believes the act has catalyzed. She describes the murder as some sort of rite of absolution that divorces her from her past sexual transgressions and allows her to restart her marriage to Amintor — the King's murder becomes, in her mind, like a second wedding, waiting, like the first, for the consummation of the wedding night. But this time, it is Amintor, not Evadne, who leaves the ritual incomplete and demonstrates the flawed nature of her logic. After telling Amintor of the King's murder, Evadne bids him, "[T]ake me to thy bed; we may not part" (5.3.151). When he declines to take her to bed, tells her to leave, and eventually begins to leave himself, Amintor denies Evadne the ritual transformation that she incorrectly hopes to find in the aftermath of her sexualized act of regicide (5.3.152–66).

Amintor's rejection of Evadne is all the more telling because his initial horror is also framed by the ritualized codes of sexual practice. His immediate response to the news of the King's murder is to say,

Those have most power to hurt us that we love;
We lay our sleeping lives within their arms.
(5.3.127–28)

While these lines certainly echo his interactions with Aspatia and his own cuckolding, they also acknowledge the inherent social contract that exists between sexual partners. While this type of agreement is to some degree made explicit in the ritualized marriage relationship, it is worth noting that Amintor sees the force of that agreement as existing in all sexual relations and also, interestingly, as more relevant than a subject's loyalty to their monarch. For Amintor, it is Evadne's misuse of the authority granted to her by her ability to manipulate the ritualized codes of the sexual relationships, as well as the additional control granted by kink practice and her own sexual competence, that makes her deeds so unforgivable.

Amintor's unwillingness to forgive Evadne for her abuse of kink practice in many ways makes the play strangely prescient regarding contemporary mores around sexual culture and the importance of consent. This added layer twists many of the traditional moral standards embedded in the revenge tragedy, specifically that revengers generally need to die solely in order to stabilize the taboo nature of private vengeance. Evadne's suicide adds a new facet to the standard expectations of the genre; her death serves as much to punish her abuse of the codes of sexual partnership as it does to stabilize her act of regicide. In addition, her sexual competence and her use of bondage and kink more generally are not in and of themselves marked as problematic; they only become so in a space where consent and care for a sexual partner are ignored. In other words, kink practice's ability to generate the access that Evadne abuses to kill the King does not lead the play to demonize alternative sexual practices. Instead, the play places that blame on Evadne, not on the kink.

Evadne's kinky sexual competence is all the more powerful because of its ability to invert both political and gender hierarchies in a period when those social structures were both extraordinarily potent. The manner in which *The Maid's Tragedy* dramatizes that power through the elision of sexuality, violence, ritual, and performance indicates just how foundational these issues are to the play's structure and offers us a glimpse into the sexual culture of the period that we rarely see in English Renaissance drama. Twenty-first-century cultures of kink are clearly aware of this same type of competence and the potential dangers that arise from its abuse, which is demonstrated by the ways that those communities emphasize the importance of consent both before and during play. Beaumont and Fletcher's play makes the case that these insights may in some form date back to at least the early modern period.

Shakespeare's (Into) Race Play

Kirk Quinsland

Perhaps one of the most remarkable things about sex is our ability to find pleasure in the unlikeliest places, including from the negation or destruction of the self. The ability of sex to transform suffering into pleasure is at the heart of many kinks; this presents serious problems for theorists who see even relatively vanilla expressions of sexuality as the shackles of a system that demands we constantly reenact our trauma. Think of Andrea Dworkin's argument that pornography inevitably dehumanizes and eroticizes violence against women, and that women cannot meaningfully consent to participate in pornography because of an oppressive sex/gender system that always already demands women's subjugation.[1] Or we can think of Catharine MacKinnon's 2021 op-ed in the *New York Times* attacking "the media's increasing insistence on referring to people used in prostitution and pornography as 'sex workers'" and revisiting her arguments against pornography from the 1980s, updated for the digital age. In the article, MacKinnon rehashes her belief in "pornography's power to make our world,"[2] an argument fundamen-

1. Andrea Dworkin, *Pornography: Men Possessing Women* (New York: Putnam, 1981).
2. Catharine A. MacKinnon, "OnlyFans Is Not a Safe Platform for 'Sex Work.' It's a Pimp," *New York Times*, September 6, 2021, https://www.nytimes.com/2021/09/06/opinion/onlyfans-sex-work-safety.html.

tally rooted in mimesis: unable to distinguish between fantasy/fiction and reality, we inevitably imitate that which we see in media, to the harm of ourselves and others. This argument springs up hydra-like in response to virtually any form of newly popularized media: in the 1950s, it was comic books; in the Satanic Panic of the 1980s, it was heavy metal, Dungeons & Dragons, and Tipper Gore's quest against *porn rock*; in the 1990s, it was violent video games. For theorists like MacKinnon and Dworkin, pornography — especially BDSM porn — is not only a reflection of misogyny but also a driver of it: there can be, this argument goes, no ethical participation in a system of pornographic production that is built entirely on the objectification of women. As Amia Srinivasan puts it, "To say that it is porn's function to *effectuate* its message is to see porn as a mechanism not just for depicting the world, but for making it. Porn, for MacKinnon and other anti-porn feminists, was a machine for the production and reproduction of an ideology which, by eroticizing women's subordination, thereby made it real."[3] To participate is to have the illusion of consent because women's consent is both always assumed and already taken for granted.

We can say much the same about kinks like race play. As defined by Kyla Robinson, "Race play is a type of consensual erotic roleplay that focuses on playing with a societal taboo; perpetuating historically situated racial, ethnic, and religious power dynamics for pleasure."[4] It can be difficult to think about kink — especially inconvenient and disagreeable kinks like race play — as positive, generative, or pleasurable. If the argumentative environment posits that sex is an inherently violent and unequal violation of the self, then there can be no ethical praxis that allow us to, in the words of BDSM educator Mollena Williams, "play

---

3. Amia Srinivasan, *The Right to Sex: Feminism in the Twenty-First Century* (New York: Farrar, Straus and Giroux, 2021), 38, emphasis in the original.
4. Kyla Robinson, "Speaking the Unspeakable: The Curious Case of Race Play in the American BDSM Community," (unpublished preprint, 2018), 1, https://doi.org/10.13140/RG.2.2.21727.97443.

with real, structural inequalities in safe and pleasurable ways: in ways that make such play *play*."[5] This discourse asks us to see kinksters as merely victims of a false consciousness that has tricked them into finding certain activities pleasurable, a position that allows no room for self-generated pleasure. The fact remains that people can, and definitively do, derive pleasure from things like submission, humiliation, and power exchange. Denying people the right to discover and practice their own consensual sexual pleasures, even if those desires have been discursively generated (as are any and all of the things we enjoy), strikes me as a denial of individual agency and an unwarranted attempt to police the sexual expression of others. In short, we do not get to tell others that they are doing sex wrong.

Even if we adopt this principle, we still run into the problem that bodies are discursively invested with meanings that are beyond the control of any individual. Hortense Spillers, focusing on the trauma embedded in Black bodies, explains that "before the 'body' there is the 'flesh,' that zero degree of social conceptualization that does not escape concealment under the brush of discourse, or the reflexes of iconography." Discourse cannot, Spillers argues, paper over the "point of convergence [where] biological, sexual, social, cultural, linguistic, ritualistic, and psychological fortunes join" and the extent to which these elements of biopolitical existence assign certain significations to specific bodies.[6] But if these associations are discursively generated, it is then possible to rewrite them. Citing Cathy Cohen's notion that deviance is where we can locate "the radical potential of queer politics," Ariane Cruz argues in *The Color of Kink* that we need to "shift our critical gaze away from the convention-

5. Catherine Scott, "Thinking Kink: The Right to Play With Race," *Bitch Media*, August 8, 2012, https://www.bitchmedia.org/post/thinking-kink-the-right-to-play-with-race-feminist-magazine-bdsm-sex.

6. Hortense J. Spillers, "Mama's Baby, Papa's Maybe: An American Grammar Book," *Diacritics* 17, no. 2 (Summer 1987): 64-81, at 67, https://www.jstor.org/stable/464747.

ally respectable to read deviance as a kind of black political strategy."[7] Cruz encourages us to adopt a "politics of perversion" that enables us to directly interrogate the problem of power at the heart of the anti-porn feminist argument that sexual encounters are inherently tied to the inequality of our sex-gender system; so too, it would seem, is race inextricable from sexual encounters because race is indelibly linked to a White-supremacist racial hierarchy.[8] To play with racial taboos in sex

7. Ariane Cruz, *The Color of Kink* (New York: New York University Press, 2016), 14.

8. Even orthography serves ideological functions. A few years ago, I came across a compelling article from Eve L. Ewing arguing that *White* should be capitalized when discussing race. Ewing explains that the choice to not capitalize "runs the risk of reinforcing the dangerous myth that White people in America do not have a racial identity. [...] When we ignore the specificity and significance of Whiteness — the things that it is, the things that it does — we contribute to its seeming neutrality and thereby grant it power to maintain its invisibility." Ewing's analysis echoes Sara Ahmed's contention that "it can be willful even to name racism: as if the talk about divisions is what is divisive. Given that racism recedes from social consciousness, it appears as if the ones who 'bring it up' are bringing it into existence," reminding us that it is all too easy for race (specifically Whiteness) to become recede into invisibility, a choice strategy for maintaining Whiteness as the so-called default. Though my subject is only American in passing, I have deliberately chosen to capitalize *White*, though the ACMRS Style Guide recommends that it should not be capitalized in reference to race. The AP Style Guide also recommends no capitalization of *White*, explaining, "we are a global news organization and in much of the world there is considerable disagreement, ambiguity and confusion about whom the term includes. [...] But capitalizing the term white, as is done by white supremacists, risks subtly conveying legitimacy to such beliefs. Some have expressed the belief that if we don't capitalize white, we are being inconsistent and discriminating against white people or, conversely, that we are implying that white is the default. We also recognize the argument that capitalizing the term could pull white people more fully into issues and discussions of race and equality." I in no way believe that failing to capitalize *White* is discriminatory, nor does my usage in any way confer any degree of legitimacy to White supremacists, but the inconsistency does seem striking and worth interrogation because of the way it draws attention away from Whiteness as a constructed racial category. Against the AP's justification, I would argue that it is precisely because of the disagreement, ambiguity, and confusion over who counts as White — one of my core arguments in this essay concerns the flexible construction of the category — that we should, as Ewing puts it, refuse its seeming neutrality and invisibility by capitalizing it. Eve L. Ewing, "I'm a Black Scholar Who Studies Race. Here's Why I Capitalize 'White,'" *ZORA*, July 2, 2020, https://zora.medium.com/im-a-black-scholar-who-studies-race-here-s-why-i-capitalize-white-f94883aa2dd3; Sara Ahmed, "Feminist Killjoys (and Other Willful Subjects)," *S&F Online* 8, no. 3 (2010), https://sfonline.barnard.edu/poly-

is to make the invisible visible in the most uncomfortable ways, but the solution cannot be to simply ban pornography or to lock away the kinks.

Race play often overlaps with and intersects with BDSM, a field which Cruz recognizes "is deeply informed by racialized sexual politics. Race is marginalized in both the scholarly literature and popular media about BDSM, contributing to the impression that it is not something black people do, or should do, and/or that race is not a salient factor in the power dynamics so essential to the practice." Yet for Cruz as for Williams, this erasure of participation and pleasure bars us from thinking about BDSM as "a productive space from which to consider the complexity and diverseness of black women's sexual practice and the mutability of black female sexuality."[9] Race play, according to this line of thinking, may then provide a productive space not just for encountering racism and racist practices but for analyzing their power as cultural narratives and the application of those narratives to individual bodies. To apply what Jesus G. Smith and Aurolyn Luykx write about interracial porn to race play, kink can "reproduce racist tropes, sexist language and heteronormative behaviours in order to counter the oppression they face from the White supremacists and to access their own erotic pleasure in the racialized space where they reside."[10] But what race play offers to participants, I will argue, does not necessarily match what outside observers might see: what observers understand as a reproduction or reinforcement of the racial order can, to the players themselves, be a source of erotic pleasure precisely because of the kink's ability to interrogate the racial order and call it into question. Race play thus presents a serious challenge for individuals and populations as biopolitical actors

phonic/print_ahmed.htm; John Daniszewski, "Why we will lowercase white," *AP*, July 20, 2020, https://blog.ap.org/announcements/why-we-will-lowercase-white.

9. Cruz, *The Color of Kink*, 10, 3.
10. Jesus G. Smith and Aurolyn Luykx, "Race Play in BDSM Porn: The Eroticization of Oppression," *Porn Studies* 4, no. 4 (2017): 433–46, at 435, https://doi.org/10.1080/23268743.2016.1252158.

while also exposing the unspoken (or unspeakable) power dynamics that White supremacy uses to try to convince us that racial categories are fixed rather than socially constructed.

Using Tamora and Aaron from *Titus Andronicus* as a test case, showing how Shakespeare has anticipated the outlines of a much later kink and highlighted some of the components of how racism is being constructed alongside the creation of the notion of race, I will argue for the importance of thinking about kink as a set of practices that are valuable precisely because they violate normative boundaries (statistical and/or ethical), and that critical practice can learn to incorporate those things that strike us as biopolitically non-expedient — or that strike us as just downright icky — through a focus on the conjoined principles of intent, consent, and pleasure. Turning our attention to this case within the context of the premodern creation of our contemporary notions of race and White supremacy, we can see how Shakespeare represents Tamora and Aaron's sexual relationship as both a violation of the "natural" order and as *ars erotica*, pleasures which need no justification. This seeming contradiction depends entirely on the observer's gaze: Shakespeare shows us that it is outsiders who police the social construction of race and raced bodies, and in so doing, demonstrates how outsiders can rewrite the signification of a sexual act. What Tamora and Aaron experience as a way of playing with and playing within systems of racial signification, the Romans read as a reinforcement of old stereotypes and boundaries, and as a degradation of a White body tarnished by its sexual association with Blackness. This contradiction in signification then illustrates the need to create space for kink/sex that is pleasurable for its consenting participants, even if it violates external ethical norms. In short, pleasure does not need to be a means to an end: pleasure is a valid end unto itself.

I. "Let her joy her raven-colored love"

The argument that Shakespeare presents us with contradictory views of Tamora and Aaron's relationship starts with a straightforward question: what race are the Goths in *Titus Andronicus*? An answer should begin with acknowledging how reductive it is to think of *race* in an early modern context as simply a manifestation of skin color. Instead, as Matthieu Chapman frames the challenge of defining the concept of race in the early modern era, "Even among scholars of race in the period, very few, if any, consensuses are reached. Everything from how race was defined in Early Modern England to who was considered a racialized being is up for debate. Whether race was defined by color, nationality, bloodlines, gender, religion, as a commodity, through culture, through encounters, or all or none of the above have all been questions with no real resolution."[11] While this multiplicity of signifiers creates a problem for the question of what we mean when we talk about race, Chapman's framing also throws open the possibilities for analyzing entire networks of signification and the ways they overlap and slide into one another. As Margo Hendricks explains, "Pre-1700 representations of race and nation were part of a systemic effort to foster social and political cohesion in England. What is more evident is that absolutes do not entirely work when reading Shakespeare's plays. We realize that sometimes race references a biological identity, whereas at other times it signifies national identity or social status."[12] These "overlapping ideological paths" are marked by "an elaborate system of linking metaphors whose rhetorical and interpretive strength lay in their fluidity."[13] These overlapping and fluid systems of signification and representation are precisely what have enabled critics

---

11. Matthieu Chapman, *Anti-Black Racism in Early Modern English Drama: The Other "Other"* (Abingdon, UK: Routledge, 2016), 2.
12. Margo Hendricks, "Race and Nation," in *The Cambridge Guide to the Worlds of Shakespeare*, ed. Bruce Smith and Katherine Rowe (Cambridge, UK: Cambridge University Press, 2016), 663-668, at 668.
13. Hendricks, "Race and Nation," 668, 663.

to think of the Goths less as a group tied to Roman history and more as stand-ins for the various national enemies of England.[14] There is no single agreement about what race "meant" or on what signifiers it was constructed, and this gives us license to observe how overlapping categories like nationality, religion, and color form the lacework of categorical differences Shakespeare employs to construct the Romans as stand-ins for the White-English and the Goths as racialized Others. This split certainly does not result in the Romans coming off well; if anything, *Titus's* Rome is a place of chaos, idle luxury, tyranny born of a succession crisis, and inflexibility of law and religion. This self-laceration has the effect of critiquing both the Romans/English and their opponents, but still insisting that while both sides might have their vices, the White side will still come out as the winners.

14. The broad consensus of this body of scholarship is that the play imagines a Rome in conflict with its enemies in the same ways that England was in conflict with its enemies. Joan Fitzpatrick has argued for overlaps between the Goths and the Irish through their shared degenerate practices around food (especially cannibalism), while Noémie Ndiaye has persuasively argued that "Spanishness can be read between the lines as Gothicness" (61) if we pay attention to Spain's perceived racial alterity and barbarism (especially cannibalism). Nicholas R. Moschovakis reads the play as a "jagged mirror for Christians, reflecting the troubles conscience of post-Reformation Europe" (473). Brian J. Harries observes that "the Rome of *Titus Andronicus* teeters on the edge between the Mediterranean Classical world and the European Middle Ages" in ways that parallel "cultural currents within the audience's own Elizabethan contemporary moment" (194–95). Similarly, John Kunat argues that, like the battles between the Goths and the Romans, "the 'others' pressing most closely on the kingdom were fair-skinned and Christian like the English themselves, who nonetheless considered these neighbouring people to be to some degree barbaric." Joan Fitzpatrick, "Foreign Appetites and Alterity: Is There an Irish Context for Titus Andronicus?" *Connotations* 11, nos. 2–3 (2001–2002): 127–45; Noémie Ndiaye, "Aaron's Roots: Spaniards, Englishmen, and Blackamoors in *Titus Andronicus*," *Early Theatre* 19, no. 2 (2016): 59–80, https://www.jstor.org/stable/90018447; Nicholas R. Moschovakis, "'Irreligious Piety' and Christian History: Persecution as Pagan Anachronism in *Titus Andronicus*," *Shakespeare Quarterly* 53 (2002): 460–86, https://www.jstor.org/stable/3844237; Brian J. Harries, "The Fall of Mediterranean Rome in *Titus Andronicus*," *Mediterranean Studies* 26, no. 2 (2018): 194–212, https://doi.org/10.5325/mediterraneanstu.26.2.0194; and John Kunat, "'I have done thy mother': Racial and Sexual Geographies in *Titus Andronicus*," in *Titus Andronicus: The State of the Play*, ed. Farah Karim-Cooper (London: Bloomsbury, 2019), 89–110.

In this section, then, I will argue that Shakespeare contributes to a White-supremacist reality that insists on the racial alterity of the Goths but also insists that the Goths can become White when it is convenient for the Romans to regard them as such, as we shall see when it comes to the judgment of Tamora and Aaron's interracial relationship. Much of the recent scholarship on the play's representations of race has understandably focused on Aaron and on the extent to which the Romans are stand-ins for the English, but less attention has been paid to the ways in which the White-Romans insist on racial differences between themselves and the also approximately White Goths.[15] And less attention still has been paid to Tamora herself, despite her ability to seemingly function equally as Goth and Roman.[16] As will become especially important in the next section of the essay, one of the prerogatives claimed by White supremacy is the power to determine not just *who* is White but *when* they can be whitened and *how* Whiteness signifies. Whiteness itself is, according to this argument, a dangerously fluid category that perpetuates itself through granting contingent access to its power. In acting as the gatekeepers for permissible sexual expression, Lavinia and Bassianus — the

15. Cf. David Sterling Brown, "Remixing the Family: Blackness and Domesticity in Shakespeare's *Titus Andronicus*," in *Titus Andronicus: The State of the Play*, ed. Farah Karim-Cooper (London: Bloomsbury, 2019), 111–33. Sterling Brown argues that Tamora "belongs to and in Rome because of a legally sanctioned marriage with the Emperor," which in turn "permits the existence of one big, white extended family that embraces cultural but not racial difference" (115). Sterling Brown's claim, I think, works if our analysis of what constitutes *race* is skin color alone; while the Goths and the Romans might both be fair-skinned, I am arguing that the Goths are racially different from the Romans, and that their inclusion/ incorporation into the White-Roman power structure is far more flexible and contingent than skin color alone would enable.

16. Cf. Kunat, "'I have done thy mother,'" esp. 97–99. Kunat writes that "the Goths embody 'whiteness' in an extreme form that opposes blackness but also partakes of its supposed barbarism" (98) and goes on to argue that Tamora's whiteness allows her to slip into the Roman power structure in a way that her son with Aaron never can. I largely agree with this analysis, though I do not think we can take Tamora's whiteness for granted. Consequently, I wish to go further by analyzing the degree to which the play treats whiteness (especially Tamora's) as a contingent property that is granted or taken away by the dominant group.

exemplars of the White-Romans — claim for themselves the ability to frame Tamora and Aaron's relationship as a violation of the social/racial order. In the process of doing so, they ignore Tamora and Aaron's own experience of the sexual component of their relationship, overwriting it in a way that denies racialized bodies their own pleasures.

The analysis that follows will be split into two parts that anticipate an important point in the later theorization of race play: so often, there is a difference between what outsiders see and what the participants experience. In the view of Lavinia and Bassianus, Tamora and Aaron's sexual relationship is simply degrading interracial sex, not race play, specifically because Tamora is capable of registering as White; sex with Aaron taints her Whitened body and marks her as a kind of race traitor. But for Tamora and Aaron themselves, their sex is kinky race play: race itself is a source of sexual energy and power through the eroticization of their racialized features and their play with and within the White-Roman socioracial hierarchy. Even as those around them insist that they are the ones who are able to determine the meaning and value of sex and race, Tamora and Aaron show us how to do race play ethically.[17]

Perhaps the most salient exploration of the racial identity of the Goths comes from Francesca T. Royster's compelling argument that in *Titus*, "Tamora's whiteness *is* racially marked, is made visible, and thus it is misleading to simplify the play's racial landscape into black and white, with black as the 'other.'" One of the play's striking features is its othering of

17. It is worth remembering Mollena Williams's story about a BDSM scene being observed by a White woman who assumed that Williams and her partner were engaged in race play. Williams responded, "That wasn't a race-play scene. That man didn't do race play. What you saw was the man to whom I was in service playing with me. What you perceived was a race play scene. I can't warn you about your own perceptions." Tamora and Aaron being viewed by Lavinia and Bassianus similarly points out the potential perception gap between players and observers: what the players are doing it not necessarily equal to how those actions are perceived by onlookers. Mollena Williams, "BDSM and Playing with Race," in *Best Sex Writing 2010*, ed. Rachel Kramer Bussel (San Francisco: Cleis Press, 2010), 70.

a woman who is conspicuously white."[18] Royster observes how "through the failed project to incorporate Tamora into the Roman social body, we can see how white supremacy is normalized and patrolled through the bodies of women."[19] What is so useful about Royster's argument is the extent to which she insists that Whiteness is not merely a default or invisible setting but instead a color tied to an identity that asks for participants in the socioracial system to police who is included and who is excluded. Lavinia and Bassianus certainly patrol these borders, insisting on Tamora's Whiteness as something that is harmed and degraded through her relationship with Aaron. Yet Aaron and Tamora understand her racial identification differently: neither sees Tamora as hyperwhite (as Royster describes her), instead persistently linking her to the liminal racial figure of Semiramis.

To return to our initial question — what race are the Goths? — perhaps the closest we can come to any firm answer is to note that while the critical literature seems to want a clear answer, perhaps the most we can say the Goths belong to an ethnic group with cultural and religious practices that depart from Roman customs but without necessarily drawing clear racial divisions along color lines. Chapman's interrogation of the differences among Moors "posit[s] that color difference was a primary constituent element of subjectivity. While texts from the Early Modern period do use overlapping terms to refer to varying darker-skinned peoples, they also allow for reading distinctions between peoples of color that aligns them structurally as human or inhuman."[20] Given Tamora's position of power as empress, the Romans have a vested interest in making sure she is read as human — as a direct contrast with a dehumanized and humiliated Aaron. Tamora is certainly capable of being humanized,

18. Francesca T. Royster, "White-limed Walls: Whiteness and Gothic Extremism in Shakespeare's *Titus Andronicus*," *Shakespeare Quarterly* 51, no. 4 (Winter 2000): 432–55, at 433, https://doi.org/10.2307/2902338. Emphasis in the original.
19. Royster, "White-limed Walls," 435.
20. Chapman, *Anti-Black Racism*, 70.

since she seems to be of the same color as the Romans, or at least the same color as Lavinia. Immediately after announcing that he will marry Lavinia, his brother's betrothed, emperor Saturninus takes possession of Tamora and recognizes her as

> a goodly lady, trust me, of the hue
> That I would choose, were I to choose anew.
> (1.1.264–65)[21]

The ambiguity here — is Tamora White like Lavinia (because Saturninus will always choose a woman of the same color), or is she recognizably a racial other (because Saturninus would prefer a non-White partner)? — is not so simple to resolve. In Henry Peachum's famous drawing of the play, Tamora and the rest of the Romans are not marked off as phenotypically different; only Aaron appears with dark skin. Aaron himself, in his rhapsodic monologue that opens act two, tells of his desire

> to wanton with queen,
> this goddess, this Semiramis, this nymph,
> this siren.
> (2.1.21–23)

It is notable that he chooses Semiramis, the Assyrian queen of Babylon, as the one human(ish) mythological figure to reach for. Semiramis is described in critical literature as a kind of in-between figure: Alison L. Beringer shows that Semiramis defies gender roles, appearing as male, female, or androgynous sometimes even within the same text.[22] Even more important here is Alice Mikal Craven's claim that Semiramis often represents an Other that draws on the "cultural projections of the black

---

21. Unless otherwise specified, all quotes from *Titus Andronicus* come from *The Norton Shakespeare*, Third Edition.
22. Alison L. Beringer, *The Sight of Semiramis: Medieval and Early Modern Narratives of the Babylonian Queen* (Tempe, AZ: ACMRS Press, 2016), 73–77.

woman … present in the period leading up to the writing of the play, but were almost exclusively fantasies rather than descriptions based on actual encounters with black women."[23] To describe Tamora as akin to Semiramis presents few easy answers; if anything, it wildly complicates any attempt to make a definitive claim about the race of the Goths. The identification makes Tamora a liminal figure residing somewhere in the vast middle of representations of gender, sexuality, and skin color. This liminality then allows Tamora to register as either White or non-White, depending on political circumstance and contextual need.

It is Tamora's racial fluidity that enables Lavinia and Bassianus to frame the sexual encounter as a dangerously transgressive violation of the social order (that is, not as race play) at the same moment that Tamora and Aaron understand the kinky pleasure potential of their meeting. Thinking they have the upper hand upon finding Tamora and Aaron together in the hunting wood, Lavinia and Bassianus mock Tamora for her "unnatural" desires in ways that her transgression is not simply cuckolding her husband but doing it with a Black man. Yet this contrast only exists if Tamora is herself White; if she is a racially Othered Goth, it is quite difficult to understand why Lavinia and Bassianus would focus so heavily on the racial nature of her trespass. Aaron's Blackness can stain and shame Tamora only within a racial hierarchy that places Whiteness on top but which regularly conflates and equates various forms of racial alterity. Lavinia states,

Tis thought you have goodly gift in horning,
And to be doubted that your Moor and you
Are brought forth to try thy experiments.
(2.3.67–69)

---

23. Alice Mikal Craven, "Representing Semiramis in Shakespeare and Calderón," *Shakespeare* 4, no. 2 (2008): 157–69, at 159, https://doi.org/10.1080/17450910802083443.

Bassianus doubles down on this insult — *experiments* suggests that the pair are thinking of interracial sex as an error, an unnatural act[24] — by telling Tamora that her "swarthy Cimmerian / Doth make your honor of his body's hue, / Spotted, detested, and abominable" (2.3.72–74), as if Aaron's Blackness is an infection whose effects will be written on her honor and by implication her body — as if race is an STI whose chief symptom is to darken her Whiteness.[25] He further asks why she is

> dismounted from your snow-white goodly steed,
> and wandered hither to an obscure plot,
> Accompanied but with a barbarous Moor,
> If foul desire had not conducted you?
> (2.3.76–79).

Along with Lavinia's exhortation that Tamora should "joy her raven-colored love" (2.3.83), this scene makes it clear that, in the eyes and through the language of the Romans, Tamora can be made White: she may remain a racial outsider as Queen of Goths, yet she is also "incorporate in Rome, / A Roman now adopted happily" (1.1.464–65), determined as racially identical to the Romans because it makes her violation of the sexual/

24. Adhaar Noor Desai argues that for Francis Bacon, experimentation provided the opportunity for "errors that are not failures" (122): as Bacon puts it, "Experience, if taken as it comes, is called accident, if sought for, experiment" (125). Adhaar Noor Desai, "Scientific Misrule: Francis Bacon at Gray's Inn," *Philological Quarterly* 98, nos. 1–2 (2019): 119–36.

25. This potential for infection creates the conditions for the destruction of the state: if Tamora's honor is made *spotted, detested,* and *abominable,* so too is her authority as Empress of Rome. As Chapman argues, reflecting on the grave threat that Black subjectivity poses to the social order, "That Aaron's incorporation into civil society coincides with the collapse of that society offers a potentially terrifying reading of the play in which Shakespeare reveals that the Early Modern English epistemology is not a divine truth, but rather a construction, and presents the possibility of a world in which the inhuman Aaron is the face of and foundation for a new paradigm that signals the end of emerging English modernity." Chapman, *Anti-Black Racism,* 157–58. For an additional discussion of the potential for White bodies to be marked by Blackness, see Miles Grier, "Are Shakespeare's Plays Racially Progressive? The Answer Is in Our Hands," in *The Cambridge Companion to Shakespeare and Race,* ed. Ayanna Thompson (Cambridge, UK: Cambridge University Press, 2021), 237–53.

racial order all the more transgressive. It is important to note that Aaron is not present for any of this, but his Blackness cannot be erased from the scene; as David Sterling Brown puts it, this discussion "reinforces just how necessary Aaron's absent presence is for assessing the value of blackness."[26] In this case, for Lavinia and Bassianus — who remain thoroughly convinced that race is ontological rather than discursive — it is Aaron's Blackness that determines and fixes Tamora's Whiteness for Lavinia and Bassianus, but in so doing, they erase the prospect that Blackness may possess an erotics of its own, separate from or outside of Whiteness.

Right after Bassianus is murdered in front of her, Lavinia momentarily switches registers, referring to Tamora as "Semiramis — nay, barbarous Tamora, / For no other name fits thy nature but thy own" (2.3.118–19), throwing together a liminally racial figure with the liminally racialized *barbarous* since the racial valences of *barbarian* are complicated.[27] Lavinia first identifies Tamora as a racial other, keeping with her steadfast insistence on reading Tamora as a threat to the social order, but quickly switches tactics: shifting away from her racial identification with Semiramis, instead Lavinia moves Tamora into the register of a barbarian, a White body who is merely a "cultural alien,"[28] perhaps as a way of insisting on a shared Whiteness that will save her life now that it is threatened. Lavinia, importantly, takes for granted her own ability to dictate the terms on which Tamora should understand herself and in so doing illustrates Ian Smith's argument that "race signifies not an abstract essence but a *doing*, a verbal performance — in both senses, grammatical and rhetorical — a continuous pursuit of subjection."[29]

26. Sterling Brown, "Remixing the Family," 121.
27. See especially Ian Smith, "Barbarian Errors: Performing Race in Early Modern England," *Shakespeare Quarterly* 49, no. 2 (1998): 168–86. Throughout the play, a number of groups are designated as barbarous: Goths (1.1.33), Scythians (1.1.149), Greeks (1.1.422), and Moors (2.3.78) all share the description.
28. Smith, "Barbarian Errors," 168.
29. Smith, "Barbarian Errors," 170. Emphasis in the original.

And Lavinia is by no means the only character in the play to insist on Tamora's Whiteness as a way of framing her relationship with Aaron as a cross-racial violation of Rome's moral/color order. In the play's fly-killing scene, present in the play's 1623 Folio version but in none of the previous quartos, Marcus strikes at a fly with his knife, an act for which Titus chastises him. But Marcus defends himself by explaining that

> it was a black ill-favored fly,
> Like to the empress' Moor; therefore I killed him.
> (3.2.67–68)

Marcus's use of the possessive in referring to Aaron seems significant: Aaron is not identified by name but instead as a racial Other who belongs to the empress, a way of figuring the relationship that invokes the racialized ownership practices of the transatlantic slave trade. Marcus's use of the possessive here works to frame that relationship as one between White master and Black slave, reminding us of the Roman understanding of the "correct" power dynamics of racial ownership. Later in the play, a Nurse arrives bearing from Tamora "*a blackamoor child*" (4.2.51.sd) to Aaron, the child's father. She exclaims that she "would hide from heaven's eye, / Our empress' shame and stately Rome's disgrace" (4.2.60–61), declaring the child to be

> a joyless, dismal, black, and sorrowful issue.
> Here is the babe, as loathsome as a toad
> Amongst the fair-faced breeders of our clime.
> (4.2.68–70)

The Nurse, like Marcus, insists on a racial difference between Tamora and Aaron: only if Tamora is White could her child with Saturninus fit in among the *fair-faced breeders*. It is because the father is Black that the recognizably Black child cannot be incorporated into Rome, emphasizing the extent to which other White-Roman characters in the play insist on understanding Tamora and Aaron's sexual relationship as a violation of the socioracial order.

But if Lavinia and the other Romans claim the prerogative to fix the race of Tamora's body, and with it the signification of her sexual relationship with Aaron as one that violates the moral/natural/color order, it is also necessary to consider what sex, and what sex in the context of racial identification, means to Tamora and Aaron. Despite their centrality to the plot, the two spend remarkably little time interacting; though they are present on stage together a few times, this scene of the thwarted encounter is their only conversation in the whole play. When apart, though, the two express considerable desire for one another along lines that emphasize the erotic delights intrinsic to race play. In Aaron's entrance monologue, apart from referring to Tamora as Semiramis, he casts their relationship as one marked by a power exchange charged by racial erotics:

Then, Aaron, arm thy heart and fit thy thoughts
To mount aloft with thy imperial mistress,
And mount her pitch whom thou in triumph long
Hast prisoner held, fettered in amorous chains
And faster bound to Aaron's charming eyes
Than is Prometheus tied to Caucasus.
Away with slavish weeds and servile thoughts!
I will be bright, and shine in pearl and gold
To wait upon this new-made empress.
To wait, said I? to wanton with this queen,
This goddess, this Semiramis, this nymph,
This siren, that will charm Rome's Saturnine
And see his shipwreck and his commonweal's.
(2.1.12–24)

Aaron's soliloquy is a remarkably complicated exploration of the power exchanges that fuel his sexual relationship with Tamora and the racial positions to which those power exchanges are attached. Aaron at first reverses the master-slave dynamic that the others have emphasized: Aaron is now the one who has held Tamora his erotic prisoner; he holds the *amorous chains* that bind her; and he insists on throwing off his *slavish weeds* in exchange for the pearl and gold riches of the Roman court. Aaron also adopts the language of the Roman practice of holding prisoners *in triumph*, reversing the expected racial dynamics to place himself as part of the Roman power structure.

But as the speech proceeds, even as he casts aside his *slavish weeds*, Aaron reverses his position to present himself as the adorned servant of the empress, subserviently placing himself back under her power and control. He may not be her slave, but he certainly seems willing to temporarily play the part for her. Yet Aaron will not be content merely to wait upon Tamora; waiting on her quickly turns to the verbal *wanton with*, a shift that signals if not equality, playing with power exchange with a woman who is a political superior, a racial other, and even a transhuman deity. And it is this wantoning that Aaron sees as the thing that will destroy the state, just as the Romans have feared. Yet this oncoming shipwreck is not going to happen, as the Romans have believed, simply because Tamora has debased herself. Instead, Aaron grants Tamora a kind of agency the Romans do not, recognizing that power comes through an ability to see the system for what it is and subversively to play with and within its conventions. Aaron later declares that the two must wait to have sex until after they have pulled off the plot to murder Lavinia and Bassianus — as he puts it, his silence and melancholy, along with his "fleece of wooly hair that now uncurls" are no "venereal signs; / Vengeance is in my heart, death in my hand" (2.2.34, 37–38). Tamora responds by calling Aaron "my sweet Moor" (2.2.51), recognizing his Black body and his *wooly hair* as elements of his erotic appeal.

After she leaves her sons to rape and murder Lavinia, she declares, "Now I will hence to seek my lovely Moor" (2.2.190), again insisting on connecting his racial identity to his sexual appeal and their sexual play.

Tamora and Aaron's relationship reveals useful principles when it comes to thinking about how Shakespeare is outlining race play long before the term existed. Of the points that I will take up in the theorization that follows, perhaps the most important is that outsiders rarely have a clear view of what goes on between two consenting adults, and yet it is outsiders who insist that they possess the power to understand the meaning of sex. Tamora and Aaron revel in their erotic play, aware of the power and racial differences between them; they violate the social order in ways that generate pleasure for them. Yet it is Lavinia and Bassianus who, along with the rest of the White-Romans, choose to whiten Tamora to emphasize the depths of her depravity. What Tamora and Aaron experience as an erotic act becomes a serious violation of the social order in a White-supremacist structure that grants itself the power to determine the signification of the acts by relying on a "generative script from which the ideological premises of racial difference can be materialized."[30] The very same act, race play, is thus made to mean two different things depending on the stance of the observers. Though what they do looks for all the world to outsiders as an unthinkable violation and a despicable form of sex — and to be sure the pursuit of murder violates the principle of consent — Tamora and Aaron are, above all else, having *fun* in a way that fosters their sexual connection and erotically plays with the meaning of racial difference within a White-supremacist regime.

II. "Now I will hence to seek my lovely Moor"

Race play can, and should, cause discomfort: "A bitchy white woman belittling her black maid. A Latino man being tied up and called racial

---

30. Smith, "Barbarian Errors," 170.

slurs. A black woman being offered for sale at a slave auction. All of these are awful in reality, but for people who are into race-play — or racialized sexual situations — they can be extremely hot."[31] Margot Weiss has argued that because Whiteness is the privileged norm, racial minority participation in BDSM is inevitably difficult because these scenes inevitably reinforce White supremacy and marginalize minorities. "Black–white pairing in domination/submission fantasies," Weiss writes, "cannot avoid the historical underpinning of such scenes"; as such, we must recognize "that it is this very history that is the source of erotic fantasy."[32] Weiss's limitation here is important: while these structures may indeed be inevitable within BDSM play, not every sexual encounter is kinky, and not all forms of contact between individuals of different races are inevitably forms of race play, even if any individual sexual encounter feels like it could arrive at kink with the faintest push.[33] What I do not want to argue (or even imply) in this section is that it is impossible for interracial sex and sexualities to exist outside the framework of race play. Following Weiss, my argument will be limited to participation in a specific form of kink that relies on violating racial systems in ways that "can be both repressive and freeing in the same instance, offering opportunities for excitement and titillation that may reify systemic oppression while also empowering marginalized subjects to disrupt these systems in

31. Anna North, "When Prejudice Is Sexy: Inside the Kinky World of Race Play," *Jezebel*, March 14, 2012, https://jezebel.com/when-prejudice-is-sexy-inside-the-kinky-world-of-race-5868600.

32. Margot Weiss, *Techniques of Pleasure: BDSM and the Circuits of Sexuality* (Durham, NC: Duke University Press, 2012), 14.

33. I also believe that it is important to acknowledge the potential for race play to exist outside of the United States. While Whiteness is the dominant/structuring force behind most race play within the US, as well as most nations with histories of colonial conquest, the United States is not the world. The possibility for non-White/Eurocentric race play absolutely exists around the world in all places with histories of racial conflict, especially if we consider formulations of race built on national, ethnic, or religious difference (Arab/Israeli, Japanese/Korean, Han/Uyghur, Bamar/Rohyingia, Spanish/Criollo/Mestizo/Indigenous, etc.).

unique ways."[34] Race play relies on active participation in (either through reinforcing or violating) existing racial systems. This does not mean that all forms of interracial sex are necessarily race play; there is absolutely room for non-kink sexual activity that does not engage with those systems and structures. We cannot, however, overlook the Lavinia/ Bassianus problem: racists, or racist pockets of the world, are likely to read even the most vanilla interracial sexual contact as destructive or demeaning simply because to a racist, any interracial sexual act is always already a violation. It has become something of a truism in anti-racist spaces that action matters more than intent, but race play may be one of the significant exceptions to this rule. When the action is a problem for non-participants, when the play is inevitably going to look racist (and will involve active invocations of racism and racist language and practice), it is up to the participants to determine whether the play violates their own boundaries and limits. Violation can feel violating, but with intent and consent, it can also create intense pleasure.

Even within BDSM communities, there is considerable discomfort around race play — "How anyone could indulge in behaviors that don't just glorify but actively eroticize this oppression is baffling to some"[35] — especially when it comes to what might be pleasurable or acceptable in private but cannot be performed or even acknowledged in public. Yet as some participants make clear, this type of play has the potential to explore race in a cathartic way. Renowned leather mother Viola Johnson spoke openly of her taboo attractions: "I can't help the fact that nice Black Jewish girls shouldn't have Nazi fantasies. I DO! Not only do I have politically incorrect fantasies, I've acted many of them out. Even worse, I've enjoyed them. They have tripped my trigger, gotten my rocks off, made me cum."[36] Johnson goes on to castigate participants in the scene

---

34. Smith and Luykx, "Race play," 433.
35. Scott, "Thinking Kink."
36. Viola Johnson, "The Love that Dare Not Speak Its Name: Playing With and Against Racial Stereotypes," *Black Leather in Color* (1994): 8-9.

who refuse to acknowledge the racialized dynamics of their relationships when such dynamics are baked into the scene, reminding us that BDSM players recognized the challenges facing non-White kinksters long before academics got around to studying the issue. Indirectly building on Johnson and directly on Weiss, Kyla Robinson argues that this refusal to acknowledge visible or present racial dynamics ends up making it difficult for people of color to even participate in kink: "By framing race play as the ultimate taboo and off-limits act, the BDSM community is feeding into neoliberal whiteness, and by refusing to acknowledge or speak about how deeply entrenched many aspects of erotic practices in general are inescapably tied to historically situated racial, ethnic, and religious traumas, there is no way forward, and no space for minorities."[37] Given the various traumas that inevitably structure race play scenes, it should come as no surprise that much of the available discourse about race play — to the extent that there even is a discourse, given the discomfort that it causes for so many — focuses on carefully negotiating scenes in advance so as to not trigger participants (or observers) and on the need for considerable aftercare and processing once the scene ends.[38]

In the review that follows, I want to recognize the biopolitical problems that race play presents both for individuals and for collectives and in doing so, to set up the final turn of this essay: that while we so often analyze a kink through the biopolitical apparatus that generates it — and then tries to control or suppress it — pleasure does not always follow the rules. If critical engagement with kink teaches nothing else, it is that pleasure can emerge out of virtually anything, however unthinkable it might be to most people.

Part of the problem with discussing race play, one which gives rise to the problem of exclusion that Robinson discusses, is that we are condi-

37. Robinson, "Speaking the Unspeakable," 2.
38. Cruz even notes that Mollena Williams "rightly acknowledges that she has 'unintentionally' become 'the poster child' for race play because so many others aren't willing to speak about it." Cruz, *The Color of Kink*, 243.

tioned by biopolitics. Susanne Schotanus writes, to "think of people first and foremost as representatives of a collective identity and only secondly as individual people with their own thoughts and convictions[,] … a person's personal decision to engage in race play then, becomes a collective problem, threatening the perceptions about the collective as well as the personal well-being of other people in this group."[39] Like Johnson and Robinson, what Schotanus recognizes is that, when it comes to kink, individual actions are likely to be read as indictments of entire communities or as ways in which individuals fail to live up to their supposed responsibilities to be good citizens of their communities. Tamora, even after becoming Empress of Rome, still remains Queen of Goths, and the play's characters insist that she violates not just herself but the White-Roman collective through her affair with Aaron, stubbornly referred to not by his own name but simply as a Moor. Along these lines, Mollena Williams has written about her frustrations with people who are unwilling to recognize that they cannot exempt themselves from the snares of sexual racism simply by not thinking about the problem: "Whenever I hear POC … insist that race 'is not an issue' and that they have no conflict or second-thoughts about engaging in kink as it pertains to Blackness, I am absolutely gobsmacked. From the stories I hear of unsolicited skin fetishism, to the 'Big Black Cock' obsession, to the incredibly inappropriate assumptions about people's roles in the dungeon or bedroom based on race, this shit is rampant."[40] For Williams, race is such a vividly obvious part of kink that ignoring it is impossible; doing so enables Whiteness to operate invisibly in ways that continue to dominate kink spaces and exclude people of color from full participation. The only option then

---

39. Susanne Schotanus, "Racism or Race Play: A Conceptual Investigation of the Race Play Debates," *Zapruder World: An International Journal for the History of Social Conflict* 4 (2017), https://doi.org/10.21431/Z3001F.
40. Mollena Williams, "Consent, Control, Compassion, and Why I Am Fucking Tired of Explaining Why 'Race Play' Is Different from Racism," *The Perverted Negress* (blog), December 18, 2015, http://www.mollena.com/2015/12/race-play-vs-racism/.

becomes to make race an openly acknowledged part of BDSM practices: to do otherwise allows White supremacy to remain uninterrogated and fester away.

Tamora's conditional Whiteness offers us insight into the dynamics of race play specifically because of how slippery it is: as my analysis of *Titus* has argued, the logic of White supremacy grants Whiteness a corrosive control over non-White sexualities to the extent that it has the power to make racial determinations over individuals, and to the extent that it denies the pleasurable possibilities of these sexualities except outside its own framework. Yet as Tamora and Aaron demonstrate, it is possible to reappropriate sexual racism and use it for pleasure. But to what extent they are fully in control of their own sexual experiences is something that we can reasonably question, especially if Tamora's identification as Semiramis makes her relationship with Aaron one that exists between two non-White bodies. In *The Erotic Life of Racism*, Sharon Holland makes a provocative claim: "Blackness, at least as it is understood in visual culture, not only produces 'erotic value' for whiteness, but it holds the very impossibility of its own pleasure through becoming the sexualized surrogate of another. In another sense, *blackness can never possess its own erotic life.*"[41] And there is an abundance of evidence for this position. In a delightfully termed *pornoethnography*, Jerry Yung-Ching Chang explores "Fire Island's race and class hierarchies" in the classic gay porn *Boys in the Sand*, explaining that "porn films are part and parcel of the modern biopolitical apparatus,"[42] and it is this engagement that enables us to use the wild popularity of interracial porn as a means of reflecting cultural attitudes toward race and sexuality. Cruz also rolls pornography into the biopolitical apparatus of race and racism, explicitly connecting

---

41. Sharon Holland, *The Erotic Life of Racism* (Durham, NC: Duke University Press, 2012), 46. Emphasis in the original.
42. Jerry Yung-Ching Chang, "The Pornoethnography of *Boys in the Sand*: Fetishisms of Race and Class in the 1970s Gay Fire Island Pines," *Women's Studies Quarterly* 43, no. 3 (2015): 101–115, at 110, https://www.jstor.org/stable/43958553.

it to race play: "In making visible the race-play fantasy, pornography is a critical venue of and for race-play performance. It is an important site of race-play analysis because of the dynamic ways it highlights both the fantasy/reality tension and the interracial dynamics that are so salient to the practice. It also brings into relief the perverse pleasures of race play."[43] In light of Cruz's analysis, it is worth another reminder that race play is a distinct phenomenon and not consubstantial with interracial sex or interracial pornography. While interracial pornography can mediate and repackage race play into a widely consumable product, interracial sexual activity requires intent, consent, and pleasure to become race play.

According to PornHub's statistics for 2021, at least six of the top twenty searched terms were explicitly racial and just as popular with women and men.[44] Men's top five favorite categories include *Japanese* (ranked first), *ebony*, and *hentai*; for women, they include *Japanese* (ranked second) and *hentai*. Breaking down the data by country, in the United States, half of the top search terms are explicitly racial: *Hentai, Ebony, Asian, Latina, BBC, Anime,* and *Black*.[45] Within interracial porn, we can see Holland's claim vividly on display, and even expanded on through the consistent fetishization of Black and Asian bodies. Interracial porn can involve bodies of any combination of races but with an important

43. Cruz, *The Color of Kink*, 77.
44. The included terms for straight porn are *ebony, Asian, Latina, BBC* (big black cock), *Black,* and *Japanese*; for gay porn, they are *Black, Japanese, Pinoy, Asian, Korean,* and *BBC*. Three additional terms, *hentai, yaoi,* and *anime*, might be included as racialized categories (*hentai* and *anime* are both in the top twenty for straight porn, and all three are in the top twenty for gay porn); while they are Japanese artforms, the characters depicted are not always necessarily recognizably racialized. It is also certainly the case that a lot of the traffic for these search terms seems to be driven by individuals looking for porn with performers who look like them: *ebony*, for instance, is the most viewed category in sub-Saharan Africa; *Arab* in Egypt, Libya, and Somalia; *Indian* in India; and *Japanese* in much of Asia, including Japan itself. "The Year 2021 in Review," *Pornhub Insights*, December 14, 2021, https://www.pornhub.com/insights/yir-2021.
45. Many countries also show search terms that fetishize populations who are subject to discrimination: *Ebony* in France; *Turkish* in Germany and the Netherlands; *Japanese* and *Korean* in the Philippines; *Asian* and *Indian* in Australia. "The Year 2021 in Review."

caveat anticipated by the conflict between Tamora/Aaron and Lavinia/ Bassianus: to be legible as *race play*, the races involved must have a history built on racism and not merely on observed racial difference. It is not really possible to engage in race play, that is, without engaging in racist and/or colonial tropes because those are the constituent parts of the discursive formation of race in the first place. As a result, anything that is legible as *race play* must be invested in perpetuating and/or perverting an existing racial hierarchy or power dynamic.

While not all interracial porn is legible as race play, certainly it is the case that much interracial porn directly engages in the language of sexual racism.[46] In a study on race and aggression in porn, Eran Shor and Golshan Golriz show that Black men were "most likely to appear in videos with titles that suggest aggression," while Asian men were "the most likely to appear in videos depicting aggression (more than two-thirds of the videos including Asian men exhibited visible aggression)" and "the most likely to appear in videos where nonconsensual aggression occurred." In the same study, it was found that "more than half of the videos containing Latina women depicted visible aggression," while "videos featuring Asian women were also more likely to include nonconsensual violence."[47] Shor and Golriz write later, "Still, one may wonder why the videos containing the Black male performer with a White woman performer were especially aggressive,"[48] but this

46. It is too simplistic to reduce all interracial pornography to White/Black racial positions, but it is also the case that this form dominates the market. "In theory, interracial porn could refer to sex between people of different races — but it doesn't. The term 'interracial' has a much different connotation when applied to adult entertainment. Within the porn vernacular, the term interracial denotes black and white and refers mostly to black guy/white girl action. In any other business this might be considered racist." Aurora Snow, "Why Porn's 'Interracial' Label Is Racist," *The Daily Beast*, April 14, 2017, https://www.thedaily-beast.com/why-porns-interracial-label-is-racist.

47. Eran Shor and Golshan Golriz, "Gender, Race, and Aggression in Mainstream Pornography," *Archives of Sexual Behavior* 48 (2019): 739–51, at 745, https://doi.org/10.1007/ s10508-018-1304-6.

48. Shor and Golriz, "Gender, Race, and Aggression," 749.

hardly seems like cause for surprise or wonder given how often inter-racial porn "specifically entails sex between a Black man and a white woman — and which often deliberately portrays Black men as racial stereotypes,"[49] often as *thugs*, insatiable *predators* on the hunt for White women, or as working-class *trade*. Thinking of pornography in this way is crucial for helping to explore/expand Holland's idea that non-White bodies do not possess their own erotic life. Interracial pornography and race play both exist in a world of "ethnosexual frontiers" made up of "erotic intersections that are heavily patrolled, policed, and protected, yet regularly are penetrated by individuals forging sexual links with ethnic 'others.'"[50] These patrolled borders inevitably impact individuals; research consistently shows that "racial stereotypes, societal beauty standards, and sexual racism can significantly affect [our] sexual and romantic lives."[51] Sexual stereotypes and racism, as well as the tendency to think of individuals as representatives of their race, make it all but impossible for Blackness to have its own erotic life because Blackness is always enmeshed in the tight nets of White supremacy.

Holland's move in response to this problem is to lean on Elizabeth Freeman's term *erotohistoriography* from *Time Binds*, which Freeman explains "is distinct from the desire for a fully present past, a restoration of bygone times. Erotohistoriography does not write the lost object into the present so much as encounter it already in the present, by treating the present itself as hybrid."[52] For Freeman, erotohistoriography does not seek to make the past present; it assumes that the past is always

49. Zoé Samudzi, "What 'Interracial' Cuckold Porn Reveals about White Male Insecurity," *Vice.com*, July 31, 2018, https://www.vice.com/en/article/594yxd/interracial-cuckold-porn-white-male-insecurity-race.

50. Joane Nagel, "Ethnicity and Sexuality," *Annual Review of Sociology* 26 (2000): 107–133, at 113, https://doi.org/10.1146/annurev.soc.26.1.107.

51. Molly Silvestrini, "'It's not something I can shake': The Effect of Racial Stereotypes, Beauty Standards, and Sexual Racism on Interracial Attraction," *Sexuality and Culture* 24 (2020): 305–25, at 320.

52. Elizabeth Freeman, *Time Binds: Queer Temporalities, Queer Histories* (Durham, NC: Duke University Press, 2010), 95.

limned onto the present, a tangle of temporalities that demand to remain entangled. For Holland, the erotohistoriography of racism constantly tried to pull us back into the past, yet it still opens up opportunities to reconfigure desire wherein we no longer have to "view them as static representations, iconographically and inextricably linked to acts that they once signified."[53] The case of Tamora and Aaron helps to illustrate this later theorization, especially through the split between the signification of their race play. For Lavinia and Bassianus, Tamora and Aaron are static representations of the past; it may be that, as Saturninus says, "lovely Tamora, queen of Goths, / ... dost outshine the gallant'st games of Rome" (1.1.320–22), but she remains Queen of Goths even after marriage — and Lavinia and Bassianus will not let her forget her place, keeping her linked to the past through their reminders that they, and not she, can determine the meaning of her body. Yet Tamora and Aaron's connection to their racial past also enables them to reconfigure those structures for themselves and for their own pleasure.

We can, in short, resist the seeming-timelessness of the history of race: even if it is the case that Blackness can *never* possess its own erotic life, we can at least recognize that "it's time to write a new chapter of our relation(s) as truly interdisciplinary, where the dangerous work of the everyday has some transformative (phenomenological?) agency."[54] Even as much of Holland's argument resists the easy move into an embrace of futurity — that everything will be better, someday, if only we can uncouple the past from the present, if only we can rewrite race only this time without racism — it positively embraces a kind of future-looking transformation that is founded on genuinely reckoning with the past and recognizing just how close to the present it really is.

53. Holland, *The Erotic Life of Racism*, 45.
54. Holland, *The Erotic Life of Racism*, 114.

III. Ars Erotica

Ultimately, the problem with race play as a kink, and the reason it remains a marginal practice even within kink communities, is the problem of futurity. Race play is so firmly planted in a past that is thoroughly imbricated in the present, always inflected by the history of racism and race relations, that it seemingly presents no opportunity for positivist growth. Every individual act of race play always reiterates and reinscribes history. Kadji Amin quotes from the French "Manifesto of the 343 Sluts" to illustrate this point: "We want to emphasize that in France, it's our Arab friends who fuck us and never the other way around. Impossible not to understand this as revenge, to which we consent, against the colonizing Occident."[55] As such, race play is an essentially unacceptable, nearly unthinkable kink: the murky ethics of actively engaging with, participating in, and newly recreating racist language, practices, and power dynamics offers nothing for the future. We can locate at least some degree of an investment in futurity in other kinks: as queer critics since Gayle Rubin and Pat Califa have argued, BDSM offers ways to reconfigure power and gender that point toward a more sex-positive and egalitarian future.[56] In cuckoldry we can see how to break free of the restrictive heteronormativity to reconfigure a future that is not built on monogamous marriage. Race play offers nothing to the future because of its persistent insistence on history, a linkage that can only embarrass by reminding us of the genuine horrors and traumas associated with racism, colorism, and colonialism.

What race play *does* offer, however, is what Tamora and Aaron so ably illustrate: sex does not have to be comprehensible to anyone outside the acts. It simply needs to provide pleasure. Yet the provision of pleasure above all raises thorny ethical objections: it is possible to misunderstand

---

55. Kadji Amin, *Disturbing Attachments: Genet, Modern Pederasty, and Queer History* (Durham, NC: Duke University Press, 2017), 77.
56. Amin, *Disturbing Attachments*, 25.

the argument as one that defends racism, or at least one that excuses participating in potentially offensive and hurtful language and practices; at worst, it could seem to enable people to defend their racism as simply a kink. Within an oppressive system of White supremacy, is there such a thing as ethical race play? As Tamora and Aaron illustrate, and as I hope my argument in this essay has made clear, consent between all participants is critical, as is some degree of reflection on the practice. There is real value, I believe, in perversion: as Cruz puts it, "The politics of perversion works to queer 'normal,' to unveil its kinks, disclose its ethical foundation, and destabilize its privileged zenith on a hierarchy of sexuality."[57] Race play can perform all of this biopolitical work, even though it does so through the most unsavory of methods; this line of argument reminds us that sometimes the only way out is through.

Amin offers another way out of the tangle, arguing that what queer theory needs now is to "cultivate a wider set of methods and tactics with which to negotiate what disturbs and disappoints and a wider range of scholarly moods than utopian hope, on the one hand, and critique on the other. Scholars might *inhabit unease*, rather than seeking to quickly rid themselves of it to restore the mastery of the critic [and] the unassailability of her politics."[58] What queer theorists need to recognize, Amin argues, is that "the alternative and the nonnormative — the terms most valued within Queer studies — *need not be politically desirable or affectively pleasurable*; at times they might be experienced as barely tolerable, or more likely, as nauseating."[59] Building off Amin's process of deidealization, of allowing unsavory sexual practices to simply be sexual practices walled off (to some degree) from biopolitics, would see us return to the idea that kink is a Foucauldian *ars erotica* rather than a *scientia sexualis*. As a *scientia sexualis*, kink must "correspond to the functional requirements

---

57. Cruz, *The Color of Kink*, 17.
58. Amin, *Disturbing Attachments*, 10. Emphasis in the original.
59. Amin, *Disturbing Attachments*, 31. Emphasis in the original.

of a discourse," but as an *ars erotica*, "truth is drawn from pleasure itself, understood as a practice and accumulated as experience; pleasure is not considered in relation to an absolute law of the permitted and the forbidden, nor by reference to a criterion of utility, but first and foremost in relation to itself."[60] For Foucault, there is necessarily some degree of secrecy and mystery around an *ars erotica*: it is something understood by the participants, passed down to new initiates, in ways that resist the regime of confessional sexuality under which we live. Maybe, Foucault suggests, not everything needs to be rigorously theorized to be considered a valid sexual practice. Maybe the point is that pleasure is a valid end unto itself, that thinking about sex as *play* enables us to explore and discover what we enjoy, and what provides pleasure can remain the private domain of the participants in the acts. Above all else, it reminds us that kink is *fun*. Sex is *fun*: have more of it.

I am grateful for the insights, suggestions, and contributions made by Benjamin Brennan, John Dixon, Mario DiGangi, Amy Guenther, Ben A. Johnson, Peter Murray, and Steven Wooley, and for the extraordinary (and extraordinarily patient) shepherding of Gillian Knoll and Joseph Gamble.

60. Michel Foucault, *The History of Sexuality, Volume 1: An Introduction*, trans. Robert Hurley (New York: Vintage, 1990), 68, 57.

PART 3
Representational Quandaries and Kinky Solutions

Early Modern Money Shots

Beatrice Bradley

In *The Color of Kink*, Ariane Cruz writes of the tension between the so-called money shot and bareback sex, asking, "If the money shot depends on visual proof of pleasure in the projection of semen *on* the body and the practice of bareback sex is contingent upon ejaculate deposited *inside* the body, how can bareback porn reconcile this representational quandary — rendering visible what is invisible while remaining a kind of authentic 'visual archive' of bareback sex itself?"[1] Cruz is glossing and responding to Tim Dean's analysis of "raw sex" in *Unlimited Intimacy*, where he writes that in bareback porn "non-normative sex comes up against the norms of representation."[2] As Cruz notes, Dean offers several

1. Ariane Cruz, *The Color of Kink: Black Women, BDSM, and Pornography* (New York: New York University Press, 2016), 192; emphasis in Cruz.
2. Tim Dean, *Unlimited Intimacy: Reflections on the Subculture of Barebacking* (Chicago: University of Chicago Press, 2009), 104; cited in Cruz, *Color of Kink*, 192. Bareback sex has different implications in 2023 from when Dean published *Unlimited Intimacy* almost fifteen years earlier. This is largely due to developments in the medical treatment and prevention of HIV, including, significantly, the widespread usage of antiviral drugs or PrEP (Pre-Exposure Prophylaxis) to inhibit exposure; see, for example, Karsten Schubert, "A New Era of Queer Politics? PrEP, Foucauldian Sexual Liberation, and the Overcoming of Homonormativity," *Body Politics* 12, no. 8 (2021): 1–41, https://dx.doi.org/10.2139/ssrn.3901719. See also Ricky Varghese, "Introduction: The Mourning After," in *Raw: PrEP, Pedagogy, and the Politics of Barebacking*, ed. Ricky Varghese (London: Zed Books Ltd, 2019), 1–20, who writes, "Might it be important to ask whether we are even barebacking anymore as a result

"solutions" to this "representational quandary" — bareback sex's depen-
dency on internal ejaculation and a cultural fixation on visibility — with
solutions often involving the displacement of ejaculate and its storage
for later consumption or the use of subtitles and verbal remarks to signal
ejaculation.[3] Dean's final example of such a substitution is a scene of urination during the end credits of a film.[4] His focus, and that of Cruz in her
close reading of his work, is not just the pornographic but specifically
pornographic cinema: both theorists follow the groundbreaking work
of Linda Williams in their collective attention to the "maximum visibility" inherent to hard-core movies as opposed to other erotic representations.[5] Dean's slippage, however, between semen and urine demonstrates
how easily hard core spills into other genres, with scenes of urination or
the flaccid penis acceptable in mainstream cinema where the money shot
is not.[6] Dean's emphasis on bareback porn as "constitut[ing] a mode of

of new technologies of sex? Is barebacking still barebacking with the invisible barrier of
chemical prophylaxes? And what does it mean to have one's life, one's sex life, always
already medicalized?" (12). In the same collection, Dean revisits *Unlimited Intimacy*, observing in the afterword a continuity in his thinking around barebacking — "It seemed to me
then, and still does now, that deciding whether bareback sex is progressive or conservative, radical or compromised, queer or otherwise makes it too easy to elide the complexity of the phenomenon" (288) — while also emphasizing the temporal distance from his
earlier writing on the subject; he asks, "Does barebacking qualify as non-normative if that
is statistically how the majority of men fuck these days?" (289) and muses, "I'm wonder-
ing whether the term 'bareback' already feels nostalgic — bareback as a look back to the
moment before pharmaceuticals, when dispensing with condoms really meant something"
(290); Tim Dean, "Afterword: The Raw and the Fucked," in *Raw: PrEP, Pedagogy, and the
Politics of Barebacking*, ed. Ricky Varghese (London: Zed Books Ltd, 2019), 285–304. I am
grateful to Joshua Barsczewski for suggesting these readings on the contemporary status of
barebacking to me.
3. Dean uses the language of "solutions" when discussing these approaches (143–44); Dean,
Unlimited Intimacy.
4. Dean, *Unlimited Intimacy*, 194.
5. Linda Williams, "Fetishism and Hard Core: Marx, Freud, and the 'Money Shot,'" chap. 4
in *Hard Core: Power, Pleasure, and the "Frenzy of the Visible"* (Berkeley: University of California Press, 1989), 93–119. For Dean's discussion of Williams in *Unlimited Intimacy*, see pages
108–11, in particular.
6. Greg Tuck observes that films such as *There's Something About Mary* (Bobby and Peter
Farrelly, 1998) include visual representations of ejaculate as a substance, even though

thinking about bodily limits, about intimacy, about power, and of course, about sex" *because of* its very "problems of representation" certainly resonates outside of hard core.[7] That is, these problems of fluidic representation are located as points of tension in other media as well, including, as is my focus here, the literary.

Quandaries

In the following chapter, I chart this "representational quandary" in early modern contexts with a renewed attention to the role of witnessing, to the erotics of an interior made hypervisible, and to the multiple locations and dislocations of pleasure in fluidic projection and exchange. I examine three representations of the female body adorned with a liquid that vacillates between aestheticized droplets and amorphous muck: Acrasia in Edmund Spenser's *The Faerie Queene*, followed by William Shakespeare's depictions in the long poem *Venus and Adonis* of Venus first in pursuit of Adonis and later anticipating his death. The fluids in question — I discuss for the most part sweat with a closing rumination on Venus's

"representations of the penis are still uncommon in cinema, whilst the direct representation of the erect penis is still prohibited" (265). Greg Tuck, "Mainstreaming the Money Shot: Reflections on the Representation of Ejaculation in Contemporary American Cinema," *Paragraph* 26, nos. 1/2 (March/July 2003): 263–79, https://doi.org/10.3366/para.2003.26.1-2.263. The British Board of Film Classification (BBFC), for example, previously held that urolagnia in film was illegal, while urination in nonsexual contexts was not, which raises questions as to how a viewer interprets various scenes of urination. The guidelines up until very recently specified that even under the rating R18 "activity which is degrading or dehumanizing (examples include the portrayal of bestiality, necrophilia, defecation, urolagnia)" was "not acceptable." "BBFC Classification Guidelines," accessed March 2021, https://www.bbfc.co.uk/about-classification/classification-guidelines; the site has since been updated to remove the above language. The Wikipedia page for the BBFC includes extensive documented reference to these guidelines. "British Board of Film Classification," *Wikipedia*, Wikimedia Foundation, last edited August 22, 2022, https://en.wikipedia.org/wiki/British_Board_of_Film_Classification.The BBFC also previously equated female ejaculate with urine. See Anna North, "Movies, Censorship, and the 'Myth' of Female Ejaculation," *Jezebel*, October 8, 2009, https://jezebel.com/movies-censorship-and-the-myth-of-female-ejaculatio-5377327.

7. Dean, *Unlimited Intimacy*, 105.

tears — are produced by the women themselves; there is no overt sex organ cited in the poetry. I am not suggesting that these scenes are literally semenic, with early modern authors wanting their readers to interpret the liquids as such.[8] Nor am I looking to allegorize sexual activity by bringing contemporary theories of pornography into contact with early modern poetry: I recognize the value of studies that emphasize the literality or, to quote Christien Garcia, the "mereness" of sex acts, with Garcia asking scholars "to consider seriously the impulse not to think about sex as more than itself."[9] Rather, I argue across this chapter that the fluidic spectacle on display in late sixteenth-century poetry generates a representational tension between the visual (droplets of pearly ornamentation) and the tactile (melting sweaty bodies). The poetry organizes

8. I moreover am not invested in whether these literary texts are or are not pornography. As Eric Langley notes, "Applying the term 'pornography' (*porno* and *graphoi*) to early-modern texts is contentious" (232n2). Eric Langley, "'Lascivious Dialect': Decadent Rhetoric and the Early-Modern Pornographer," in *Decadences: Morality and Aesthetics in British Literature*, ed. Paul Fox (Stuttgart: ibidem Press, 2014), 231–55. *Venus and Adonis* in particular has long been associated with the pornographic. Chantelle Thauvette gives a comprehensive history of both the poem's reception and the term "pornography" in "Defining Early Modern Pornography: The Case of *Venus and Adonis*," *Journal for Early Modern Cultural Studies* 12, no. 1 (Winter 2012): 26–48, https://www.jstor.org/stable/23242178. See also Katherine Duncan-Jones, "Much Ado with Red and White: The Earliest Readers of Shakespeare's *Venus and Adonis* (1593)," *The Review of English Studies* 44, no. 176 (1993): 479–501; cited in Thauvette, "Defining Early Modern Pornography," 29. Theorists such as Williams locate "pornography" as originating with the invention of cinema, and Renaissance scholars have similarly argued that the use of the word to apply to early modern erotica is anachronistic. See Williams, *Hard Core*, 36–37. In her introduction to *The Invention of Pornography*, Lynn Hunt traces pornography to early modern contexts while still associating it with "the culture of modernity" (11). Lynn Hunt, "Introduction," in *The Invention of Pornography: Obscenity and the Origins of Modernity, 1500–1800*, ed. Lynn Hunt (New York: Zone Books, 1993), 9–46; cited in Thauvette, "Defining Early Modern Pornography," 37. Ian Fredrick Moulton dismisses the term in the first paragraph of *Before Pornography*, writing, "In particular, 'pornography' is too historically specific a term to be much use in a discussion of the early modern period, for the erotic writing of the sixteenth and seventeenth centuries — whatever its explicitness — is different in both form and content from the genres of pornography as they developed in later periods" (3). Ian Frederick Moulton, *Before Pornography: Erotic Writing in Early Modern England* (Oxford: Oxford University Press, 2000).

9. Christien Garcia, "Merely Barebacking," in *Raw: PrEP, Pedagogy, and the Politics of Barebacking*, ed. Ricky Varghese (London: Zed Books Ltd, 2019), 263–84, at 264.

its language of fluidic projection and exchange — the formal staging of ejaculate — with a set of terms and focal points that align its pleasures with contemporary porn's use of the money shot.

This chapter employs the term "ejaculate" to refer to a range of liquids produced by the body in a sexualized context. In doing so, I echo early modern usages of "ejaculate" to apply to all fluids, including but not exclusively semen, that are "eject[ed] from the body."[10] It is worth noting that contemporary scholarship's analysis of the money shot has also expanded as porn grows more accessible and diverse, from Williams's understanding of the money shot as definitively heteronormative to Dean's analysis of the act in the context of sex between men at the height of the AIDS crisis to Cruz's attention to Black female sexuality in performances that employ the Sybian and other "mechanized phallic devices" to stimulate ejaculation.[11] Enduring debates around squirting — whether the liquid produced is urine *or* vaginal ejaculate — demonstrate how easily bodily fluids collapse into each other, not only in the humoral theory of the past but also today.[12] Indeed, this indeterminacy is built into the appeal of fluidic projection and exchange. A camera lens's close focus on the face, chest, or other body part — as with poetic presentation of the

10. *Oxford English Dictionary* (hereafter *OED*) *Online*, s.v. "ejaculate (*v.1.b*)": "To eject fluids, etc. from the body." The *OED Online* cites John Banister's *The Historie of Man*, published in 1578, as the first usage of "ejaculate" in such a context. Banister uses the term repeatedly in his medical writing, for example referring to "the eiaculation of sperme" (Aaiiiir). John Banister, *The Historie of Man* (London, 1578).

11. Cruz, *The Color of Kink*, 171.

12. Gail Kern Paster explains that "Galenic humoralism proposed a structural homology among all forms of evacuation, including the bodily release of male and female 'seed' in sexual climax," and she goes on to provide a reading of Ben Jonson's *Bartholomew Fair* that brings together female ejaculate, spit, and urine (39). Gail Kern Paster, *The Body Embarrassed: Drama and the Disciplines of Shame in Early Modern England* (Ithaca, NY: Cornell University, 1993). For modern contexts, see North, "Movies, Censorship, and the 'Myth' of Female Ejaculation." Cruz quotes the adult performer William Margold as declaring, "The one thing a woman cannot do is ejaculate in the face of her partner. We have that power," to then offer the riposte, "Countless female squirters have proved Margold wrong, and hardcore pornography has provided evidence of women's ability to ejaculate (and do so in the face of her partner)" (192–93). Cruz, *Color of Kink*.

liquid as stylized droplets — obfuscates, at least momentarily, both the source and the substance of the ejaculate. In early modern thought, John Donne illuminates a capacious interplay between fluids (sweat, semen, and menstrual blood) in his aptly titled poem "The Comparison," which, like *The Faerie Queene* and *Venus and Adonis*, was likely written in the last decade of the sixteenth century.[13] Donne's speaker first compares "the sweat drops" on his "mistress' breast" to "almighty balm" and "pearl carcanets," before attacking his friend's beloved for the "rank sweaty froth" on her "brow" that resembles, according to the poet, "the spèrm'tic issue of ripe menstr'ous boils."[14] The "breast" and "brow" are important loci in generating spectacle and indeed pleasure in visual media: Cruz's definition of the "typical" money shot emphasizes the particularity of the site of ejaculate on "the face, mouth, buttocks, stomach, and/or breasts."[15] In "The Comparison," the locations of "breast" and "brow" attach to Donne's reference to "spermatic" — that is, "resembling sperm" — to produce a semenic substance that adorns both women, an early modern rendering of the contemporary sexual innuendo of the "pearl necklace."[16] These scenes of fluidic projection and exchange in late sixteenth-century poetry constitute sites of erotic pleasure that are largely disassociated from the specificity of the substance — my readings, not unlike Donne, perform an elision of sweat, semen, and tears — and detached from the acts that produce it, sexual or otherwise.

13. Robin Robbins dates "The Comparison" as composed between 1593 and 1596. See John Donne, "The Comparison," *The Complete Poems of John Donne*, ed. Robin Robbins (New York: Routledge, 2013), 299–305, at 299.
14. Donne, "The Comparison," lines 3, 4, 6, 7, and 8.
15. Cruz, *The Color of Kink*, 189.
16. Robbins notes, "The analogy is with the secretion of the sperm-whale rather than semen" (301n.8). Donne, "The Comparison." However, I find that the pairing of "spèrm'tic" with "issue" (a word with clear reproductive resonances), as well as the general tenor of the poem, indicates that a reader should understand "spèrm'tic" as semenic. For the extensive early modern usages of the word in reference to semen, see *OED Online*, s.v. "spermatic (adj. 1–5)." The *OED Online* defines the slang usage of "pearl necklace" as "semen ejaculated on to a sexual partner's neck or chest." *OED Online*, s.v. "pearl necklace (n)."

My point in the above elision of fluids is that a lack of specificity is integral to many facets of erotic life, facets that not only include practices of kink that prioritize sensory overwhelm and/or disorientation but also the staging of the money shot itself. This is evident in Williams's account of the money shot as "an obvious perversion — in the literal sense of the term, as a swerving away from more 'direct' forms of genital engagement — of the tactile sexual connection," as well as in Dean's description of the "multiple displaced money shot" that ritualizes the accumulation of ejaculate and "mak[es] apparent how sex involves persons who are not physically present — except as fragmentary, material traces."[17] As an example, Dean cites the "Devil's Dick," the "recipe" for which involves "collecting multiple loads of ejaculate in a single condom, freezing the contents, and then using as a dildo the super-sized cum popsicle that results."[18] Throughout this chapter, I attend to the "swerves" and "displacements" of early modern poetry — the "perversion" that makes the money shot such a rich area of exploration in conversations around kink — with the understanding that the act's representation in contemporary hard-core cinema participates in, rather than pioneers, a long-standing tension in fluidic representation between visual appeal and sensory overwhelm.[19] In doing so, I work to recuperate mislaid histories of erotic spaces, pleasures, and indeed fluids that reveal cracks in normative models of desire

17. Williams, *Hard Core*, 101; Dean, *Unlimited Intimacy*, 141.

18. Dean, *Unlimited Intimacy*, 141. The film *Breeding Season* (TIM, 2006) and its use of the instrument is also discussed in Garcia, "Merely Barebacking," 268; and Lee Edelman, "Unbecoming: Pornography and the Queer Event," in *Post/Porn/Politics: Queer-Feminist Perspective on the Politics of Porn Performance and Sex Work as Cultural Production*, ed. Tim Stüttgen (Berlin: b_books, 2009), 195–211, at 207–208.

19. Williams observes in *Hard Core* that hard core is "a genre more like other genres than unlike them" (269); her discussion of *Fred Ott's Sneeze* in her chapter on the "prehistory" of hard core likewise demonstrates how the genre can be brought to bear upon other bodily acts outside the category of the explicit (51–53).

and reciprocity, which so often focus on the genital and on exclusively penetrative sex.[20]

Vocabularies

Consider the final reveal of Acrasia in Book 2 of *The Faerie Queene*. Guyon, the so-called Knight of Temperance and protagonist of the Book, travels across twelve cantos in search of the aforementioned enchantress. His objective, along with that of his companion in the quest (referred to textually as the Palmer), is to ensnare Acrasia and render her seductive powers ineffective. At long last, in the final canto, Guyon and the Palmer make their way into her lush and intoxicating habitat — the Bower of Bliss that will be destroyed by the Book's end — and discover "the faire Witch" looming over her sleeping lover, Verdant.[21] Acra-

20. In the context of heterosexual pornography, Lisa Jean Moore writes, "The sex act itself is centered around the male penis and orgasm. Only when that happens does conventional wisdom tell us that sex has occurred" (73). Lisa Jean Moore, "Overcome: The Money Shot in Pornography and Prostitution," chap. 5 in *Sperm Counts: Overcome by Man's Most Precious Fluid* (New York: New York University Press, 2007), 71–91. Even in nonnormative forms of pornography, such as various representations of kink, the genitals often remain a cinematic focus.
21. Edmund Spenser, *The Faerie Queene*, ed. A. C. Hamilton (Harlow: Pearson Education Limited, 2006), 2.12.72. All subsequent references to *The Faerie Queene* are taken from this edition and cite book, canto, and stanza parenthetically. Patricia Parker, *Literary Fat Ladies: Rhetoric, Gender, Property* (New York: Methuen, 1987), writes of the romance genre's tendency toward delay: "'Romance' is characterized primarily as a form which simultaneously quests for and postpones a particular end, objective, or object" (4). Guyon's ultimate demolition of the Bower has been much discussed by critics, as has Acrasia's intoxicating allure. See, among many others, Angela D. Bullard, "Tempering the Intemperate in Spenser's Bower of Bliss," *Spenser Studies* 31–32 (2018): 167–87; Dennis Austin Britton, "Ovidian Baptism in Book 2 of *The Faerie Queene*," chap. 2 in *Becoming Christian: Race, Reformation, and Early Modern English Romance* (New York: Fordham University Press, 2014), 59–90; Helen Cooney, "Guyon and His Palmer: Spenser's Emblem of Temperance," *The Review of English Studies* 51, no. 202 (May 2000): 189–92; Holly Dugan, "Bowers of Bliss: Jasmine, Potpourri Vases, Pleasure Gardens," chap. 6 in *The Ephemeral History of Perfume* (Baltimore: Johns Hopkins University Press, 2011), 154–81; Rebecca Helfer, "Misprision and Freedom: Ruining and Recollecting the Bower of Bliss," chap. 6 in *Spenser's Ruins and the Art of Recollection* (Toronto: University of Toronto Press, 2012), 299–318; Wendy Beth Hyman, "Seizing Flowers in Spenser's Bower and Garden," *English Literary Renaissance* 37, no. 2 (Spring

sia remains drowsily unaware of the intruders, who, in turn, gape at her. The text luxuriates in an aestheticized sweat that trickles down her body, highlighting her nudity and in fact magnifying her allure:

Her snowy brest was bare to ready spoyle
Of hungry eies, which n'ote therewith be fild,
And yet through languour of her late sweet toyle,
Few drops, more cleare then Nectar, forth distild,
That like pure Orient perles adowne it trild,
And her faire eyes sweet smyling in delight,
Moystened their fierie beames, with which she thrild
Fraile harts, yet quenched not; like starry light
Which sparckling on the silent waues, does seeme more bright.
(2.12.78)[22]

Spenser is reworking Torquato Tasso here, transforming the Italian poet's description of a generalized beautiful sweat (*i bei sudor*) in *Jerusalem Delivered* into a mode of ornamentation.[23] Acrasia is first likened to stone

2007): 193–214; and Ayesha Ramachandran, "Clarion in the Bower of Bliss: Poetry and Politics in Spenser's 'Muiopotmos,'" *Spenser Studies* 20 (2005): 77–106.

22. I include a similar paragraph and analysis of the stanza in the essay "How to Do Things with Sweat," which appears in a forthcoming issue of *Shakespeare Studies*.

23. Torquato Tasso, *Gerusalemme Liberata* (Milan: Ulrico Hoepli, 1898), 16.18.4. Anna Wainwright provides a nuanced reading of Tasso's enchantress Armida and discusses the sweat that whitens her face in *Jerusalem Delivered* (192). Anna Wainwright, "'Tied Up in Chains of Adamant': Recovering Race in Tasso's Armida Before, and After, Acrasia," *Spenser Studies* 35 (2021): 181–212, https://doi.org/10.1086/711936. For a discussion of Acrasia's sweat, see Michael Schoenfeldt, who argues that "for Spenser [sweat] is always at the core of moral effort," before he then identifies Acrasia's perspiration as evidence of just how hard "vice works in the pursuit of pleasure" (46). Michael Schoenfeldt, *Bodies and Selves in Early Modern England: Physiology and Inwardness in Spenser, Shakespeare, Herbert, and Milton* (Cambridge, UK: Cambridge University Press, 1999). Joseph Campana notes that Acrasia "appears soaked in the sweat of her sordid play," and he more broadly connects the general liquidity of Books 1 and 2 of *The Faerie Queene* — there is, for example, a prevalence of fountains — to a sensuous male pleasure in repose. Joseph Campana, *The Pain of Reformation: Spenser, Vulnerability, and the Ethics of Masculinity* (New York: Fordham University Press, 2012), 130. Finally, Stephen Guy-Bray, in an essay specifically focused on Acrasia's

— her skin is described as "alablaster" in the preceding stanza (2.12.77) — but the "Few drops" that "trill" or flow down her body are not the gathered drops of condensation on a marblesque surface: the fluid is produced "*through* languour of her late sweet toyle," excreted and "distild" (emphasis mine). The drops that decorate Acrasia's "bare" chest at once construct an insistently exoticized white body — the "Orient perles," sharing the language of Donne's "pearl carcanets," amplify the already over-determined whiteness of the enchantress's "alablaster" skin and "snowy brest" — and shimmer "more cleare then Nectar." These contrasting comparatives and shifting metaphorical resonances, from "Nectar" to "perles" to "silent waues," together chart the impetuous course of desire as it moves from containment to overflow. The fluid streams down Acrasia's body but also down the stanza, accumulating in the final line as no longer a "Few drops" but instead "silent" oceanic "waues."

Spenser at no point uses the word "sweat" nor does he provide a locus of origin; the fluid merely emanates "forth."[24] Upon sustained engagement with the text — the density of the language and its refusal to clarify locate the reader too as voyeur in the necessary close reading of the stanza — the references to "toyle" and its resulting exhaustion signal the fluid as perspiration. But whatever forms of erotic labor produced the moisture remain outside the scope of the narrative. The only mode of

sweat, argues that the fluid is only seemingly attractive but in truth a foul substance: he reads perspiration as linking Acrasia to Duessa in Book 1, another malevolent enchantress whose monstress form reveals breasts that leak "filthy matter" (1.8.47). Stephen Guy-Bray, "Spenser's Filthy Matter," *The Explicator* 62, no. 4 (2004): 194–95, https://doi.org/10.1080/00144940409597218.

24. J. K. Barret, *Untold Futures: Time and Literary Culture in Renaissance England* (Ithaca, NY: Cornell University Press, 2017), observes in *The Faerie Queene* Spenser's "habit of putting pressure on when we know, from something as simple as withholding the name of the character for several stanzas to something as complex as the status of the present moment in the narrative itself" (67). The refusal to name sweat in the narrative (although located explicitly elsewhere in the text) appears just such a pressure point. Barret later argues for a poetic pleasure in Spenser that is "associated equally with not knowing and accessing the possibility of knowing" (79).

exchange in the above stanza is that of visual pleasure: Acrasia's "sweet smyling" eyes flash with "delight" — in line with premodern accounts of vision, her eyes emit "fierie beames" that reflect off her damp breast — and spectators' "Fraile harts" are "thrild" in response.[25] The pleasures of observing a sweating body are overwhelmingly familiar in contemporary culture. Think, for example, of Britney Spears in the "I'm a Slave 4 U" music video; the slicked bodies of fitness magazines; or even a Gatorade commercial where tantalizing beads of moisture whet the thirst.[26] These pleasures, however, are predominantly one-sided. Sweat does not explicitly signify the satisfaction of desire as does the expulsion of other bodily fluids. Yet in the Bower of Bliss, Acrasia's sweat does just that. The substance is visual proof of the enchantress's pleasure projected on her body, the liquid magnifying her "sweet smyling ... delight" that is itself a residue from a similarly "sweet" labor now past.

Despite the stanza's prioritization of the visual, there is something tantalizingly edible about the pronounced "sweetness" of the Bower. The language of "Nectar" extends beyond its insistent visual register — the poem underscores the liquid's exceptional clarity as it is "more cleare then Nectar" — to incorporate the suggested taste of bodily fluids. Sixteenth- and seventeenth-century dictionaries define "nectar" as a rarefied beverage, that which is ingested with great pleasure: "excellent

25. In his essay on the subject of early modern paradigms of vision, Eric Langley provides an account of shifting concepts, where the theory of the "eyebeam" is ultimately supplanted; he identifies in Spenser the "eye-emitted ray paradigm," where "both the eye and the object viewed are emitting tangible physical beams or visual currents, one at the other, which meet and merge in the coalescence of sight, a coalescence that in the love-lyric assumes an erotic charge, an implicit sense of proto-sexual mingling" (343). Eric F. Langley, "Anatomizing the Early-Modern Eye: A Literary Case-Study," *Renaissance Studies* 20, no. 3 (June 2006): 340–55, https://doi.org/10.1111/j.1477-4658.2006.00161.x.

26. In "I'm a Slave 4 U," Spears employs familiar language from BDSM, where the person in the submissive role is often referred to as the "slave" and thus the property of the "dominant." Spears comes in uncomfortable proximity to referencing chattel slavery in her music video's use of sweat that reinscribes the linkage between the fluid and hard labor. Britney Spears, "I'm a Slave 4 U," October 25, 2009, YouTube music video, 3:23, https://youtu.be/Mzybwwf2HoQ.

wine" or, more frequently, "the drink of the gods."[27] Erotic poetry of the same period associates the delicacy with the kiss, where lovers taste "nectar" on each other's lips. For example, Thomas Stanley writes in his mid-seventeenth-century poem "The Enjoyment" of his desire for his love object:

> To cool my fervent Thirst, I sip
> Delicious Nectar from her lip.[28]

Later, an anonymous author similarly uses such language in a 1685 poetry collection, where the speaker describes ostensibly his lover's mouth — referred to as a cavity, "the lovely odiferous Cell" — as "fill[ed]" with "delicious Nectar."[29] Even a didactic text, the 1740 *A Dialogue Between a Married Lady and a Maid,* which seems to operate simultaneously as an instructional to those persons new to sexual activity and as erotica for a larger audience, employs "Nectar" as a term to mediate its explicit content. The young maid in question, Octavia, details an encounter between herself and her new husband where she directly refers to her own ejaculate as "delicious Nectar":

> putting his Finger into my C–t, and stirring gently up and down, towards the upper Part of it, he made me spend so pleasantly, such a Quantity of the delicious Nectar, that it flew about his Hand, and all wetted him … I was struck with a mighty Confusion at my own Lust,

27. Richard Huloet provides the Latin translation for "Wine called nectar, an excellent wyne;" Richard Huloet, *Huloet's dictionarie* (London, 1572), zzvir. For texts that define "nectar" as the drink of the gods, see, among others, Henry Cockeram, *The English dictionarie* (London, 1623), H2r; Thomas Elyot, *The dictionary of syr Thomas Eliot knyght* (London, 1538), Ovr; and John Florio, *A vvorlde of words, or Most copious, and exact dictionarie in Italian and English* (London, 1589), V6r.

28. Thomas Stanley, "The Enjoyment," *Poems by Thomas Stanley, Esquire* (London, 1651), b7v.

29. Anonymous, "Kissing his Mistris," *Poems by several hands, and on several occasions collected by N[ahum] Tate* (London, 1685), S5r.

and blushing, and hiding my Face, I said, that if he felt any Moisture, it was that which he put into me, and not any that I had send out.[30]

After the relative opacity of "nectar" in earlier writings, the direct approach of the above passage is refreshing (to draw on the language of thirst and liquidity throughout this chapter) in that there is little doubt as to what the speaker refers. This is not to say, however, that the dialogue retrospectively locates Acrasia's "Nectar" as vaginal or, for that matter, semenic. I am invested in maintaining the Spenserian refusal to name any particular fluid, as I read the stanza's lack of specificity as integral to its understanding of pleasure. Instead, I wish to emphasize that, for one, "nectar" is actively employed in a vocabulary of sexualized fluids — a vocabulary with a long history, vacillating degrees of particularity, and a fixation on ingestion. Secondly, I read the choreographed disorientation of the above passage as reminiscent of the mood in the Bower. Octavia's own "Confusion" at her body's arousal prompts her to trouble the fluid's source of origin altogether. Despite the fact it is evident that she, like Acrasia, is the source of the "Moisture," Octavia attempts to ascribe its production to her husband ("that which he put into me"), as opposed to that which she herself expelled ("not any I had send out"). In the Bower of Bliss, the liquid's stylized presentation — replete with metaphorical language such as "Nectar" — similarly blurs distinctions between Acrasia's own excretions and those that might be deposited by others. "Hungry eies" lurk *in potentia* as active participants in this scene of fluidic display.

The language's movement from "more cleare then Nectar" to "pure Orient perles" generates its own representational tension not only in the confusion of the liquid's source of origin but also in the contrasting

---

30. Anonymous, *A Dialogue Between a Married Lady and a Maid* (London, 1740), 36. Earlier, Octavia praises the "heavenly Nectar" women are "provided with" (32). I was introduced to this passage in a talk by Valerie Traub at the University of Pennsylvania, titled "Racializing Subjectivity in the 17th-Century Erotic Narrative," where Traub provided a reading of Octavia's "blushing." Valerie Traub, "Racializing Subjectivity in the 17th-Century Erotic Narrative," 2023 Phyllis Rackin Lecture, University of Pennsylvania, March 1, 2023.

descriptive features that probe the bounds of metaphor. How can the substance be both exceptionally "cleare" and pearly white? What does it mean for Acrasia to be at once an emblem of "pure" whiteness and associated with materials of the "Orient"? If, as Amber Jamilla Musser argues, "liquidity ... is something that emanates from flesh and is therefore inseparable from the processes of racialization," the shifting and often contradictory resonances of the stanza's language correspond with and indeed mobilize the construction of Acrasia's indeterminate yet exoticized racial identity in the Bower.[31] The ornamentation of the pearl is demonstrative of Kim F. Hall's foundational work on the lyric and particularly Petrarchan emphasis on whiteness as constitutive of early modern beauty — the "pure" pearl reaffirms the fairness of the "faire Witch" — whereas the attachment of "Orient" destabilizes the normativity of said whiteness.[32] As Arthur L. Little Jr. observes in the context of Tamora in Shakespeare's *Titus Andronicus*, the exceptionalism of whiteness "isn't always ... a case of who has presumably the whitest skin," and "hyperwhiteness," especially when it corresponds with "hypersexuality,"

---

31. Amber Jamilla Musser is writing in reference to two African statues — a nkisi and a bieri — that continue to produce palm oil centuries after they were first carved (101). Amber Jamilla Musser, "Sweat, Display, and Blackness: The Promises of Liquidity," *Feminist Media Histories* 7, no. 2 (2021): 92–109, https://doi.org/10.1525/fmh.2021.7.2.92.

32. In *Things of Darkness: Economies of Race and Gender in Early Modern England* (Ithaca, NY: Cornell University Press, 1996), Kim F. Hall writes, "Coral and pearl are not just metaphors. They appear prominently in both domestic manuals and art treatises: the acquisition of these items figured prominently in English trade practices. Often, the very materials that made women 'fair' (in both art and cosmetics), like the perfumes that made them sweet, are the fuel for colonial trade ... whiteness is not only constructed by but dependent on an involvement with Africans that is the inevitable product of England's ongoing colonial expansion" (253); I am also thinking in particular of Kim F. Hall, "'These bastard signs of fair': Literary Whiteness in Shakespeare's Sonnets," in *Post-Colonial Shakespeares*, ed. Ania Loomba and Martin Orkin (London: Routledge, 2003), 64–83. Britton writes in his reading of Book 2 of *The Faerie Queene*, "There are different types of bodies in Book 2, and specific bodies, like Acrasia's ... are racially and religiously marked" (70). Britton, "Ovidian Baptism in Book 2 of *The Faerie Queene*."

can itself be read as a perversion of the norm.[33] Acrasia's "Orient perles" make paradoxical claims to identity and also to race as a category. The descriptor at once insists on a fiction of racial essentialism so totalizing that even the pores produce a white fluid, while simultaneously parodying the very designation of "alablaster" skin: sweat is not really white but, of course, neither is flesh.[34]

The stanza ends with a dazzling, overwhelming brightness. Acrasia's "fair eyes" reflect off her glistening body

> like starry light
> Which sparckling on the silent waues does seem more bright.
> (2.12.78)

This "sparckling" reinforces the pearlescence of the liquid, underscoring the stanza's use of the term "Orient" to signal qualities that are, as Miriam Jacobson notes, both "lustrous and white."[35] The luster that "seem[s]" to radiate from the enchantress's body is resonant with Anne Anlin Cheng's reading of "shine" in the context of "orientalized feminin-

33. See Arthur L. Little Jr., "Is It Possible to Read Shakespeare through Critical White Studies?", in *The Cambridge Companion to Shakespeare and Race*, ed. Ayanna Thompson (Cambridge, UK: Cambridge University Press, 2021), 276–77.
34. On whiteness in the context of Shakespeare, Richard Dyer observes, "Whiteness, really white whiteness is unattainable. Its ideal forms are impossible … Whiteness as an ideal can never be attained, not only because white skin can never be hue white, but because ideally white is absence: to be really, absolutely white is to be nothing" (78); Richard Dyer, *White: Essays on Race and Culture* (New York: Routledge, 1997). Dyer's discussion as to how sweat is "something inappropriate to ladies, that is, really white women" points to Acrasia's complicated representation in the Bower (78).
35. Miriam Jacobson extensively discusses the term "Orient" as "lustrous and white," and she observes, "There is more to an orient pearl than meets the eye. As jewels, pearls are valuable, fungible imports. Furthermore, orient pearls are simultaneously bright white (which, in reference to skin color, marks one as Western) *and* foreign. In the figure of the orient pearl, the Western ideal of spotless virginity gets reconfigured as an Eastern material object" (163, 165–66; emphasis in original text). Miriam Jacobson, *Barbarous Antiquity: Reorienting the Past in the Poetry of Early Modern England* (Philadelphia: University of Pennsylvania Press, 2014).

ity."[36] In her analysis of Anna May Wong's performance in the 1929 film *Piccadilly* — which features a scene in which Wong dons "an ornamental costume of glittering gold" and dances for an audience — Cheng identifies the refractive shine as functioning not only as a mode of allurement but also as "armor," overwhelming the spectator with its glare.[37] Through this staging, Cheng continues, "the 'Oriental woman' as objet d'art has been derealized. Shine offers less a description or quality of light than an active mode of relationality: a dynamic medium through which the organic and inorganic fuse, and through which the visual spills into the sensorial."[38] Cheng herself recognizes a long prehistory to her reading of the twentieth-century silent film as she acknowledges that "woman as ornament is an old trope" and later describes Wong's performance as a "revision" of Botticelli's fifteenth-century *Birth of Venus*.[39] In Spenser, too, the "starry light" and "sparckling" liquidity of the passage facilitate that which shine "offers" Cheng: Acrasia's own shine, both "thril[ling]" and self-protective in its capacity to arrest the spectator, functions as "an active mode of relationality" that brings the enchantress into a dynamic visual interplay with the attendant "Fraile harts" of the Bower.[40] When, to quote Cheng, "the visual spills into the sensorial," it navigates a representational tension not unlike that of Dean and Cruz. In fact, Cheng identifies "the exhilarating eruption of the visual into other realms" as precisely that which produces "the intense visual pleasure" of the film.[41]

---

36. Anne Anlin Cheng, "Shine: On Race, Glamour, and the Modern," *PMLA* 126, no. 4 (2011): 1022–41, at 1026, https://doi.org/10.1632/pmla.2011.126.4.1022. See also Anne Anlin Cheng, *Second Skin: Josephine Baker & the Modern Surface* (Oxford: Oxford University Press, 2010). I am grateful to Jessica Rosenberg for suggesting Cheng's work on "shine" to me.

37. Cheng, "Shine," 1024, 1031.

38. Cheng, "Shine," 1034.

39. Cheng, "Shine," 1034, 1036.

40. Cheng differentiates between the "pearlized, feminized" surfaces of white femininity, "the shine of animalistic and corporeal sweat" associated with racialized bodies, and the metallic gleam of Wong in the film. Cheng, "Shine," 1031. Acrasia's "sparckl[e]" combines all three modes, again pointing to the instability of her representation in the poem.

41. Cheng, "Shine," 1034.

Cheng's language of "eruption" joins with "spills" to suggest just how climactic sensorial displacement can be. The pleasures of the Bower, pleasures organized around the visual, are generated in this stanza by the "eruptive" movement of the liquid down Acrasia's body ("Nectar" to "perles" to "sparckling ... waues"), an erotic fluidity that is inextricable, as Cruz's work unpacks in the contemporary, from the processes of racialization. An attention to the stylized representation of fluids in transtemporal and transmedial contexts thus asks readers to rethink how visibility functions in both poetic practice and hard-core cinema. In the following section, I suggest that early modern poetry offers an immediacy in this transition from visual splendor to immersive tactility that videography and particularly hard-core cinema is forever approximating yet unable to fully achieve.

Boundaries

Shakespeare seems to recognize in Spenser the erotic potential of perspiration. He reworks the image of a beautiful woman made more desirable by her sweat in *Venus and Adonis*, the 1593 long poem closely following the 1590 edition of *The Faerie Queene*.[42] In the epyllion, Shakespeare introduces touch to what in Spenser is a visual phenomenon. *Venus and Adonis* catalogs a proliferation of "solutions" to the "representational quandary" that I have been analyzing throughout this chapter. In the poem, the first interaction between the titular pair is when the goddess reaches out and grabs Adonis by his moist hand:

> she seizeth on his sweating palm,
> The precedent of pith and livelihood,
> And trembling in her passion, calls it balm,

---

42. Shakespeare's reception of *The Faerie Queene*, particularly in *Venus and Adonis*, has been much noted in scholarship. See, for example, Judith Anderson, "*Venus and Adonis*: Spenser, Shakespeare, and the Forms of Desire," chap. 13 in *Reading the Allegorical Intertext: Chaucer, Spenser, Shakespeare, Milton* (New York: Fordham University Press, 2008), 201–13.

Earth's sovereign salve to do a goddess good.
(25–28)[43]

The boy's wetness is cited as evidence of his fleshy vitality, with sweat demonstrating not only his "livelihood" — which is to say, liveliness — but also his "pith." The *Oxford English Dictionary* offers the metaphoric definition of "pith" as the "spirit or essence" of a being, but here, coupled with the reference to "sweating," the word also invokes its primary, material definition: the "soft internal tissue" of Adonis that is turned inside out by the end of the poem.[44] Venus's reaction to the boy's perspiration is peculiar.[45] She labels it a "balm" that can "do a goddess good," despite the fact that, as an immortal being, she has no need for curatives nor somatic improvement. Venus fails to specify just what the fluid *does*, and the verb's sexual implications echo.[46] Her interpretation of Adonis's moist

43. William Shakespeare, "Venus and Adonis," *Shakespeare's Poems*, ed. Katherine Duncan-Jones and H. R. Woodhouse (New York: Bloomsbury Publishing, 2007). All subsequent references to the poem are taken from this edition, and line numbers are cited parenthetically.

44. See *OED Online*, s.v. "pith (n.2)," 4.a, for abstract uses and *OED Online*, s.v. "pith (n.1)," 1–2.a, for concrete uses. The erotic resonances of Adonis's death, such as the phallic implications of the boar's tusks, have been much emphasized in scholarship of the poem. Melissa E. Sanchez describes Adonis's encounter with the boar as "much kinkier" than his interactions with Venus. see Melissa E. Sanchez, *Shakespeare and Queer Theory* (New York: Bloomsbury Publishing, 2019), 120. Richard Rambuss observes, "The coupling of the boar and the boy stands as one of the most graphically sexual figurations in Renaissance poetry of male/male penetration, of tusk in groin, of male body 'rooting' male body" (249). Richard Rambuss, "What It Feels Like For a Boy: Shakespeare's *Venus and Adonis*," *A Companion to Shakespeare's Works*, vol. 4, ed. Richard Dutton and Jean E. Howard (Malden: Blackwell Publishing, 2003), 240–58.

45. Marcela Kostihová writes of Venus in the poem, "One of the most appalling fixations of the supposedly heavenly creature is on earthly bodily fluids, which she inexplicably celebrates" (71). Marcela Kostihová, "Discerning (Dis)taste: Delineating Sexual Mores in Shakespeare's *Venus and Adonis*," in *Disgust in Early Modern English Literature*, ed. Natalie K. Eschenbaum and Barbara Correll (New York: Routledge, 2016), 69–81.

46. Shakespeare uses the verb "to do" in a sexual context in *Titus Andronicus*, for example, a play first performed in 1594; Aaron tells Chiron, "Villain, I have done thy mother" (4.2.78). See William Shakespeare, *Titus Andronicus*, ed. Jonathan Bates (New York: Bloomsbury Publishing, 1995).

hand positions the substance as a contradictory signifier: rarefied and precious ("sovereign salve") but also markedly human ("earthly").

Later in the poem, Venus employs the boy's sweat quite literally as "precedent," "an example to be followed or copied," when she again attempts to seduce the uninterested Adonis.[47] She calls upon the allures of her own sweaty touch, announcing,

My flesh is soft and plump, my marrow burning;
My smooth moist hand, were it with thy hand felt,
Would in thy palm dissolve, or seem to melt.
(143–55)

Just as Adonis's "sweating palm" evidences his "pith," Venus's "moist hand" makes sensible her own insides, her "marrow burning." She modifies "marrow" — an exact synonym for "pith" — with "burning," her desire permeating all inner recesses and bubbling to the surface, promising a sweat suggestive of more than just vitality.[48]

Shakespeare's emphasis on "melt[ing]" as facilitated by Venus's "smooth moist hand" experiments with the ornamental function of sweat in the Bower and provides an alternative erotic representation of the same fluid. The goddess promises a dissolution of boundaries that "would" occur if Adonis would deem to grasp her hand in his, but this promise is cautioned with the counterfactual use of the subjunctive and the acknowledgment that their bodies would only "seem to melt" in joining. Sweaty palms generate, in Venus's language, the sensory experience

47. See *OED Online*, s.v. "precedent (*n*)," 4.a.
48. Gail Kern Paster writes that although Hamlet's phrase "'the pith and marrow of our attribute' [1.4.22] ... [is] often glossed in the abstract as 'reputation,' [it] seems to me more material, even perhaps more specifically *liquid* than that ... Both words ["pith" and "marrow"] bring reputation solidly into a material realm inhabited equally by plants, animals, and humans, giving reputation a spongy core, even a backbone with *a fleshy or liquid interior*" (258, emphasis mine). Gail Kern Paster, "The Pith and Marrow of Our Attribute: Dialogue of Skin and Skull in *Hamlet* and Holbein's *The Ambassadors*," *Textual Practice* 23, no. 2 (2009): 247–65.

of melting into another body that is in distinction from a literal dissolution of boundaries. It is easy to make comparisons with the money shot as theorized by contemporary scholars and the "Nectar" of Acrasia, the "Waues" she produces, and the "languour" that suffuses the Bower.[49] But the mechanisms that make visible the seemingness of "melting" in sexual activity are also key to the displaced money shot. In his discussion of the "Devil's Dick" — this denotes, as referenced earlier in the chapter, a frozen condom filled with the semen of multiple men to be used as a self-lubricating dildo — Dean writes of a performer, Dylan, who is penetrated with such an object, "As seventy-three loads of ejaculate melt into his orifices and over every surface, it becomes impossible to tell whose semen is inside him and whose is outside; he is pervaded by the erotic traces of others."[50] This confused pervasiveness is that which Venus promises in her language of "dissolve" and "melt," with "seem" communicating the pleasures of an entanglement in which it is "impossible to tell" the internal from the external. Clasped moist hands make legible to the reader the fluidic exchange of sexual activity that is otherwise hidden, interior. In even the most explicit forms of pornography, fluidic exchange, as opposed to the projection of fluid, is almost always kept from sight, deposited rather than external.

If the ecstatic melting of clasped sweaty hands offers a "solution," to paraphrase Dean, to representing the mechanics of internal ejaculation, this poetic practice nevertheless does not necessarily generate the "maximum visibility" that Williams and Dean identify as the appeal of the money shot. Williams describes the money shot as entailing a "shift from a tactile to a visual pleasure at the crucial moment of … orgasm," whereas

---

49. Cruz, for example, explores the "volume" of the fluid and the eroticization of women's exhaustion as "worn out" from orgasm (with a focus on squirting-as-spectacle). See *The Color of Kink* and her discussions of "volume" on page 193 and fatigue on pages 190, 203. See Williams, *Hard Core*, 100–103, and Dean throughout *Unlimited Intimacy*, though particularly his discussion of *Plantin' Seed*, 138–39.

50. Dean, *Unlimited Intimacy*, 142–43.

Dean explores the temporary visibility of a "compromise shot" where "the guy pulls out immediately before cumming, so that the camera can record his climax, but then quickly reinserts his penis to finish ejaculating inside."[51] A successive shifting from the tactile to the visual (or vice versa) has largely been absent from this chapter: the representation of Acrasia is that of visual pleasure, which is markedly distinct from the tactility of sweaty hands in *Venus and Adonis*. Shakespeare's poem, however, does ultimately provide such a shift between registers, right as Adonis's death comes into focus. The goddess fears, correctly, that her love object has died, but she stirs herself to hope that a huntsman's yell is that of the boy. In her frenzied state, Venus falters in her weeping, and Shakespeare describes her tears with a language that is now familiar to a reader of this chapter:

> her tears began to turn their tide,
> Being prisoned in her eye like pearls in glass;
> Yet sometimes an orient drop beside,
> Which her cheek melts, as scorning it should pass
> To wash the foul face of the sluttish ground,
> Who is but drunken when she seemeth drowned.
> (979–84)

The stanza begins with an emphasis on the visual — the "pearls" and "orient drop" recall the liquid that adorns Acrasia in the Bower — only to shift into the tactile as the liquid "melts" on her cheek and then splatters onto the face of another. Shakespeare reverses the movement of Acrasia's sweat from "Nectar" to "perles," with Venus's flushed cheek facilitating a transition from "pearls" to further liquidity. This is a near literalization of what contemporary readers would label a money shot: the copious fluid produced by Venus is projected in excess onto the visage of another,

---

51. Williams, *Hard Core*, 101; Dean, *Unlimited Intimacy*, 131.

"wash[ing] the foul face of the sluttish ground."[52] Although the language of "foul" and "sluttish" revels in degradation — even if just to emphasize the dirt of the earth's floor — there is simultaneously the indication of pleasure, ecstasy.[53] The feminized ground responds not with suffering (she merely "seemeth drowned") but instead with a "drunken[ness]" suggestive of revelry or delight. The last line in fact itself offers a gloss of hard core where the seeming too-muchness of physical exploits, that is, of "taking it" or being overwhelmed in some capacity, is identified in the poem as both illusory ("seemeth" recalling Venus's promise of her hand that would "seem to melt") and the potential source of pleasure.[54]

Conclusion

Whose pleasure is it? The problems of fluidic representation, from early modern poetry to contemporary hard-core movies, seem to consistently pose this question.[55] It is significant that although Venus in the above

52. Williams includes tears alongside "sexual fluids" and blood in movies as all part of "a system of excess," when she asks, "Is it simply the unseemly, 'gratuitous' presence of the sexually ecstatic woman, the tortured woman, the weeping woman — and the accompanying presence to the sexual fluids, the blood and the tears that flow from her body and which are presumably mimicked by spectators — that mark the excess of each type of film? How shall we think of these bodily displays in relation to one another, as a system of excess in the popular film? And finally, how excessive are they really?" (5–6). Linda Williams, "Film Bodies: Gender, Genre, and Excess," *Film Quarterly* 44, no. 4 (Summer, 1991): 2–13.

53. For the suggested degradation of the money shot, sex advice columnist Dan Savage writes, "Facials are degrading," before continuing, "that's why they're so hot." See Dan Savage, "Savage Love," *Chicago Reader*, April 9, 2009, https://chicagoreader.com/columns-opinion/savage-love-22/; see also Samantha Cole, "'The Money Shot': How Porn Made Cum So Valuable," *Vice*, September 30, 2020, https://www.vice.com/en/article/bv8q45/history-of-the-money-shot-cum-fetish.

54. There are 220 hits for "drown" on PornHub, with the first hit reading: "BEST, BIGGEST FACIAL IN THE WORLD! Giggling blonde drowning in Cum Facefuck." The title, like Shakespeare, eroticizes the hyper-quickness of a move between pleasure and pain ("giggling" to "drowning" not unlike "drunken" to "drowned"), https://www.pornhub.com/video/search?search=drown, last accessed February 19, 2021.

55. See Williams, *Hard Core*, 95. In his reading of Williams, Dean writes, "In [her] account, the spectacle of male ejaculation substitutes for what cannot be seen: porn's ubiquitous money shots compensate its straight male viewers for the missing visual testimony of women's

stanza weeps, her fluidic expulsion slows, "turn[ing]" its "tide" in "joy[ful]" response to the belief that Adonis is still alive (977). There is an aura of mutual delight here that is wholly absent from the goddess's predatory interactions with Adonis himself. Venus's tears are perhaps the most extreme, which is to say, the most overtly kinky representation of fluidic projection discussed in this chapter. The complex power play in the interspecific mixing of divinity with the personified earth; the affective cacophony of the goddess's happy tears, the weighing doom of the narrative, and the "scorning" cheek; and finally, the dizzying pathways of the liquid as it falls to the ground all position the stanza as transgressive or at the very least surprising. How to code the money shot more generally is a real question.[56] The act has become a commonplace in pornography across genres, that without which the movie cannot be fully seen to come to a satisfactory close, and thus is normative in porn if not in practice. My emphasis here is not so much whether scenes of fluidic projection and exchange were considered normative (or nonnormative) in early modern thought but rather how the problems of fluidic representation function to suggest not only climax — both in terms of narrative structure and as a physiological response — but also a displace-

---

erotic pleasures" (108–9). Dean, *Unlimited Intimacy*. Cruz problematizes this claim in her extended attention to squirting (esp. 193). Cruz, *The Color of Kink*. See also Dean's remark as to "how the convention of aiming his ejaculate at someone else obscures the degree to which the man having an orgasm is overcome by a bodily action that he ultimately cannot control" (107). Dean, *Unlimited Intimacy*.

56. For example, Chyng Sun, Matthew B. Ezzell, and Olivia Kendall argue that what they label "EOWF" ("ejaculation on women's face") is "a sexual act largely constructed and popularized through the pornography industry"; they draw this conclusion because "there is no evidence that EWOF has been a common sexual practice, and no known sexual behavior surveys include the act as a measured sexual practice" (1711). See Chyng Sun, Matthew B. Ezzell, and Olivia Kendall, "Naked Aggression: The Meaning and Practice of Ejaculation on a Woman's Face," *Violence Against Women* 23, no. 14 (2017): 1710–29. However, the omission of sexual behavior surveys to include the money shot does not necessarily prove that the act is not "a common sexual practice" nor do the authors specify what other "evidence" they would be looking for beyond these surveys to confirm the prevalence or absence of the money shot in daily life.

ment of pleasure and control, eliding distinctions between characters who involuntarily produce the fluid and those who come into contact with it.[57] These fluids are the "erotic traces of others" in their lingering presence, dazzling ornamentation, and capacity for dissolution: stylized representations of fluidic projection and exchange glimmer with potential, a tantalizing shattering of somatic boundaries promised yet restrained, "prisoned ... like pearls in glass."

———————

I am grateful to Joseph Gamble and Gillian Knoll for their organization of the Shakespeare Association of America 2021 seminar "The Kinky Renaissance" and for their important suggestions and impeccable coordination in editing this collection. During the seminar, I received incisive feedback from participants, and I owe particular thanks to Stephen Spiess and Lisa Robinson, whose comments shaped not only the direction of this chapter but also my work more broadly. I also wish to thank Joshua Barszczewski, Ryan Campagna, Timothy Harrison, Sarah Kunjummen, Sarah-Gray Lesley, Jeffrey Masten, and Brandon Truett, who read this paper in various drafts and provided generous and transformative responses. Finally, Mario DiGangi as shepherd for ACMRS Press provided nuanced and detailed feedback that sharpened this chapter and its arguments; I am very grateful.

---

57. Madhavi Menon writes of *Venus and Adonis*, "Instead of focusing on the success of a teleological approach to desire, the poem ponders what it might mean for such studies to fail or rather, what it might mean for studies of sexuality to take seriously not the idea of teleological success but that of failure" (498); Madhavi Menon, "Spurning Teleology in *Venus and Adonis*," *GLQ: A Journal of Lesbian and Gay Studies* 11, no. 4 (2005): 491–519. While I would not describe the poem as ending in failure, Menon's attention as to how *Venus and Adonis* — and I would add Book 2 of *The Faerie Queene* — disrupts normative teleologies of desire resonates with my readings here.

Fletcher's Golden Showers

Heather Frazier

John Fletcher's *The Tamer Tamed* and *The Captain* are full of women who sexually dominate men with their urine. In fact, at least three of Fletcher's plays, two-coauthored with Francis Beaumont, involve women emptying or threatening to empty their chamber pots on men in scenes that twenty-first-century readers might register as kinky.[1] Although these plays feature the subversive trope of sexual domination through urine, they deploy this kinky trope to conservative effect. In *The Tamer Tamed* and *The Captain*, women threaten to dump their urine on

---

1. Although this article focuses on Fletcher's use of the chamber pot in a sexual context in *The Tamer Tamed* and *The Captain*, this trope frequently appears in a sexual context in other literature in the period. See, for instance, Ben Jonson's 1612 court masque *Love Restored*, in which a group of men position themselves underneath a staircase so that they can gaze upwards to see under the skirts of the women standing on the staircase above them. The men subsequently receive punishment for their transgression, as the women urinate on them while they look upwards. Ben Jonson, *Love Restored*, in *Ben Jonson: Selected Masques*, ed. Stephen Orgel (New Haven, CT: Yale University Press, 1970), 116–27, at lines 102–7. Even when this trope appears in a context that is not explicitly sexual, it nonetheless often expresses male anxieties that women might usurp domestic authority. See, for example, the frequent early modern allusions to Xanthippe, Socrates's shrewish wife who dumps urine on his head. John Harrington, *A Nevv Discourse of a Stale Subiect, Called the Metamorphosis of Aiax* ... (London: Imprinted by Richard Field, 1596), 78–79, Early English Books Online, https://www.proquest.com/books/nevv-discourse-stale-subiect-called-metamorphosis/docview/2248584507/se-2.

men who have disrupted the early modern family model by refusing the ideals of procreative and companionate marriage.[2] In Fletcher's now-obscure marriage comedy *The Captain*, the contents of women's chamber pots are dumped on a male suitor's head as he stands beneath a window. In dumping urine on him, *The Captain*'s women incite a confrontation that compels Jacamo, the eponymous captain, to renounce his misogyny and confess his love for Franck, the play's female protagonist. This scene, which positions women on the top and a man on the bottom, reflects the broader sexual dynamics of the play, at least in the first several acts, which feature multiple instances of women's sexual dominance of men. Although this event might seem unusual in the context of marriage comedy, *The Captain* is far from the only play in Beaumont and Fletcher's oeuvre to feature female characters throwing or threatening to throw the contents of their chamber pots on misogynistic men. Fletcher also uses the chamber pot as a plot device in his better-known marriage comedy and response to early modern shrew-taming literature, *The Tamer Tamed*. In both plays, communities of women band together to subdue men who threaten contemporary ideals of companionate marriage through their misogyny. Thus, Fletcher's female characters perform the kinky act of dumping urine on unruly men to discipline them into appropriate domesticity, but once the men submit to their traditional roles, the women embrace roles as submissive wives. In sanctioning the women's

2. In addition to *The Tamer Tamed* and *The Captain*, see *The Wild-Goose Chase*. When Pinac courts Lilia, a servant warns him of her capriciousness and that she will likely throw a chamber pot at him if she becomes cross:

> 'May be she'll call ye sawcy scurvey fellow,
> Or some such familiar name: 'may be she knows ye,
> And will fling a Piss-pot at ye, or a Pantofle,
> According as ye are in acquaintance; if she like ye,
> 'May be she'll look upon ye, 'may be no,
> And two monthes hence call for ye.

See John Fletcher, *The Wild-Goose Chase a Comedie ...* (London: Printed for Humpherey Moseley, 1652), 17, Early English Books Online, https://www.proquest.com/books/wild-goose-chase-comedie-as-hath-been-acted-with/docview/2264211006/se-2.

sexual dominance, Fletcher challenges contemporary cultural narratives that paint women's erotic domination as deviant, but at the same time, the women's erotic domination ultimately advocates for a view of marriage in which wives remain subordinate to their husbands.

The Chamber-Pot Trope in Shrew-Taming Literature

Fletcher is deeply indebted to other sixteenth- and seventeenth-century popular literature for his use of the chamber pot as a central plot device. Seventeenth-century English ballads cast the chamber pot as a site of erotic dominance. Ballads such as "Poor Anthony's Complaint" and "Mirth for Citizens" feature wives dominating their husbands with sex and urine. "Poor Anthony's Complaint" resembles other ballads about scolding wives from the period, in that it features a first-person speaker complaining of his wife's tyrannies in a familiar arc. He begins by lamenting that she does not allow him sufficient time to finish his dinner, that she serves him scalding broth, that she scolds him while he "rock[s] Bearn in the Cradle," and most significantly, that she urinates on him as he attempts to sleep. As Poor Anthony lies in bed, his wife intends to "take the pot" to urinate but instead takes a "Leaky Cullender" and "all bepist [him] sweetly," soaking both him and their bed in her urine and calling him a cuckold when he confronts her.[3] Whereas "Poor Anthony's Complaint" only hints that his wife's urinary indiscretions proceed to sexual improprieties with another man through its allusion to cuckoldry, the speaker of "Mirth for Citizens" identifies his wife's extramarital affairs as one of his chief degradations. Even more significantly, he connects her adultery with her practice of requiring his service while she uses the chamber pot. The speaker's wife in this ballad declares her mas-

---

3. Anonymous, "Poor Anthony's Complaint / And Lamentation against his miseries of / marriage, meeting with a scolding wife" (Printed for J. Conyers at the Black Raven in Fetter-lane, c. 1662–92), English Broadside Ballad Archive, https://ebba.english.ucsb.edu/ballad/31889/xml.

tery over the household the morning following their marriage, requiring her husband to wait on her and retaliating with a cudgel when he threatens to beat her with a stick. However, even her beatings pale beside the humiliation of waiting upon her and her paramour in their bed as they relieve themselves:

> Another thing troubles my head
> and grieves me worse than this,
> When her Comrade is with her in bed
> I must reach her the pot to piss.[4]

Like "Poor Anthony's Complaint," the speaker of "Mirth for Citizens" presents a hyperbolic list culminating in sexual degradation. Although he employs the image of the chamber pot to obvious comic effect, it nonetheless suggests a cultural anxiety that unruly wives might overmaster their husbands with their bodily fluids and lust.

The women's choice of punishment in the ballads is by no means unusual within the context of sixteenth- and seventeenth-century literature. Medieval and early modern texts are rich in accounts of women emptying their chamber pots upon men — for disciplinary purposes and otherwise. Socrates's wife represents the archetype of the shrew in many verse and prose works. Xanthippe appears most famously in Chaucer's *Canterbury Tales* in the Wife of Bath's narratives of the shrewish women in her husband's book, among them "How Exantippa cast pisse up on [Socrates's] hed." In his study of urinary comedy in medieval and early modern texts, Shawn Normandin argues that the Wife of Bath's example demonstrates medieval fears about women's speech, fears that are linked to the portrayal of urine as "a convenient sign of female debasement" and

---

4. Abraham Miles, "Mirth for Citizens: Or, A Comedy for the Country … " (Printed for P. Brooksby, c. 1672–1696), English Broadside Ballad Archive, http://ebba.ds.lib.ucdavis.edu/ballad/37229/xml.

"a humorous emblem of female prolixity."[5] For Normandin, medieval and early modern writers describe female urination both to acknowledge and diminish contemporary anxieties about women's bodies since urine occupies a medial position in the hierarchy of excrement that privileges *feces* and *menstrual blood* as more revolting substances and therefore more capable of influencing masculine behavior: "The triviality of piss, which rarely achieves the satiric intensity of shit, contains the threat of female treachery by debasing its agents."[6] However, if texts such as the Wife of Bath's prologue nullify female resistance to male authority by trivializing chamber-pot discipline, the comic texts of the English Renaissance seem to reverse this trend. Although plays such as *The Tamer Tamed* and *The Captain* cast urine-throwing as a primarily female activity, they contradict the idea that it carries less power than feces-throwing, especially since these plays typically connect the practice to even more taboo sexual desires, such as incest.[7]

Underlying male attempts to trivialize female "leakiness" is a visceral fear of the uncontained female body, as well as an anxiety that women

5. See Shawn Normandin, "The Wife of Bath's Urinary Imagination," *Exemplaria* 20, no.3 (2008): 244–63, at 247–48, https://doi.org/10.1179/175330708X334538.

6. Normandin, "The Wife of Bath's Urinary Imagination," 248.

7. Even those texts that seem to debase women for their urinary excess often treat the chamber-pot trope as a mark of female agency. Consider, for instance, John Taylor's prose description of a woman emptying her chamber pot: "A Neat Gentleman ... going hastily through the gate that leads into the Pallace at Westminster, suddenly, a woman (or maid) did chance to cast out a dish or pot of newmade warm water, some tale whereof lighted in the Gentlemans shooes, and withall besparkled his silke stockings; at which, very angerly he said, *Thou filthy base sluttish Queane, Canst thou not see, but throw thy stinking pisse into my shoes and hose?* To whom she answered, Sir, I am sorry that I have done you any wrong, but yet you have done me a great deal more injury then I have done to you, for I would have you know, that I am no such *Slut* as you call'd me, neither do I keep pisse til it stinkes, but I *always throw it away fresh and fresh as I make it*" (emphasis in the original). John Taylor, *Bull, Beare, and Horse, Cut, Curtaile, and Longtaile. VVith Tales, and Tales of Buls, Clenches, and Flashes ...* (London: Printed by M. Parsons, for Henry Gosson, 1638), Early English Books Online, https://www.proquest.com/books/bull-beare-horse-cut-curtaile-longtaile-vvith/docview/2240892079/se-2.

might weaponize the stereotypes imposed upon them.[8] In staging the women's threats to empty their chamber pots upon the men in *The Tamer Tamed*, Fletcher directly responds to the popular shrew-taming work most influential to his plot, *The Taming of the Shrew*. In Shakespeare's version, Petruchio alludes to Xanthippe in listing the qualities of the shrew he would be willing to marry in order to secure a large fortune (*Shrew* 1.2.65–72).[9] In comparing Katherine to Xanthippe, Petruchio opens the possibility that a wife will eventually subdue him with a chamber pot, even though his punishment is deferred until Fletcher's response to Shakespeare's play. Maria replaces Petruchio's first wife in the role of shrew so readily perhaps because Fletcher's characters never name Katherine directly.[10] She fills the void left by Katherine's death. Indeed, his first marriage seems to have primed him to submit more readily within his second marriage. As commentators such as Lucy Munro note, Fletcher casts Katherine's subjugation as much less final than Shakespeare's ending suggests.[11] In the first act, we learn that his first wife's specter continues to haunt Petruchio in his sleep:

> the bare remembrance of [her]
> . . . .
> Will make him start in's sleep, and very often
> Cry out for cudgels, cowl-staves, anything,
> Hiding his breeches out of fear her ghost

8. In *The Body Embarrassed*, Gail Kern Paster argues that the early moderns represented women as fundamentally "leakier" than men. Gail Kern Paster, *The Body Embarrassed: Drama and the Disciplines of Shame in Early Modern England* (Ithaca, NY: Cornell University Press, 1993).

9. William Shakespeare, *The Taming of the Shrew*, ed. Barbara Hodgdon (London: Arden Shakespeare, 2010). The parenthetical citation above refers to act, scene, and line number.

10. As Lucy Munro notes in her introduction to the New Mermaids edition of the text, Katherine's name does not appear in Fletcher's version. John Fletcher, *The Tamer Tamed*, ed. Lucy Munro (London: Methuen Drama, 2010), ix. All in-text parenthetical citations refer to this play by act, scene, and line.

11. Fletcher, *The Tamer Tamed*, ix.

Should walk and wear 'em yet.
(*Tamer* 1.1.31, 33–36)

Whereas Shakespeare's Petruchio never threatens Katherine with physical violence, Fletcher suggests that Petruchio resorts to the more conventional shrew-taming methods after starvation and sleep deprivation
fail to subdue Katherine entirely.[12] The explicit violence omitted from
The Taming of the Shrew is perhaps imagined here as taking place in the
interval between Katherine's final speech and her early death. Not only
does this passage anticipate Maria's own resolution to wear the breeches
within her household, but it also works to justify her preemptive measures of barring Petruchio from his house and placing him under quar-
antine. When Maria first embarks on her tamer-taming, she does not
take pleasure in denying Petruchio sexual satisfaction. She characterizes
her plan to delay the consummation of her marriage as "Fasting [her]
valiant bridegroom" and denying herself the "delights" and "pleasure"
of the bedchamber, her rhetoric mirroring Petruchio's strategy of taming his first wife in its dual focus on self-denial and fasting the tamed
spouse (*Tamer* 1.2.120–21).[13] Maria's compatriot Bianca goes even further in reclaiming Petruchio's rhetoric when she alludes to the untamed
wife as a "free haggard," or falcon,

Which is that woman that has wing, and knows it,
Spirit and plume — will make a hundred checks
To show her freedom, sail in every air
And look out every pleasure, not regarding
Lure nor quarry, till her pitch command

---

12. See the most famous extant ballad example, *A Merry Jest of a Shrewd and Curst Wife*, in which
the husband beats his shrewish wife before wrapping her wounded body in a salted horse-
hide. See "A Merry Jest of a Shrewd and Curst Wife Lapped in Morrel's Skin, for Her Good
Behavior," in William Shakespeare, *The Taming of the Shrew: Texts and Contexts*, ed. Frances
E. Dolan (New York: Bedford, 1996), 254–88.
13. See also Shakespeare, *The Taming of the Shrew*, 4.1.177–200.

What she desires …
(*Tamer* 1.2.150–56)

Here Bianca redefines Maria's defiance as an expression of *freedom* rather than of self-denial, stating that the free falcon will disregard her keeper's *lure*[s] and desired *quarry* in favor of her own *pleasure* and *What she desires*. After hearing Bianca's celebration of the *free haggard* who looks after her own pleasure, Maria enters into the spirit of the taming more fully, imagining herself "Turn[ing] him, and bend[ing] him as [she] list" and "mould[ing]" him to such a degree that even "aged women" without "teeth and spleen may master him" (*Tamer* 1.2.173–75). Her tamer-taming endeavor, which begins as a necessity, becomes a source of pleasure.

Unlike the shrew-taming ballads of the period, *The Tamer Tamed* sides with the disobedient wife who must resort to urinary violence to assert her agency. At the start of the play, Maria's docility runs counter to the tempestuousness of Petruchio's erstwhile wife, so much so that Petruchio's friends express pity at the prospect of an obedient woman further flattened by a domineering husband. Tranio imagines Maria's future as Petruchio's wife in the first scene of the play:

She must do nothing of herself, not eat,
Sleep, say 'Sir, how do ye', make her ready, piss,
Unless he bid her.
(*Tamer* 1.2.45–47)

If she continues in her seeming docility, Petruchio will impose such tight control on her person that he will regulate all of her bodily functions, both alimentary and excretory. In response, she can only answer Petruchio's expectation of total bodily control down to her *piss* by weaponizing her body and its products.

Erotic Domination to Restore the Marital Hierarchy

In spite of Maria's successful rebellion, Fletcher certainly does not present his readers with a progressive view of gender in *The Tamer Tamed*. After all, his comic resolution magically reverses Petruchio's declaration of submission. She begins the play as "the gentle, tame Maria" and ends as an obedient wife (*Tamer* 1.2.75). However, the play allows women to assume positions of sexual dominance in the service of correcting transgressive familial bonds and improper erotic desires. After Petruchio accedes to Maria's demands at the end of the play, she renounces her former defiance in favor of wifely submission to a husband's appropriate authority:

> As I am honest,
> And as I am a maid yet, all my life,
> From this hour, since you make so free profession,
> I dedicate in service to your pleasure.
> (*Tamer* 5.4.54–57)

After the *ramping tricks* that Maria enacts throughout the narrative, such an ending allows for a comfortable return to Petruchio's mastery. In one sense, Maria's vow upon her honesty and maidenhood, or her continued celibacy, invites the audience to think of the play's ending as properly the beginning of the marriage.[14] Now that Petruchio has suffered his comeuppance, he will assert mastery again, albeit in a gentler form and on condition of his continued commitment to companionate behavior. *The Tamer Tamed* allows Petruchio the last words, as well as the privilege of instructing husbands about the proper way to approach marriage, as he asserts:

---

14. The term *honest* here clearly refers to Maria's sexual honesty, a trope common within the period.

> I have my colt again, and now she carries,
> And, gentlemen, whoever marries next,
> Let him be sure to keep him to his text.
> (*Tamer* 5.4.88–90)

Within his formulation, Maria's rebellion against improperly exercised male authority only facilitates his proper exercise of marital governance, as well as her own appropriate position within the marriage as the *colt* who *carries*. However, Maria's use of the conditional within her own vow clearly recalls the terms of her previous disobedience since she only offers her *service* on the condition of her husband's *free profession* of reciprocal love. She might revert to her previous dominance if he balks at his new role, but she remains fundamentally aligned with the conservative strictures placed on wives.

The Captain uses the chamber pot trope to similar effect, casting Franck, a gentlewoman, in a sexually dominant role only long enough to curb her would-be suitor Jacamo's misogyny. While *The Tamer Tamed* positions its principal marriage at the beginning of the drama, with the chamber-pot scene following later, *The Captain* adopts the more conventional narrative in marriage comedy, staging its marriages at the end. In spite of their differences in narrative structure, both plays punish characters for their transgressive erotic relationships with urinary degradation. In a dynamic that closely resembles Maria's and Bianca's interactions, *The Captain*'s tamers, Franck and Clora, conspire to douse Jacamo in urine when he refuses to believe Franck's protestations of love. However, the play precedes this final act of domination with a prolonged series of erotic foreplay in which Franck, Clora, and other characters participate. While the chamber pot brings together Franck and Jacamo in a more conventional marriage, the erotic domination leading up to the chamber pot displaces sexual agency onto other characters, particularly Clora. Although Franck accepts that she must dominate Jacamo in order to win him, she derives no enjoyment from her friends' subsequent order that a chamber pot be poured on his head. On the other hand, Clora takes considerable pleasure first in dominating Jacamo with verbal taunts and later in plotting his urinary humiliation. In the play's third act, Clora's brother Fabritio formally introduces Jacamo to Franck and Clora, although Franck has already fallen in love with Jacamo before their first meeting. Jacamo enters into the acquaintance with misogynistic rudeness based on the conviction that no woman could ever find him attractive. While Franck answers his rudeness with polite admiration, Clora answers it with sarcasm and mocking compliments, ordering Jacamo to "be merry," as it would be a "pitty" for a "faire man of [his] proportion" to "have a soule of sorrow" (3.3.75–76).[15] When Jacamo becomes angry at what he perceives as Franck's derision and Clora's genuine ridicule, Franck finds his anger attractive, and Clora pretends to agree, stating that she "[could] kisse him," an action that Jacamo carries out later in the play (*Captain* 3.3.118).

Although Clora assumes the role of misogynist tamer for Franck's benefit, for her, the role provides its own erotic reward and source of pleasure. The next scene in which she, Franck, and Jacamo meet confirms and justifies her erotic involvement in Franck and Jacamo's kinky courtship, as well as the erotic involvement of Franck's brother Frederick. When Jacamo next visits Franck's house, he declares his love for Franck before kissing her, Clora, and finally Franck's brother Frederick, as he mistakes Frederick for a "sweet woman" (*Captain* 4.3.61). After the trio laugh at Jacamo for his mistake, he brandishes his sword at Frederick in a gesture that reinforces the homoerotics of the kiss. Frederick then pretends to be wounded so that the servants will drag Jacamo from the house. As Mario DiGangi argues in his reading of the play, Fletcher in this scene uses the *homoerotic disorder* of Jacamo's mistaking Frederick

---

15. Francis Beaumont and John Fletcher, *The Captain*, ed. L. A. Beaurline, in *The Dramatic Works in the Beaumont and Fletcher Canon*, vol. 1, ed. Fredson Bowers (Cambridge, UK: Cambridge University Press, 1966), 541–670. All in-text parenthetical citations refer to this play by act, scene, and line number.

for a woman "as a striking emblem for heteroerotic disorder." Jacamo's resultant "humiliation" after the kiss "finally allows him to recognize and accept the sincerity of Frank's love."[16] His *humiliation* in this scene also anticipates his later urinary humiliation.

Ultimately Clora, rather than Franck, devises the plan that shocks Jacamo into listening to Franck's declaration of love; she suggests that one of the household maids pour either a bowl of water or the contents of a chamber pot on his head. However, Clora's brother Fabritio diminishes the women's erotic agency when he adds his own instructions for how the urine should be gathered. Rather than merely instructing a maid to dump a chamber pot on Jacamo's head, Fabritio suggests that the maids should gather as much urine from as many women in the household as possible and empty it on Jacamo's head in order to "anger" him enough to draw him into the house and force him to listen to Franck's declaration of love:

> Take all the women-kind in this house, betwixt the age of one, and one hundred, and let them take unto them a pott or a bowle containing seven quarts or upwards, and let them never leave, till the above named pott or bowle become full, then let one of them stretch out her arme and power it on his head, and *Probatum est*, it will fetch him, for in his anger he will run up, and then let us alone.
> (*Captain* 5.2.42–49)

Although this passage differs from *The Tamer Tamed*'s chamber-pot discipline, in that the women actually throw the "watrish humours" on the offending man (*Captain* 5.3.7), it nonetheless highlights the repeated concern with female community and urinary discipline found in Fletcher's canon. In both instances, communities of women organize against a man whose misogyny threatens an early modern ideal of companionate

---

16. Mario DiGangi, *The Homoerotics of Early Modern Drama* (Cambridge, UK: Cambridge University Press, 1997), 149–50.

marriage, and they punish his hatred by confronting him with one of the bodily fluids most offensive to his misogynistic worldview: their urine. However, Fabritio's insistence that the urine be gathered by *all the women-kind in this house* shifts Franck and Clora's gesture from a kinky register, as it reinforces the fate for which all women are destined and which Jacamo's misogyny obstructs: procreative matrimony.

Franck, Clora, and Fabritio act according to an "approv'd receipt" for tamer-taming, and Fabritio even prescribes this degrading urine rinse as medicine, suggesting that the women's *watrish humours* can treat Jacamo's unbalanced humors and discipline him into matrimony.[17] The same *watrish humours* that elicit Jacamo's initial *anger* also cure his aversion to productive marriage, as the women's urine draws him into the house and Franck's tears convince him of her devotion. After the maids empty their urine on his head, Jacamo enters the stage lamenting the women's contempt for him:

> I ever knew no woman could abide me,
> But am I growne so contemptible, by being
> Once drunke amongst 'em, that they begin to throw
> Pisse on my head? For surely it was pisse.
> (*Captain* 5.3.1–4)[18]

What Jacamo takes as contempt for his drunkenness, Franck transforms into a mark of affection and intimacy, watering his *pitty* with her tears

---

17. Contemporary medical texts frequently prescribe recipes including urine for ailments such as head injuries and baldness. See Peter Levens, *A Right Profitable Booke for all Diseases Called, the Pathway to Health ...* (London: Printed by I. Roberts for Edward VVhite, 1596), Early English Books Online, http://www.proquest.com/books/right-profitable-booke-all-diseases-called/docview/2240892214/se-2; and Pope John XXI, *The Treasurie of Health Contayning Many Profitable Medicines ...* (London: William Copland, 1560), Early English Books Online, https://www.proquest.com/books/treasurie-health-contayning-many-profitable/docview/2240935101/se-2.

18. The stage directions indicate that Jacamo smells himself here, presumably to ascertain that the maids have emptied urine, and not water.

even as the maids water his head with their urine (*Captain* 5.4.34). Indeed, the plotters render the urine and the tears equivalent, since both substances signal Franck's authenticity and discipline Jacamo into exhibiting the *pitty* appropriate in a man (*Captain* 5.4.35).[19] The women's brief expression of dominance only facilitates Jacomo's transformation into the productive husband and master of his household. Franck's collaboration with Clora, Fabritio, and the maids intensifies Jacomo's humiliation, providing an audience to witness his degradation, but it also displaces her dominating gesture onto other agents, particularly Clora, who first derives pleasure from ridiculing Jacomo before receiving his kiss and then finally colludes to dump urine on his head. What may register as kinky and subversive on first glance, partnering with Clora to subdue Jacamo, also allows Franck to slip back into the role of *gentlewoman*, now settled into a traditional pairing.

While Maria's pleasure in taming Petruchio differs from Franck's comparative passivity, she also relies on a community of women to help dominate her lover. As Petruchio prepares to consummate his marriage, his friend Sophocles warns him that Maria and the women have barricaded the men from the house and that Petruchio should not attempt to enter lest he be "beaten off with shame" as Sophocles was with "a waterwork" flying "from the window with" considerable "violence" (*Tamer* 1.3.89, 92–93). When the women use their chamber pots as ammunition, they mock the early modern patriarchal assumption articulated by Gail Kern Paster in *The Body Embarrassed*, the "discourse [inscribing] women as leaky vessels by isolating one element of the female body's material expressiveness — its production of fluids — as excessive."[20] They turn the discourse about their bodily excess into a weapon against men who assert that women require the strictures of marriage to exercise control

---

19. Franck's brother Fredrick enjoins Jacamo to trust Franck's earnestness: "Behold how the teares flow, or pitty her / Or never more be call'd a man" (5.4.34–35).
20. Paster, *The Body Embarrassed*, 25.

over their bodies. Maria's improper decision to abstain from consummation directly challenges Petruchio's marital sovereignty since it delays a crucial portion of the marital contract — the sexual act that cements the bond and promises children.[21] Sophocles describes her preparations for a siege in terms of the body's excretory and sexual functions: her "chamber's nothing but a mere Ostend" with "pewter cannons mounted" in "every window" ready to emit "waterwork[s]" (*Tamer* 1.3.92, 96–97). This reference to the siege at Ostend denotes the women's usurpation of military authority, but it might also be read as engaging the bawdy connotations of the Low Countries, given the presence of chamber pots and the "Long tongues" lining the "lower works" (*Tamer* 1.3.101).[22] Indeed, the women's barricade resembles the urinating vulva, as medical literature of the period often likens the clitoris to the tongue and assigns it the same functions as the penis: it contains the urinary passage and imparts sexual pleasure.[23] Maria's defiance perverts Petruchio's expectation of their wedding night as she simultaneously withholds her body from the desired consummation while also challenging her husband's supremacy by asserting her own sexual mastery and forestalling Petruchio's ejaculation with the threat of her own. Her armed barricade underscores and corrects the perverse bond that Petruchio forms with her father, illustrated most notably in the men's conversation prior to the wedding night.

21. A marriage was considered complete only if it was consummated. Petronius invokes the process of legalizing marriage through consummation when his younger daughter elopes with Roland, as he asks Livia, "Hast thou lain with him?" and his son-in-law, "And hast thou done the deed, boy?" (*Tamer* 5.4.73–74).

22. *Low Countries* often functions as a slang term for the genitals. See Eric Partridge, *Shakespeare's Bawdy*, (Milton Park, UK: Taylor & Francis, 2005), 198. As Valerie Traub notes in *The Renaissance of Lesbianism*, early modern medical practitioners such as Charles Estienne describe the clitoris as "a little tongue," and medical texts debated whether or not the clitoris had a urinary or an erotic function. Valerie Traub, *The Renaissance of Lesbianism in Early Modern England* (Cambridge, UK: Cambridge University Press, 2002), 88.

23. See Traub, *The Renaissance of Lesbianism*, 88.

Urinary Discipline and Incestuous Desire

Fletcher's marriage comedy *The Tamer Tamed* and Beaumont and Fletcher's *The Captain* are idiosyncratic in their juxtapositions of incestuous desire with the chamber-pot trope in early modern literature as evinced by Petronius's intimate interest in Maria and Petruchio's impending consummation of their marriage. Petronius's conversation with Petruchio and his friends before the aborted wedding night rehearses Maria's urinary punishment of her husband, hinging as it does on images of impotence and sexual defeat. This discussion resembles other comic wedding night ribaldry in that it cements masculine bonds through the ridicule of female sexuality, but it deviates in at least one important respect — Maria's father joins the other men in teasing Petruchio about his daughter's impending deflowering. Indeed, Petronius allies himself with Petruchio at Maria's expense, taking vicarious enjoyment in the prospect of the marriage's consummation. After Petruchio solicits wagers upon his sexual prowess, Petronius chivvies him to the marital bedchamber in a manner that suggests his own pseudo-incestuous interest both in his daughter's erotic desire and his son-in-law's sexual prowess, stating:

> Will you to bed, son, and leave talking?
> Tomorrow morning we shall have you look,
> For all your great words, like St. George at Kingston,
> Running a-footback from the furious dragon
> That with her angry tail belabours him
> For being lazy.
> (*Tamer* 1.3.18–22).

This description of Petruchio / St. George running from Maria / the dragon raises the question of why Petronius is horrified at his daughter's later rebellion when he finds the imagined prospect of her sexual domination of her husband so titillating. As many critics observe, Petronius aligns himself with Petruchio's misogynistic perspective of marriage, but this passage suggests an even more specific motive for his misogynistic identification with Petruchio.[24] Even before she demonstrates her disobedience, Petronius's address evinces a desire to cut Maria from the family structure — to acquire Petruchio as a "son" in a way that allows him to disown (de-sire) his daughter's monstrous femininity, figured here as the dragon that threatens Britain's nationhood and the patrimonial order. When he compares Maria to a monster, he not only follows a long tradition of identifying the dragon with disordered female desire but also anticipates the later terms through which he articulates her disobedience.[25] In placing the phallic "tail" on his daughter instead of her husband, he unknowingly invokes the "monstrous" desire for sexual authority that Maria expresses in her threat to release urine upon Petruchio and his cohorts.[26] Petronius can take pleasure in his pseudo-incestuous imaginings of Maria's insatiable desire precisely because he refuses

24. See, for instance, David Bergeron's study of *The Tamer Tamed* and *The Taming of the Shrew* as *Querelle des Femmes* literature. David Bergeron, "Fletcher's *The Woman's Prize*, Transgression, and *Querelle des Femmes*," *Medieval and Renaissance Drama in England* 8 (1996): 146–64, http://www.jstor.org/stable/24322255.

25. See, for instance, Jacques Olivier's *A Discourse of Women, Shewing their Imperfections Alphabetically*, which states, "As a Jewel of Gold in a Swines Snout, so is a fair woman without discretion: a Dunghill for her Nastiness and Filthyness, a whorish woman shall be trodden down as the Dung in the Street: a Wind for her levity, he that holds her as if he held the wind: a Scorpion for her mischievousnesse, he that keeps a lewd woman is as he that cherisheth a Scorpion: a Dragon for her cruelties, it is better to dwell with a Lyon and a Dragon, then to cohabit with a naughty woman." Jacques Olivier, *A Discourse of Women, Shewing their Imperfections* ... (London: Printed for Henry Brome, 1662), 6, Early English Books Online, https://www.proquest.com/books/discourse-women-shewing-their-imperfections/docview/2240926442/se-2.

26. See John Fletcher, *The Tamer Tamed*. When Maria refuses to leave her father's house for Petruchio's bed, Petronius "charge[s]" her "by the duty of a child" to obey him:
    This is monstrous!
    That blessing that St. Dunstan gave the devil
    If I were near thee I would give thee —
    Pull thee down by the nose.
    (1.3.187–88, 197–200)

to identify with her on a filial basis — because he casts her instead as wife to his son.

When Maria subverts the men's expectations of what form her sexual dominance will take by threatening to dump urine on Petruchio and his friends, she redresses this convoluted triad and returns both Petruchio and Petronius to their appropriate roles. Petruchio's friends unknowingly prefigure Maria's taming methods in their replies to his arrogant call for wagers about the outcome of his wedding night. The men unsurprisingly fill their wedding-night jocularity with phallic metaphors, emphasizing the penis's erotic, as well as its urinary, function. Thus, immediately following Petronius's comparison of Petruchio to St. George, Tranio imagines Petruchio's defeat at the hands of Maria: his impotency will be such that "any privy saint, even small St. Davy" will be able to "lash him with a leek" (*Tamer* 1.3.25–26).[27] Leaving aside the obvious pun upon the size and function of the root vegetable, the metaphor aligns sexual play with urinary discipline, as it evokes *leek*'s homonym *leak* alongside the phrase *privy saint*.[28] The play's answer to the men's inappropriate exchange closely aligns with medical literature of the period. Sixteenth- and seventeenth-century herbals prescribed the leek as a diuretic, with some medical texts noting the leek's impact upon the sexual and reproductive functions in its ability to engender erotic desire.[29] The pots launched from Maria's chamber windows likewise act

---

27. For the practice of wearing leeks on St. David's Day, see, for instance, *The Welsh-Mens Glory, Or, the Famous Victories of the Antient Britans Obtain'd upon St. David's Day* (London: Printed by Thomas Dawks, his Majesties British printer, at the west-end of T', 1684), Early English Books Online, https://www.proquest.com/books/welsh-mens-glory-famous-victories-antient-britans/docview/2240899958/se-2.

28. See *Oxford English Dictionary Online*, s.v. "leak (*v.*)," 2.c.

29. Citing Dioscorides, Thomas Hill writes that the leek "moveth and provoketh the venerial acte" since it counteracts coldness, "procureth thirst and inflameth the bloud." Similarly, leek juice mixed with wine might "aide forwarde the delivery of childe." Just as the leek could elicit sexual desire and purge the body of children, it could also purge the body of urine. In his seventeenth-century herbal, John Gerard also cites Dioscorides in describing the leek's diuretic properties, stating that the vegetable "provoketh urine mightily, and

as physic to one of the play's principal ills, Petruchio's unnatural alliance with Petronius's misogynistic order.[30] In her taming project, Maria realizes the men's joking predictions of Petruchio's impotency, but instead of defeating him with her excessive sexual desire, as the men imagine in their previous exchange, she defeats him with a related bodily function, urination. A golden shower becomes the appropriate punishment for failed erotic play, since even the inferior Welsh patron saint *Davy* can *lash* Petruchio in this manner. However, Maria substitutes the men's desired form of sexual dominance for an undesirable form of erotic mastery from their point of view, as it represents a form that will not admit consummation. When Maria decides to delay the consummation of her marriage, she effectively halts her passage from her father's authority to her husband's rule, rebelling against her father's inappropriate desire to lay claim to her sexuality as much as she rebels against Petruchio's oppressive government. Her scheme to tame Petruchio is successful partly because she remains in limbo between her father's and Petruchio's guardianship until the sexual act.

Although Fletcher's association between incest and urinary dominance is unusual, it is perhaps unsurprising given sixteenth- and seventeenth-century medical theories regarding the composition of semen

bringeth downe the floures." In this way, early modern medical treatments combine urinary purgation and erotic catharsis. Thomas Hill, *The Gardeners Labyrinth Containing a Discourse of the Gardeners Life ...* (London, By Henry Bynneman, 1577), 88, Early English Books Online, https://www.proquest.com/books/gardeners-labyrinth-containing-discourse-life/docview/2248559510/se-2; and John Gerard, *The herball or Generall historie of plantes ...* (London: Printed by Adam Islip Ioice Norton and Richard Whitakers, 1633), Early English Books Online, https://www.proquest.com/books/herball-generall-historie-plantes-gathered-iohn/docview/2240902621/se-2.

30. In her study of the play, Holly Crocker discusses Petruchio's tyranny as analogous to a disease as evinced by Maria's declaration that he has contracted the plague: the "scene is fascinating for the ways in which it connects the maladies of tyrannical marriage with representations of contagious disease in early modern Europe." Holly Crocker, "The Tamer as *Shrewd* in John Fletcher's *The Woman's Prize: Or, The Tamer Tamed," Studies in English Literature, 1500–1900* 51, no. 2 (2011): 409–26, at 416, https://www.jstor.org/stable/23028082.

and urine, both bodily fluids intimately linked with *venery*.[31] Although Fletcher does not feature any consummated acts of *venery* in relation to the plays' representations of incestuous desire, contemporary remedies for the effects of excessive lust nonetheless reveal a peculiar logic to the plays' urinary discipline. Particularly in *The Tamer Tamed*, the women answer the men's inappropriate expressions of desire with the threat of an emptied chamber pot. Just as incestuous desire threatens to displace seminal fluid into an inappropriate vessel (the daughter), the women threaten to retaliate with a related bodily fluid.

However, *The Captain*'s subplot reveals the limits of how far women can go in expressing sexual dominance, even as it associates a similar chamber-pot trope with another incestuous dynamic. While *The Tamer Tamed*'s father exhibits inappropriate interest in his daughter's sex, *The Captain*'s father becomes the object of his daughter's erotic desire. When the widow Lelia, the subplot's female protagonist, summons a sea captain famed for his bravery to her house to seduce him, she discovers that she has summoned her father. Instead of recoiling at the revelation of his identity, Lelia continues her attempts to seduce him without knowing that Angilo, one of her suitors, witnesses the exchange. Angilo has just bribed Lelia's maid to hide him in her chamber after she answers his knock at the door. The maid warns him that Lelia will retaliate against him for dissuading his friend from pursuing her by emptying the contents of her chamber pot on his head:[32]

---

31. Fletcher's association is unusual within the Renaissance but not unique. Lorenzo Lotto's *Venus and Cupid* features Cupid urinating upon a reclining Venus. As Patricia Simmons notes in her discussion of the painting, the erotic resonances of the painting, with its implicit emphasis upon *fertilization*, are apparent. See Patricia Simmons, "Manliness and the Visual Semiotics of Bodily Fluids in Early Modern Culture," *Journal of Medieval and Early Modern Culture* 39, no. 2 (2009): 331–73, at 360, https://doi.org/10.1215/10829636-2008-025.

32. Lelia's father never receives a name within the narrative; he is simply *Father*, the figure who must curtail Lelia's rampant sexuality.

And if it shall happen that you are in doubt of these my speeches, insomuch that you shal spend more time in arguing at the dore, I am fully perswaded that my Mistris in person from above, will utter her mind more at large by way of urine upon your head, that it may sink the more soundly into your understanding faculties.

(*Captain* 4.4.28–33)

The maid deems *urine upon* [his] *head* an appropriate punishment for the transgression of interfering in Lelia's sexual pursuits. However, Lelia's incestuous desire takes precedence as a more serious offense, and he escapes punishment to become her father's ally in marrying her off to a respectable suitor. Together, they negate her incestuous desire and expressions of sexual dominance by matching her with an appropriate husband.

Ultimately, the conservative messages of both plays limit the extent to which the women characters can express sexual dominance within marriage. *The Tamer Tamed*'s men, who fantasize about Maria dominating Petruchio through her voracious sexual appetite, but who cannot accept Maria's chosen mode of dominance, demonstrate the limitations of female sexual dominance in the play's register. The men in *The Captain*'s subplot override the maid's fantasy of Lelia dumping urine on Angilo's head and circumvent Lelia's previous sexual agency by forcing her to marry. Clora, who takes pleasure in dominating and humiliating her friend's suitor Jacamo, enters into marriage with the man who had been unfaithful to her, becoming, in his words, a "piece of" him (*Captain* 5.4.19). While the play justifies Clora's and Franck's domination of Jacamo as facilitating his transition into productive matrimony, the final act removes that justification as both the misogynistic Jacamo and the unfaithful Julio have assumed the roles of productive husbands by the end of the play. Similarly, the final act of *The Tamer Tamed* characterizes Maria's previous acts of dominance as *tricks*, temporary measures designed to subdue Petruchio's misogyny. After securing Petruchio's vow to renounce his tyranny, Maria promises that she will "Never" again resort to her "old tricks," finally submitting to his authority and his "pleasure" (*Tamer* 5.4.52, 57). Even as Fletcher intensifies the subversive potential of the women's golden showers by juxtaposing them with aberrant forms of sexuality such as incest, he dampens that potential by authorizing a return to female submission.

Pandora, Kneeling

Gillian Knoll

> I want someone to tell me what to wear in the morning …
> I want someone to tell me what to wear every morning. I want
> someone to tell me what to eat, what to like, what to hate, what to
> rage about, what to listen to, what band to like, what to buy tickets
> for, what to joke about and what not to joke about. I want someone
> to tell me what to believe in, who to vote for, who to love and how
> to tell them. I want someone to tell me how to live my life, Father,
> because so far, I've been getting it wrong. And I know that's why
> people want people like you in their lives, because you just tell them
> how to do it.
> — Fleabag, *Fleabag* ("Articles of Faith," season 2, episode 4)

These lines, spoken by the main character of the award-winning Amazon
Prime comedy *Fleabag,* have been posted, pinned, and tweeted many
times over (a Google search for the first sentence produces over thirty
thousand results).[1] Memorable not only for their content but also for
their context, they convey in almost equal measure the protagonist's dis-
arming vulnerability and a palpable sexual charge. The scene is set in a

---

1. Google search completed on October 12, 2023.

confessional, the speech addressed to a priest with whom the main character shares an undeniable erotic connection. She is drunk, infatuated with this priest, pleading and tearful by the time she reveals to him what she really wants: "to be told how to live my life, Father … Just tell me what to do, just fucking *tell me what to do,* Father." Both a confession and an invitation, Fleabag's lines draw from the priest a one-word reply that is as startling as it is suggestive: "Kneel."[2]

"Kneel," he commands, and she obeys, and a scene that should by all rights amount to little more than a kinky cliché (sex with a priest in a confessional — *really?*) instantly ensnared the hearts and imaginations of fans and critics. *GQ Magazine* dubbed it "the greatest moment of TV this year" and "the most erotic use of Catholic imagery since Madonna's 'Like a Prayer' video."[3] Google reported an uptick in searches for "sex with priest" after the episode aired, and searches on PornHub for "religious" reportedly increased by 162% after the "Hot Priest" was introduced on the series. Articles in mainstream media publications appeared with titles like "The Hot Priest in 'Fleabag' Says Kneel, and It's Never Sounded Sexier" (*The New York Times*) and "Kneel! How the Whole World Bowed Down to Fleabag … and Her Hot Priest" (*The Guardian*).[4] I was even able to locate a tote bag for sale on RedBubble with "Kneel?" printed

2. *Fleabag*, season 2, episode 4, "Articles of Faith," directed by Harry Bradbeer, written by Phoebe Waller-Bridge, aired March 25, 2019, https://www.amazon.com/gp/video/detail/B0875FRLWQ, 00:24:09.

3. David Levesley, "Andrew Scott Talks Us Through Fleabag's 'Kneel' Scene," *British GQ Magazine*, September 4, 2019, https://www.gq-magazine.co.uk/men-of-the-year/article/andrew-scott-fleabag-kneel.

4. See Kathryn Shattuck, "The Hot Priest in 'Fleabag' Says Kneel, and It's Never Sounded Sexier," *The New York Times*, May 17, 2019, https://www.nytimes.com/2019/05/17/arts/television/fleabag-andrew-scott-hot-priest.html; and Laura Snapes, "'Kneel! How the Whole World Bowed Down to Fleabag … and Her Hot Priest," *The Guardian*, December 23, 2019, https://www.theguardian.com/tv-and-radio/2019/dec/23/kneel-how-the-whole-world-bowed-down-to-fleabag-and-her-hot-priest. Results from Pornhub and Google searches are reported in Snapes, "'Kneel'!."

above a photo of Phoebe Waller-Bridge's face, her eyes turned dreamily upward at the word. Below it, the response reads, "Yes, Daddy."[5]

Kneel. What can account for the erotic force of this simple word, this single syllable? After the priest issues his mandate once, twice, and a third time, the seconds tick by in silence as Fleabag slowly places her drink on a ledge and descends to her knees. At long last, she looks up and waits … for what? Absolution? Compassion? Direction? The sound of a zipper? The rustling of clerical robes? The possibilities are intentionally tantalizing; but if mainstream representations of sex have trained us to be future-oriented — to dwell on what happens next — a kinky reader knows that *it does not matter what the protagonist is waiting for.* What she wants, she has already secured: she has been told what to do.

My essay explores the creative potential of this fantasy as it shapes the protagonist of a much different comedy, John Lyly's *The Woman in the Moon* (1597). Lyly's play explores the eroticized experience of being controlled, a vessel, a hollow thing — someone guided, inhabited, even possessed by an outside influence. This is the condition of a (sexual) submissive, a label that has been used broadly to describe someone who finds pleasure in yielding control. Although some submissives ("subs" in kinky parlance) derive pleasure from receiving pain from a Dominant (Dom/Domme), others define their role more generally as a form of erotic receptivity. They might be on the receiving end of any number of bedroom practices (being bound, beaten, humiliated, enslaved, ordered, denied, etc.), but there is no single practice that defines a sub. In this way, submission extends beyond the conventionally "sexual." As Robin Bauer notes in his ethnographic work on queer BDSM intimacies, "Many partners experienced many erotic practices not directly as sexual, but as cre-

---

5. Please buy this tote bag: fleabagmemes, "FLEABAG Kneel. Yes, Daddy. Tote Bag," Redbubble.com, accessed December 14, 2022, https://www.redbubble.com/i/tote-bag/FLEABAG-Kneel-Yes-Daddy-by-fleabagmemes/66533522.A9G4R.

ating an erotic atmosphere."[6] Because this form of kink is less tethered to gender identities or particular sex acts, it can account for forms of intimacy currently undertheorized in queer studies, such as heterosexual intimate relationships with a female sub. My essay's methodology falls in line with work by scholars such as Melissa E. Sanchez and Joseph Gamble, who propose a queer feminist reexamination of sexual practices and attitudes that might traditionally be perceived as normative, such as heterosexual intercourse. I follow Gamble's persuasive call to bring "a queer analytic to sexual practice that might seem the furthest thing from 'queer.'"[7]

Offhand, the premise of John Lyly's *The Woman in the Moon* "might seem the furthest thing from 'queer.'"[8] The play's central character, Pandora, begins as an unnamed "lifeless image" (1.1.57) that the deity Nature animates at the request of four shepherds who long "to propagate the

6. Robin Bauer, *Queer BDSM Intimacies: Critical Consent and Pushing Boundaries* (London: Palgrave Macmillan, 2014), 48. Bauer also explores this subject from a phenomenological perspective, which defines "desire as reaching out toward the world with one's body" (49).

7. Joseph Gamble, "Practicing Sex," *The Journal for Early Modern Cultural Studies* 19, no. 1 (2019): 85–116, at 94, https://doi.org/10.1353/jem.2019.0013. See also Melissa E. Sanchez, "'Use Me But as Your Spaniel': Feminism, Queer Theory, and Early Modern Sexualities," *PMLA* 127, no. 3 (2012): 493–511, https://doi.org/10.1632/pmla.2012.127.3.493.

8. Prior to queer studies of Lyly over the past two decades, most scholarship on Lyly's corpus was decidedly straight and vanilla, focusing on political allegory and prose style. I am delighted to be contributing to a queer/kinky renaissance in Lyly criticism, most of which has focused on his play *Galatea*. See for example Valerie Traub, *The Renaissance of Lesbianism in Early Modern England* (Cambridge, UK: Cambridge University Press, 2002); Simone Chess's *Male-to-Female Crossdressing in Early Modern English Literature: Gender, Performance, and Queer Relations* (New York: Routledge, 2019), 138–66; and the pioneering work on *Galatea* by Andy Kesson and Emma Frankland, "'Perhaps John Lyly Was a Trans Woman?': An Interview about Performing *Galatea*'s Queer, Transgender Stories," *The Journal for Early Modern Cultural Studies* 19, no. 1 (2019): 284–98, https://doi.org/10.1353/jem.2019.0048. My own book explores queer forms of eroticism in Lyly's dramatic corpus. See Gillian Knoll, *Conceiving Desire: Metaphor, Cognition, and Eros in Lyly and Shakespeare* (Edinburgh: Edinburgh University Press, 2020).

issue of our kind" (1.1.42).[9] Created to satisfy the desires of men by way of reproductive sex, Pandora might be seen as a heteronormative fantasy incarnate, imbued with a singular purpose: "I make thee for a solace unto men" (1.1.91). To perfect her creation, Nature endows Pandora with gifts from each of the seven planets. But when the planets discover that Nature has stolen their best qualities, their plan for revenge is to dominate Pandora:

> Let us conclude to show our empery,
> And bend our forces 'gainst this earthly star.
> Each one in course shall signorize awhile,
> That she may feel the influence of our beams,
> And rue that she was formed in our despite.
> (1.1.133–37)

Throughout the remainder of the play, each planet takes a turn at filling Pandora with a different ruling passion, from melancholy to madness and mutability, until change itself becomes her defining quality.

Pandora may begin as a heteronormative fantasy, but she quickly embodies a different, kinkier fantasy of utter submission. Lyly's entire play might be seen as a "what if" scenario analog to Fleabag's longing to be, in effect, a receptacle. Each of the god-planets dominates Pandora by filling her with their "influence," and Pandora's job is, essentially, to take it — more precisely, to *feel* it, to "*feel* the influence of [their] beams." On the one hand, this sounds like the language of the humoral body, filled with liquid passions that govern mood, personality, and behavior.[10] On the other, kinkier hand, this is the language of BDSM, of fantasies that

9. All citations of Lyly's *The Woman in the Moon* are from John Lyly, *The Woman in the Moon (The Revels Plays)*, ed. Leah Scragg (Manchester, UK: Manchester University Press, 2006). Parenthetical citations refer to act, scene, and line number.
10. Gail Kern Paster describes humoral bodies as "earthly vessels defined by the quality and quantity of liquids they contain" (6). See Gail Kern Paster, *Humoring the Body: Emotions and the Shakespearean Stage* (Chicago: University of Chicago Press, 2004).

feature a submissive being filled with the ejaculate ("influence," from the Latin *influere*, to flow in)[11] of multiple dominant partners. That Pandora is initially created to "propagate the issue of our kind" with *four* male shepherds (more on Nature's kinky arithmetic later); that she is essentially used in turn by various Dom/mes who plan to "spot her innocence" (1.1.232) by filling her with their "influences"; that she engages in offstage sexual encounters with every mortal character in the dramatis personae; that her increasingly besotted servant, Gunophilus, spends a good deal of the play breaking the fourth wall to delight in the erotic spectacle Pandora makes of herself: all of this tells a kinky story, the story of Pandora as a sexual submissive. A kinky methodology creates space for this story to run alongside, and to intertwine with, more familiar narratives of early modern cosmology, medieval dramaturgy, and humoral embodiment.

The *Oxford English Dictionary* (*OED*) *Online* lists the first recorded use of "submissive" in 1974 as a noun designating a sexual identity,[12] and one aim of this essay is to elongate that historical arc by exploring the rich history, in lived experience and in artistic representation, of the sexual submissive as an embodied way of being. Applying the term "submissive" to Pandora's character — and in general, approaching Lyly's play with a kinky methodology — illuminates some of Pandora's most extraordinary and unique features as a character on the early modern English stage. Leah Scragg singles her out because "the rapid shifts of disposition that Pandora undergoes through the influence of the planets make far greater demands on the performer than any other Lylian role," and Andy Kesson boldly asks, "Does any other character in early modern theatre, or even

---

11. See *Oxford English Dictionary Online*, s.v. "influence, n.," September 2023, https://doi.org/10.1093/OED/1751993208.

12. Entry B2b under "submissive, adj. and n." reads, "A person who plays the submissive role in (sadomasochistic) sexual activity." (The earliest example is from M. M. Hunt's *Sexual Behavior in 1970s* [1974]). *Oxford English Dictionary Online*, s.v. "submissive (*adj. and n.*)," July 2023, https://doi.org/10.1093/OED/2537623946.

in theatre full stop, have this much bodily fun?".[13] The language and conventions of BDSM can function like a grammar that shapes, and helps us trace, the eroticism that runs through the scenes of Pandora's domination. BDSM also recasts what might be seen as an utterly passive condition as a submissive's art, and craft, of eroticized feeling. As the planets "bend [their] forces 'gainst" her, Pandora skillfully bends back. She bends so consummately under the control of each planet throughout the play that she outdoes them, effectively beating them at their own game.

If a Dominant controls the "what" of a scene, a submissive's skill is to modulate the "how." Lyly's play follows this script, with the planets dictating "what to like, what to hate, what to rage about," but Pandora dictating *how* she likes, hates, and rages: "how to live my life," in Fleabag's words. Pandora's "how" is utterly constitutive of her character in *The Woman in the Moon*, a play that dramatizes the process of identity formation by exploring the various roles of nature and nurture, matter and form, in the creation of a self or character. In the end, Pandora finally has a chance to choose her own future course, but even before act five, she develops a sense of self through her experiences as a submissive, an identity based on the mythos from which she takes her name. Pandora, all-gifted, turns out to be a virtuoso in receiving gifts. Submissives are the ones who "take it" in a sexual encounter, and Pandora is no exception. But her example helps us see that taking it can be a gift, a form of self-giving that is also self-making.

Scene Setting

Much has been made of how practitioners of BDSM or "kink" are admirably practised in a forthright, explicit, pragmatic approach to

---

13. See Leah Scragg, introduction to John Lyly, *The Woman in the Moon (The Revels Plays)*, ed. Leah Scragg (Manchester, UK: Manchester University Press, 2006), 34; and Andy Kesson, "The Women in the Moons," *Before Shakespeare* (blog) March 10, 2018, https://beforeshakespeare.com/2018/03/10/women-in-the-moons/.

> consent ... The risk is that these boundaries — assertions of what
> we want and who we are — become a fixed part of oneself, rather
> than a strategic stance; that they begin to settle and harden, when
> one of the pleasures of sex is precisely its changeability, its ability to
> unfold in ways unpredictable to us; our own capacity to end up
> somewhere we had not expected.
> — Katherine Angel, *Tomorrow Sex Will Be Good Again:*
> *Women and Desire in the Age of Consent*

A BDSM scene is set through explicit negotiations between play partners, but Pandora hardly ever speaks or acts on her own in *The Woman
in the Moon*. As Kesson observes, "Every utterance and action Pandora
makes between her first speech and the final scene is made under the
direction of one of the god-planets."[14] Perpetually intoxicated with planetary moodiness, Pandora clearly cannot consent to her treatment in the
play. Her lack of consent makes Pandora's situation crucially different
from that of a submissive partner in a BDSM encounter. What makes
Lyly's play kinky is not its faithful replication of a real-world BDSM
relationship (whatever this might look like in its various premodern or
modern configurations) but instead its commitment to unrealness. *The
Woman in the Moon* is, at its core, a creation myth. Aestheticized, fantas-
tical, sometimes hyper-theatrical, Lyly's play dramatizes a mythology of
how a submissive might come to be: the qualities with which the gods
fill her, the way she receives and manifests them, the skill she culti-
vates through various erotic encounters, and the way she experiences the
world — or, in Pandora's case, the cosmos.

Pandora suffers a universe of feeling throughout the play, and Lyly
takes great pains to present this universe as fictive. His protagonist exists
out of time and place (the play is set in Utopia, literally, "no place"), and

14. Andy Kesson, "'It is a pity you are not a woman': John Lyly and the Creation of Woman,"
Shakespeare Bulletin vol. 33, no. 1 (2005): 33–47, at 41–42, https://doi.org/10.1353/shb.
2015.0001.

she is dominated not by the staffs and crooks of four mortal shepherds but by the gauzy influences of gods. Even Lyly's dramaturgical style is somewhat out of time. Scragg notes that the play appears "to revert to a style of dramaturgy already outdated when the play was composed." The divided stage, in which a higher sphere is devoted to supernatural beings and a lower sphere features mortals, along with a host of other features, "point to an emblematic representation of experience in terms of a series of 'shows', at one with the procedures of early Tudor drama."[15] The cumulative effect of this "emblematic representation" is something along the lines of a BDSM scene, bounded and discrete, artful and contrived. Because Lyly's play is bounded not so much by its place or genre as fictiveness, we can approach it as a fantasy that invites us to read with and for pleasure[16] and to toggle between now and then, tracing erotic connections that do not always obey the spatial-temporal logics of either historicism or presentism. Taking my cue from Lyly's play, I too thread together different "series of 'shows,'" arranging them side by side to see how they play — play with and off each other. The robust form of *The Woman in the Moon*, with its sequence of emblematic representations that explicitly invite us to *interpret* them (to read both "into" and across) frees us to explore the critical pleasures of identification and resemblance, coincidence and resonance. Not least among these pleasures is *noticing* Pandora and Fleabag, centuries apart, kneeling and waiting.

First up in Lyly's aestheticized "series of shows" is Nature's display of dominance, wherein Lyly goes full bore with the kinky quality of the

---

15. Scragg, introduction to *The Woman in the Moon*, 15–16.
16. A kinky methodology also engages in the kind of reparative reading practice that Christine Varnado calls for at the end of *Shapes of Fancy*, in which critics acknowledge "the seeking of pleasure, both as an end in itself and as an intrinsic element of knowledge production, in relation to texts" (259). See Christine Varnado, *Shapes of Fancy: Reading for Queer Desire in Early Modern Literature* (Minneapolis, MN: University of Minnesota Press, 2020). Varnado draws from Eve Kosofsky Sedgwick's "Paranoid Reading and Reparative Reading: Or, You're So Paranoid, You Probably Think This Introduction Is about You," in *Novel Gazing: Queer Readings in Fiction*, ed. Eve Kosofsky Sedgwick (Durham, NC, and London, UK: Duke University Press, 1997), 1–40.

power imbalance in the scene of Pandora's making. Gazing proudly on her creation, Nature recalls her plan "to make it such as our Utopians crave" (1.1.59), affirming Pandora's status as an "it," an object of "crav[ing]." The scene of Pandora's "quickening" (1.1.68) has the appearance of a BDSM tableau — probably not the sort of "emblematic representation" Scragg had in mind when she described the play's dramaturgy, but emblematic all the same. As Nature prepares to imbue the image with "life and soul" (1.1.67), she instructs her two handmaidens, Concord and Discord, to

> hold *it* fast, till with my quickening breath
> I kindle seeds of sense and mind.
> (1.1.68–69, my emphasis)

The implied stage directions suggest that each handmaiden holds the lifeless Pandora with force ("fast"), perhaps one on each side of her, while Nature brings her lips to Pandora's to "kindle" her/its "sense."[17] While it is impossible to pin down exactly what transpires between creator and creation in this exchange, it is clear that Nature displays her dominance as she kindles Pandora, who is at once frozen in a submissive pose, bound and utterly receptive, a vessel of pure feeling.[18]

Apparently Nature has feelings of her own; certainly she relishes her power to enkindle. If Pandora, all-gifted, is defined by her seemingly infinite capacity to receive, Nature might be as readily defined by her aggressive manner of giving:

---

17. For punning connotations of "sense," see Angelo's aside in Shakespeare's *Measure for Measure*, when he is overcome with lust for Isabella: "She speaks and 'tis / Such sense that my sense breeds with it" (2.2.141–42). Cited from William Shakespeare, *Measure for Measure* (*The Pelican Shakespeare*), ed. Jonathan Crewe (New York, NY: Pelican Books, 2017).

18. See Colby Gordon, "A Woman's Prick: Trans Technogenesis in Sonnet 20," in *Shakespeare/Sex: Contemporary Readings in Gender and Sexuality*, ed. Jennifer Drouin (London: Bloomsbury, 2020), 269–89, for an analysis of Shakespeare's "transfeminine version of the creation myth" (273), another mythology "governed by an infatuated Nature" (283).

Thou art endowed with Saturn's deep conceit,
Thy mind as haught as Jupiter's high thoughts,
Thy stomach lion-like, like Mars's heart,
Thine eyes bright-beamed, like Sol in his array,
Thy cheeks more fair than are fair Venus' cheeks,
Thy tongue more eloquent than Mercury's,
Thy forehead whiter than the silver Moon's.
Thus have I robbed the planets for thy sake.
(1.1.95–102)

Nature cannot sustain for long the equanimity of her balanced similes ("as haught as," "lion-like, like Mars's heart"). Carried away by her display of power, she finally boasts that she has "robbed the planets" of their gifts in an effort to make Pandora greater — "more fair," "more eloquent," and even "whiter" — than her unwilling benefactors. Lyly's play here installs whiteness among its cosmic superlatives, blanching even Pandora's "bright" eyes and "fair" cheeks in its pallid hue.[19] Thus "endowed" with this dazzling array of properties and powers, Pandora is nonetheless soon reminded of her subservience to the deity's demands: "see thou follow our commanding will" (1.1.92).

Nature's "commanding will" exposes her kinky bent even before the queer erotic charge passes between the two female characters during Pandora's "quickening." The deity sets an ensnaring scene for Pandora, binding her into a thick web of desires remarkable not only for their volatility but for their sheer quantity. Nature's kinky arithmetic, what with its 4 lovelorn shepherds 1 infatuated servant 7 affronted gods,

19. For a recent account of "the overwhelming whiteness of BDSM," and more generally the role of race and racialized gender in kink communities, see Katherine Martinez, "The Overwhelming Whiteness of BDSM: A Critical Discourse Analysis of Racialization in BDSM," *Sexualities* 24, no. 5–6 (2021): 733–48, https://doi.org/10.1177/1363460720 932389. See also Ariane Cruz, *The Color of Kink* (Durham, NC: Duke University Press, 2014); and Amber Jamilla Musser, *Sensational Flesh: Race, Power, and Masochism* (New York: New York University Press, 2014).

also reveals the Dommey (sometimes sadistic) potential embedded in the playwright's own scene setting. The creation deity is repeatedly conflated with Lyly in the opening scene, where Nature is "author of the world" (1.1.31), "author of all good" (1.1.87), and "author of your lives" (1.1.123). Why does Pandora's "author" (Lyly? Nature? Or both?) create such a stark imbalance, and why does no character in Lyly's play call attention to it? It is assumed that the four shepherds will duke it out for Pandora's affections, but it is difficult to puzzle out *any* vanilla reason behind this odd calculus, especially because we learn early on that Nature has been crafting several images in her workshop. Lyly's stage directions indicate that curtains are drawn to reveal *"Nature's shop, where stands an image clad, and some unclad"* (1.1.56.1). Why does Nature surround Pandora with naked "images" (paintings? sculptures? actors?) but not kindle three more of them to join Pandora as mates for the remaining shepherds? Queer studies of early modern literature and culture have, as we would expect, made a case for nature's queerness, and Lyly's play falls in line with much of this important work.[20] But *The Woman in the Moon* makes a compelling case that Nature is kinky, too.

Topping from the Bottom

> Submission, I soon learned, was also a kind of power ... I had a
> choice, a craft, whether he ascends or falls depends on my willing-
> ness to make room for him, for you cannot rise without having
> something to rise over. Submission does not require elevation in

20. The plenary session on "Queer Natures: Bodies, Sexualities, Environments" at the 2017 Shakespeare Association of America's annual meeting in Atlanta presented important work on this topic by Karen Raber, Joseph Campana, Vin Nardizzi, and Laurie Shannon. See Karen Raber et al., "Queer Natures: Bodies, Sexualities, Environments," (plenary panel session, Shakespeare Association of America, Atlanta, GA, April 7, 2017), https://www.youtube.com/watch?v=YVgx9-6wTOE. Lyly's *Galatea* is cited in Laurie Shannon, "Nature's Bias: Renaissance Homonormativity and Elizabethan Comic Likeness," *Modern Philology* 98, no. 2 (2000): 183–210, https://doi.org/10.1086/492960.

order to control. I lower myself. I put him in my mouth, to the base,
and peer up at him, my eyes a place he might flourish. After a while,
it is the cocksucker who moves. And he follows, when I sway this
way he swerves along. And I look up at him as if looking at a kite,
his entire body tied to the teetering world of my head.
— Ocean Vuong, *On Earth We're Briefly Gorgeous*

Kneel. For the protagonist of Ocean Vuong's *On Earth We're Briefly
Gorgeous*, this is a self-reflexive act: "I lower myself." Vuong's novel tells
a complex story of action and passion, doing and being, and among the
most arresting features of that story is the expansive verticality of the
kite image. By kneeling so low, Vuong's protagonist makes his Dom soar.
There is something about the submissive's groundedness, the "teetering
world" he makes of his head, that frees the Dom to stretch infinitely
upward. Peering down at the submissive's eyes, the Dom finds more than
a mere reflection of himself — he finds "a place he might flourish."[21] Pandora becomes such a place for the god-planets, an "earthly star" (1.1.135)
that reflects their best qualities but also makes each of them glow more
brightly. Like the protagonist of Vuong's novel, Pandora adopts the set of
practices known in the kink community as "topping from the bottom."
The Woman in the Moon's vertical economy makes this practice uniquely
visible; dramaturgically, the planets sit on high and gaze down on Pandora until the end, when she ascends to the top, taking her place in the
moon. But Pandora tops from the bottom in other ways, too. Ontologically, she is characterized by her receptivity to planetary influence, yet
she outperforms those planets at various points in the play. Dramati-
cally, she holds all the power; like *Fleabag*'s kneeling protagonist, whom
the camera almost never leaves, Pandora's submission takes center stage
throughout the play. And sexually, although Pandora is defined by her
receptivity, we see her aggressively beat one suitor, bed down three oth-

---

21. Ocean Vuong, *On Earth We're Briefly Gorgeous* (New York: Penguin, 2019), 118.

ers in quick succession, and flip some of the scripts the god-planets write for her.

The first two planets script Pandora as a receptacle to "fill" (2.1.3), but in both scenes, she bursts with feeling — and in both scenes, she brings others to their knees. While Saturn plans to inflict a "melancholy mood" (1.1.144) that makes her "self-willed and tongue-tied" (1.1.149), Pandora reacts with eloquence and precision, giving a voice to her supposedly "tongue-tied" melancholy:

> What throbs are these that labour in thy breast?
> What swelling clouds that overcast my brain?
> I burst unless by tears they turn to rain.
> (1.1.171–73)

Pandora's action verbs — throbs, swelling, overcast, burst — characterize her less as a container than as a conduit who overflows with feeling. When at last, her melancholy does silence her, Pandora's stage action speaks volumes. Perhaps Lyly's most memorable stage direction is the delightfully ambiguous *"she plays the vixen with everything about her"* (1.1.176.1), which Scragg glosses as "acts shrewishly, ill-temperedly."[22] Kesson writes of this "extremely unusual" turn of phrase, "Once again, the play hands over decision-making to its performer, and asks them to go crazy."[23] Perhaps it is the actor's virtuosic improvisation that draws from the four besotted shepherds their own dramatic display of supplication. Showering her with praises, they *"all kneel to her"* (1.1.184.1). She, in turn, *"hits [Stesias] on the lips"* (1.1.188.1) and *"strikes [Learchus's] hand"* (1.1.194.1). Pandora's aggression here is a virtuosic expression of her submission to Saturn. She follows his script to the letter, since her "self-will" is what drives her "tongue-tied" stage actions, but she also exceeds this script. Effectively gagged, Pandora discovers a new improvisational

22. Lyly, *The Woman in the Moon*, 62.
23. Kesson, "The Women in the Moons."

language of striking, hitting, and playing the vixen — of topping from the bottom — through which she absorbs and owns the melancholic feeling he imparts.

Lyly explores the sexual power of this aggressive receptivity in the following scene, in which Jupiter initially describes Pandora as a vessel, comparing her to his other conquests: "in this one [Pandora] are all my loves contained" (2.1.18). As soon as he confronts Pandora, however, Jupiter changes his tune and figures himself beneath her, claiming to be

> High Jove himself, who, ravished with thy blaze,
> Receives more influence than he pours on thee,
> And humbly sues for succour at thy hands.
> (2.1.24–26)

If Pandora spends much of the play topping from the bottom, here we see "High Jove" bottoming from the top, even capitulating to Pandora's demand to "give me thy golden scepter in my hand" (2.1.41) and finally fleeing the scene altogether in fear of "jealous Juno" (2.1.80). When Pandora redirects her newfound power toward her servant Gunophilus, she plays with scripts and postures familiar within BDSM scenes, commanding the "base vassal" to

> honour me with kneel and crouch,
> And lay thy hands under my precious foot.
> (2.1.85–87)

More important than this display of power is the pleasure it apparently affords Pandora. When Gunophilus confesses his "feeble[ness]" and "holy fear" of her, she answers, "thou pleasest me" (2.1.100); then, receiving the four doting shepherds, "I please myself in your humility" (2.1.145). Pleasure was never on the menu when Jupiter began his reign; he planned only to "fill her with ambition and disdain" (2.1.3). Pandora's self-reflexive declaration, "I please myself," signals her conversion of the planets' proprietorship into pleasures entirely her own. Like Vuong's "I lower myself," Pandora is both subject and predicate, top and bottom, finding in submission not only "a kind of power," but a kind of pleasure, too.

Slut Training

> Slut training is a BDSM process where a dominant partner teaches the consenting submissive partner to behave in a sexually unrestricted or "slutty" way … It ideally results in a holistic transformation involving what they wear, how they act, and how they think.
> — "Slut Training," *Kinkly.com*

> Great sluts are made, not born.
> — Janet W. Hardy and Dossie Easton, *The Ethical Slut*

While many BDSM rituals intensify the hierarchies that separate a Dominant from their submissive, "slut training" is a murkier, boundary-blurring practice. How does the teacher hold onto the reins when they are instructing their student to "be loose" (3.2.66), to use Pandora's phrase? And how does anyone teach "sexually unrestricted" behavior in the first place? Scholars like Valerie Traub and Gamble have argued persuasively that sexual knowledge is not like other kinds of knowledge because, as Traub writes, "there is much about sex that we *don't know*: of what acts sex consists, what pleasures it affords, what difficulties it encounters, and what inventiveness it engenders."[24] Slut training is thus a somewhat opaque pedagogical encounter (e.g., defining "sexually unrestricted" behavior — unrestricted from *what*, exactly?), and if the teacher does

---

24. Valerie Traub, *Thinking Sex with the Early Moderns* (Philadelphia, PA: University of Pennsylvania Press, 2016), 123 (Traub's emphasis). See also Joseph Gamble on "sexual-logistical knowledge" in "Practicing Sex."

their job well, the student's erotic "inventiveness" might soon take them both off book.

Perhaps this is why Venus confines herself to a relatively simple script when she ascends in act three of *The Woman in the Moon*. "I'll have her witty, quick, and amorous," she declares,

> Delight in revels, and in banqueting,
> Wanton discourses, music, and merry songs.
> (3.2.2–4)

The love goddess takes a hands-off approach to slut training (Venus is one of the few characters whose hands are not on Pandora in this scene). She sketches the "what," but leaves it to Pandora to manifest the "how." How, for example, might Pandora embody Venus's "amorous[ness]," a supple word that leaves room for improvisation, as Jeffrey Masten has shown in his research on the word's active and passive connotations in the *OED*? To be amorous might mean that Pandora is (actively) "inclined to love," but also that she is (passive) "loveable, lovely," a condition already woven into her identity as a purpose-built love object.[25] If Pandora has been passively amorous from the start of the play, the experience of slut training licenses her to lean into this condition — to "incline" actively.

Venus does not so much write a script, then, as create conditions that quicken Pandora's kinky inventiveness and improvisation. She frames her control over Pandora as a kind of enforced freedom. "Let her to the world" (3.2.18), Venus proclaims, and in response Pandora falls in love with the world — or at least, all the people in it. She woos her servant Gunophilus ("I am lovesick for thee" [3.2.83]) and seduces all the shepherds except Stesias, whom she married in the previous scene, but now asks herself, "Must I be tied to him? No! I'll be loose" (3.2.66).

---

25. For a fuller account of "amorous," see Jeffrey Masten, *Queer Philologies: Sex, Language, and Affect in Shakespeare's Time* (Philadelphia: University of Pennsylvania Press, 2016), 157–59.

Thus loosened, Pandora embodies Venus's "witty, quick, and amorous" in her own way — by becoming singularly bossy. Observing that the shepherds "look like water nymphs" (3.2.148), she emasculates each of them in turn, comparing one to "Nature in a man's attire" (3.2.149), then another to "young Ganymede, minion to Jove" (3.2.150). Robbing her suitors of any opportunity to woo her, she devotes herself to orchestrating what Kesson calls "a six-person sex free-for-all."[26] Not sex but Pandora's sexual dominance is everywhere present in the scene, even at the level of language. Rarely figuring herself as passive in her offstage sexual escapades, she takes charge of each action verb:

> Now have I played with wanton Iphicles,
> Yea, and kept touch with Melos. Both are pleased.
> Now, were Learchus here! But stay, methinks
> Here is Gunophilus. I'll go with him.
> (3.2.224–27)

Venus may rule on high, but Pandora rules on the ground, to the extent that her sexuality can take a violent turn:

> Thus will I hang about Learchus' neck,
> And suck out happiness from forth his lips.
> (3.2.257–58)

When Pandora is not engaging in offstage sexual rendezvous, she is busy organizing them, an activity that appears to offer its own pleasures. First she arranges to meet each shepherd separately — "Meet me in the vale" (3.2.156), "go to yon grove" (3.2.169), and so on — but then she coordinates a banquet where her lovers can fight over her. She sets the time and place, she orders Gunophilus to manage various details, and she navi-

---

26. Andy Kesson, "*The Woman in the Moon* Onstage," *Before Shakespeare* (blog), August 19, 2017, https://beforeshakespeare.com/2017/08/19/the-woman-in-the-moon-onstage/.

gates the tense conversation among her jealous lovers in a series of asides ("Knows not Melos I love him?" [3.2.299] she whispers to one, then to another, "Hath Iphicles forgot my words?" [3.2.301]). Scragg has called this "the most intricately plotted scene in the Lylian corpus,"[27] and it would seem that this distinction owes something to Lyly's kinky collaborators. Who is doing the plotting? Within the scene's fiction, "banqueting" (3.2.3) is Venus's design, but the "how" of the banquet belongs to Pandora, who carefully caters it onstage and thus exceeds the fiction, bending it to her self-will. Lyly's script depends on Nature's, hers depends on the planets', the planets' on Pandora's improvisational art. Apparently this "most intricately plotted scene" is the work of many kinky minds and hands, its pleasures and powers diffused and distributed among Dom/mes and sub alike.

If Venus's mode of "slut training" looks familiar, it is because we have already seen it in the play's opening scene. Venus's art reflects Nature's own art of scene setting, of creating conditions, of binding in order to loosen. Pandora's Dommes set the parameters — Nature's kinky math, Venus's scripted "banqueting" — but they leave it to her to activate the potential eroticism within the scene. That Pandora decides to invite all her lovers to a banquet right on the heels of her private sexual trysts with each one (and with her servant) suggests that she shares in the pleasures of Nature's kinky math. That she wants to "entertain" (3.2.237) multiple lovers at once suggests that intricate plotting affords its own erotic delights, as Venus, Nature, and evidently Lyly himself all know. Such pleasure may not align with the stereotype of a slavish, passive submissive, but Pandora's submissiveness is defined by responsiveness, not slavishness, by a capacity to take what she is given, absorb it, and make it her own.

27. Lyly, *The Woman in the Moon*, 90.

Subspace

> It can look so many ways ... almost like being both
> in yourself and outside yourself simultaneously.
> — Quinn B., kink educator and founder of
> Unearthed Pleasures, "A Beginner's Guide to Subspace"

By the time Pandora is subjected to Luna's influence, she has been dominated by six planets and given herself up to an impressive range of passions: melancholy, disdain, anger, gentility, lust, and duplicity. When the moon goddess ascends, she promises to add to this list "Newfangled, fickle, slothful, foolish, [and] mad" (5.1.5). In some respects, Luna's script for Pandora is a rehash of Lyly's; one gets the sense that Pandora has been auditioning for this role from the start of the play. But if she contains multitudes in acts one through four, those multitudes multiply in act five, in which Pandora's mood changes as quickly as her mind:

> Where is the larks? Come, we'll go catch some straight!
> No, let us go a-fishing with a net!
> With a net? No, an angle is enough.
> An angle? A net? No, none of both.
> (5.1.25–28)

Luna's script reduces Pandora to a creature of *want*; Pandora can hardly pronounce one object of her desire before the next one claims her. The men around her describe Pandora as "lunatic" (5.1.69, 93) "foolish" (5.1.120, 136), and "stark mad" (5.1.191), but a kinky reader might descry in what Scragg calls Pandora's "sexually laden stage raving"[28] something akin to "subspace."

---

28. Scragg compares Pandora's language with Ophelia's sexually charged language in act four, scene five of *Hamlet*. See Lyly, *The Woman in the Moon*, 128.

Not all submissives experience subspace, and those who do characterize it so variously that it escapes easy definition, but kink educator Quinn B.'s broad description of "being both in yourself and outside yourself simultaneously" captures many of its flavors.[29] For some submissives, subspace is a state of high suggestibility and vulnerability, a psychic space as much as a material one. Some describe it as a metaphysical state, "a kind of profound and divine loss of self."[30] For others, subspace is more of a physical condition induced by pain and characterized by an increased pain tolerance. Some submissives describe it as a high, an intense euphoria often followed by "sub-drop," a depleted state that has been associated with a reduction of adrenaline, oxytocin, and serotonin.[31] Not all of these accounts fit Pandora's situation, but the play's descriptions of Pandora's altered state (e.g., Gunophilus's "What a sudden change is here!" [5.1.22]) present an opportunity to reflect more closely on what it is that Luna does to Pandora. In subspace, a submissive is likely to crave *more* — more of whatever constitutes their submission, more pain or humiliation, more restrictions or commands, or more intense edgeplay or roleplay. And under Luna's sway, Pandora manifestly wants more. Her desires are remarkable both for their plasticity (an angle! no, wait — a net!) and their abundance:

But shall I have a gown of oaken leaves,
A chaplet of red berries, and a fan
Made of the morning dew to cool my face?
How often will you kiss me in an hour,

29. See "A Beginner's Guide to Subspace," *Healthline.com*, accessed 16 December 2022. https://www.healthline.com/health/healthy-sex/subspace-bdsm.

30. Julie Fennell, "'It's all about the journey': Skepticism and Spirituality in the BDSM Subculture," *Sociological Forum* 33, no. 4 (2018): 1045–67, at 1060, https://doi.org/10.1111/socf.12460.

31. See "What is Sub-drop?" in "A Beginner's Guide to Subspace," *Healthline.com*, accessed December 16, 2022, https://www.healthline.com/health/healthy-sex/subspace-bdsm.

And where shall we sit till the sun be down?
(5.1.35–39)

She wants *so much* and *so many*, articulating each desire in such fine-grained detail that we can hear how she anticipates Fleabag's "I want someone to tell me what to eat, what to like, what to hate, what to rage about, what to listen to, what band to like, what to buy tickets for, what to joke about and what not to joke about." For both Fleabag and Pandora, their objects of desire, though carefully specified, matter less than the attendant affect, the posture, and the *condition* of wanting.

Subspace is intoxicating, and Pandora's inebriated state leads her to pursue her desires aggressively. Still, the overall effect is one of submission. Pandora inarguably submits to Luna, as she submitted to the other planets, but here she seems mostly enslaved to her own whims. Moreover, her language and behavior comport with accounts of subspace by BDSM practitioners who describe it as an altered state of consciousness. "I get high"; "You end up in this incredibly strong rush so you just don't have control anymore"; "It is almost that I lose consciousness. Not that I get tired but I give up."[32] Under Luna's domination, Pandora's final stage direction is *"Dormit"* (5.1.209.1). One gets the sense that her slumber is a mix of giving up and giving in. Pandora sleeps through about fifty lines of angry dialogue among her jilted lovers, who are at the point of killing her when the planets finally intervene, at which point *"She awakes and is sober"* (5.1.258.1).

It is easy to imagine that Pandora's drunken slumber is a way of tapping out, of removing herself from the intensity of Luna's domination (and her lovers' violent display). But when Nature returns to the stage and allows her creation finally to choose which "one of [the planets']

---

32. Interviews quoted in Charlotta Carlström, "Spiritual Experiences and Altered States of Consciousness: Parallels between BDSM and Christianity," *Sociological Forum* 33, no. 4 (2018): 749–66, https://doi.org/10.1177/1363460720964035. Carlström cites sociological research on *"reality slips"* in her work on Christian glossolalia and BDSM subspace (761).

seven orbs ... she shall be placed in" (5.1.276), Pandora settles on Luna, "the lowest of the erring stars" (5.1.2). There is something about sub-space, apparently, that draws Pandora back: "it content[s] me best" (5.1.315). Her final choice of the play is to become at turns "idle, mutable, / Forgetful, foolish, fickle, frantic, mad" (5.1.313–14), in short, to aban-don herself to each new feeling that strikes her. She has been doing this all along, but in *freely* choosing submission ("awake and sober"), Pandora embraces the constitutive and creative power and pleasure of receptiv-ity.

Pandora, Kneeling

> Perhaps this was everything: thus to kneel ... : to kneel: and
> thereby hold one's own outward willing contours tightly reined
> — Rainer Maria Rilke, "The Donor"[33]

Lyly's stage directions call for Pandora to kneel only once in *The Woman in the Moon*, during the scene of her creation. Kneeling is her third scripted stage action of the play, but it is the first thing she does under the speech prefix "Pandora" in Lyly's quarto. Until she kneels, she is only "the Image," and until she kneels, "the Image" is rather unsteady. Her first scripted action, after Nature decides to "let her stand, or move, or walk alone" (1.1.77), reads, *The image walks about fearfully* (1.1.77.1). Kesson singles this out as "an unprecedented early modern stage direction, a cue for a player to walk as a new creature in a terrifying world."[34] Pandora begins the play with the freedom of motion, with a menu of options for how to comport herself and make her way in the world. For how long does Pandora's "fearful" stage business persist? It might go on for

---

33. Quoted in Karmen MacKendrick, *Counterpleasures* (Albany, NY: SUNY Press, 1999), 79. Rilke's original reads, "zu knien: daß man die eigenen Konturen, / die auswärtswollenden," with "Konturen" usually translated into English as contours or outlines.
34. Kesson, "It is a pity," 41.

as many as ten lines of dialogue, until Nature commands her handmaid Discord to "unloose" Pandora's "tongue, to serve her turn" (1.1.83), which prompts Lyly's next set of stage directions (figure 9.1): *"Image speaks,"* and then, *"Pandora kneeling"* (1.1.86–87.1).

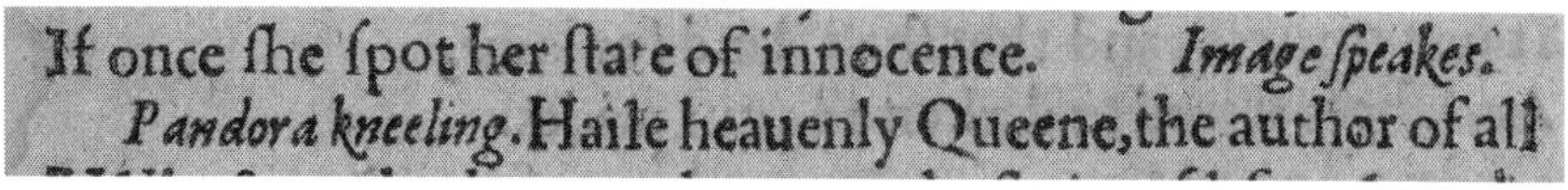

If once fhe fpot her ftate of innocence.   *Image fpeakes.* **Pandora kneeling.** Haile heauenly Queene, the author of all

Figure 9.1. *The vvoman in the moone. : As it was presented before her Highnesse. / By Iohn Lyllie maister of Artes* (London: William Jones, 1597), sig. A3r. Detail from RB 62382, The Huntington Library, San Marino, California. Reproduced with permission.

Given a voice "to serve her turn," Pandora uses it to serve her author. And then she kneels, a gesture of submission that serves Pandora too. Kneeling seems to gather her, to "hold [her] own outward willing contours tightly reined," in Rilke's words. In choosing to lower herself, to draw herself in, Pandora takes shape and earns her name.

Kneeling is not an altogether atypical response to what we might call an existential crisis, Pandora's sudden awareness (she talks of her "understanding soul" [1.1.89]) of herself as a created being. Across time and place, another character who undergoes a similar crisis is Fleabag. Among Fleabag's many struggles is a peculiar metaphysical quandary that grips her in the episodes with the priest, involving her status as a fictional character. As she becomes more intimately connected with the priest, the wry asides she has been delivering to camera throughout *Fleabag* suddenly and alarmingly open themselves to the priest's ears. Surely this new development heightens her awareness of her condition as a created being who answers to an "author" of one kind or another.[35] And this awareness draws her almost magnetically toward the priest,

---

35. Fleabag's crisis is doubly complex because the character, played by Phoebe Waller-Bridge, is also the writer/creator of the series.

someone with the power to see and hear her, to "tell [her] what to" do. It is what brings her to her knees.

Rilke's poetic conceit of kneeling as self-binding would likely resonate with many submissives. Bondage, and even pain, can define a person by making them feel their shape, sharpening their edges, and creating sensation at the body's contours, whether in the push back against restraints or in the sting of flesh. Imani Davis's poem "Kink" speaks to this shaping power:

> I never thought restraint would be my thing.
> Then you: the hole from which my logic seeps,
> who bucks my mind's incessant swallowsong
> & pins the speaker's squirming lyric down
> with ease.[36]

For Davis and their "Kink," bondage is what imparts a "measured" iambic form on their "squirming lyric"; it wraps

> knuckles tight around
> a bratty vers.

It is a kind of kneeling, a pinning down and gathering in. If *The Woman in the Moon* is not kinky in any other way, it is at least kinky in this, its form. It is John Lyly's only play written in verse, and at its center is a brat.[37]

---

36. I am grateful to Joseph Gamble for sharing this poem with me. Davis's opening lines set a familiar scene: "The *moon* assumes her voyeuristic perch / to find the rut of me, released from sense" (my emphasis), Imani Davis, "Kink," *Poem-a-Day*, Academy of American Poets, February 3, 2023, https://poets.org/poem/kink?mc_cid=031c76dab8&mc_eid=307c62b1f7.

37. Jillian Keenan, author of *Sex with Shakespeare: Here's Much to Do with Pain, but More with Love* (New York: William Morrow, 2016), self-identifies as "what the kink community calls a 'brat' — someone who is a bottom, but has a play style that is more sassy or combative" (94).

I don't think Lyly's verse restrains bratty Pandora in quite the way Davis imagines the poetic form containing their "bratty vers." Pandora never kneels in her final scene (in fact all of the mortal characters have knelt before her by this point in the play, to her palpable delight) but neither does *the Image walk ... fearfully.* Something gathers Pandora when she is at last given the opportunity to choose her own course, because when she settles on Luna, she declares that

> change is my felicity,
> And fickleness Pandora's proper form.
> (5.1.307–8)

Like Davis's speaker, Pandora locates her pleasure — her "felicity" — in having a "proper form." But for Pandora, that form is fluid and "mutable" (5.1.313). What gives her shape is receptivity, her desire and capacity to feel.

If Lyly's play is a mythology of a sexual submissive, it might also be a story of anyone who has found pleasure in feeling influence. As Katherine Angel writes, "Relationality and responsivity characterize all human interactions, whether we admit it or not …. Why consider as a flaw the act of yielding, the fact that we *are* susceptible to others? Feelings, sensations, and desires can lie dormant until brought into being by those around us."[38] In Pandora's character and situation, Lyly stretches Angel's "relationality and responsivity" to a cosmic extreme. This is what kink offers us in its extremes — the ability to see with a magnifying glass the subtle eroticism in gestures, postures, and language that we encounter every day. In the fleeting, inexplicable rush of sensation we can feel from an exceptionally good hug, for example, we might sample the pleasures and freedoms of being bound to the bedframe. As Karmen MacKendrick writes,

---

38. Angel, *Tomorrow Sex Will Be Good Again,* 149. Angel's emphasis.

All one can do is to give oneself over to pleasure, and it will take one beyond oneself, or not. In this giving over, the distinctions between "normal" and "perverse" pleasure begin as differences of degree, or more clearly of intensity, and this intensification at some level becomes indistinguishable from a difference in kind.[39]

Such differences seem sharply drawn in *The Woman in the Moon*, with its mythological context and its cosmic cast of characters, but MacKendrick makes the case that they coalesce in the act of "giving over" to pleasure. Giving over: this is Pandora's submissive art, itself a source of pleasures both strange and familiar. Lyly's origin story locates such pleasures in our *aptitude* for yielding to the force of another body — in the act of leaning (even for an instant) into a too-tight embrace, of softening against a hard edge and being shaped by someone else's desire. For Pandora, the moon is just such a shaping force that helps to "hold one's own outward willing contours tightly reined," even as those contours shift and change.

39. MacKendrick, *Counterpleasures*, 12.

Aftercare

Christine Varnado

Is This a Room

I was privileged to serve as the respondent to the first "Kinky Renaissance" conversation, a seminar at the 2021 Shakespeare Association of America (SAA) meeting. That was the second all-virtual SAA conference, the one everyone knew would be virtual from the start. For many of us it marked one year of intellectual isolation, save the fleeting disembodied contact with others' tinny, walkie-talkie voices and talking heads in Zoom boxes on our computer screens. Virtual panels and seminars provided a tantalizing taste of intellectual stimulation — the content of brilliant, groundbreaking new work, without the community engendered around it. Virtual talks felt like a one-way channel, with no way for listeners to give anything back to the speaker by laughing or murmuring assent, and no way to process our thoughts about the ideas we had heard collectively, by reacting to a shared experience together in time and space. If you had something to say to someone, you could say it in an email after the fact.

Eviscerated from the experience were all of the structures and energies that scholarly exchange shares with performance — a special ordering of time and space, bodies brought into proximity for a ritualized purpose, a repertory cast of recurring and new characters moving through the space, and a visual vocabulary of costumes and props that telegraph the genre of scene we're in, as well as aiding characterization. And, hardest of all to put into words and hence, I think, most missed, was what, to me, is the performance itself: the academic conference's convention-bound yet idiosyncratic, improvisatory dance of verbal and affective contacts — the open weave of addressing others and being addressed; the searching dynamics of receptivity that govern taking, holding, and ceding the floor in a multi-person conversation, in which there is time and space to think aloud, to change positions; the free-floating agency and occult, multi-layered constraints around joining, inviting others into, and leaving, fleeting conversational trios and quartets and quintets whose content could swing wildly afield of anything anyone had said on a panel; and, everywhere, the potential for surprise, for encountering someone or something new that might become, perhaps through many iterations over time, incorporated as a vital element of one's being. It's repetition with revision, iterated over years and decades of scholarly life; it's a *form*, as formative of texts (like this one) and authors (like me) as any other. And, like all forms, the kinds of community it materializes and the ways of thinking it produces are particular to it and can't be engendered apart from the physical practice of the form.

This description of the affordances the academic conference shares with performance is also, of course, a description of the structural features it shares with scenes of group erotic interaction — of the resemblance that informal conference socializing bears to attending a kinky party, where everyone is there for the same larger purpose, though each is doing different things in a different order, with different configurations of people, together in space and time. A conference is, in this sense, a group erotic dynamic, in which pleasure — and pain, both pleasurable and just plain painful! — are generated collectively across a group of people together, interacting with one another in different groupings and power dynamics, at a variety of scales and levels of formality. And the conference *scene* is just as constituted by a specific subculture and its performance traditions as any kink party scene is. Its players are bound together by a set of structuring conventions, idiosyncratically understood and enacted by each one. This collective invention within the bounds of generic constraint makes the scene, the iteration of which makes the form.

There's a reason some snarkily compared the difference between leading a discussion about literature on Zoom versus in person to the difference between watching porn and having sex (or, an analogy I like even better: the difference between producing an episode of a cooking show, and cooking and sharing a meal). Was it better than nothing? Was it better than getting and spreading COVID-19, before anyone was vaccinated? Yes and yes. But the elements of embodied, improvisatory performance, and of collective pleasure generated through a thousand shifting contacts framed by a larger *scene*, couldn't be replicated in the digital simulacrum of the form. Caroline Levine says this about how the affordances of forms are produced in *Forms*: "One cannot make a poem out of soup or a panopticon out of wool. In this sense, form and materiality are inextricable, and material is determinant."[1]

Something that happens during a virtual intellectual event is that, at the end of the session's allotted time, everyone logs off and the Zoom meeting ends. The brief portal into contact, conversation, and community abruptly closes, and you are left, very suddenly, alone, staring at your computer screen, your cluttered desk, the wall. It feels absolutely horrible. It's a specific, highly predictable sinking feeling, caused by the absolute lack of social denouement after the climax of the panel's conclusion (last question, last word, thanks to all the participants, applause). For someone who has just put themselves and their ideas before others,

1. Caroline Levine, *Forms: Whole, Rhythm, Hierarchy, Network* (Princeton, NJ: Princeton University Press, 2015), 9.

expended energy in the aspirational self-gratification-through-gratify-ing-others of a performance they hope was well-received, this emotional drop can be particularly severe. It's called the *drop*, and it's a well-documented and much-discussed occurrence after power exchange or BDSM sex play. It's caused by the neurochemical ebbing of endorphins and other material transmitters of pleasure, stress, and excitation from the brain and body, and it's exacerbated by inadequate aftercare — the practice of intentionally communicating with one's partners to process the intensity of a BDSM scene after it concludes.[2]

What happens in a room just after a ritualized performance — whether a sex act, a lecture, or a seminar discussion — is an integral part of the ritual. It is not the cessation of form; it is convention-bound precisely in its transition to a more dispersed, informal mode of being together, in which no one is addressing the whole group and anyone can say anything they want to anyone else. A pent-up charge of affective, erotic, and social energy is discharged in this moment. Both the tension in which audience members were silently holding themselves, and the tension with which the performers were remaining "on," are released. It's a moment of decompression, in which the complex power imbalances that structure the ritual, dividing people into their specialized roles, are (partially) equalized. But this restorative diffusion of power requires the players/participants in the event to *be* together, to collectively participate in what I would call the academic form of aftercare.

All of this is to say that the world we live in, the world of desire and power and being in configurations with others, the world of politics and pedagogy and thought, presents situations all the time that we need a kinky analysis, or kink theory, to fully understand. Why do I feel so awful after giving a talk on Zoom? Ask a kinky person. Read some BDSM theory. Watch and learn.

---

2. "Aftercare," *BDSM Wiki*, accessed February 17, 2023, https://bdsmwiki.info/Aftercare.

Sex, But Make It Fashion

My reading just above, of the formal structures that link an academic conference, a performance, and a sex party, is an example, I think, of the kind of analysis this volume sparks. These essays invite us to think kink not only as a set of topics or subcultural activities but as a methodology, a reading practice, an analytic. This move of extrapolating, from the history and practices of a marginalized sexual subculture, the methodological tools and interpretive techniques that culture has cultivated, and using them to analyze material beyond that subcultural archive, echoes queer theory's early leap of deploying methods of reading honed in gay and lesbian studies to analyze the rest of the supposedly not-gay universe (finding, of course, much queerness there).[3] In making this move, kink as method offers itself as the odd, outré cousin of queer method, taking its place on an *L Word*–style hookup chart of critical influences and intersections that now includes asexual, trans, and disability reading practices as well.

In what follows, I want to sum up the particular quality to this set of essays that, I think, amounts to a kink methodology. Much like queerness or asexuality, as scholars advancing those methodologies have taught us,[4] kink is there if you know how to read for it. And once you see it, you can't un-see it. The question becomes, then, what does a kinky reading practice do? What are its qualities? What does it recognize, what does it bring out, what kinds of interventions does it enable, what does it *get* us in literary studies?

3. See Eve Kosofsky Sedgwick's "Introduction: Axiomatic," in *Epistemology of the Closet* (Berkeley and Los Angeles: University of California Press, 1990), 1–63, especially "Axiom 6: The relation of gay studies to debates on the literary canon is, and had best be, torturous" (48).
4. See Stephen Guy-Bray, *Shakespeare and Queer Representation* (Abingdon, UK: Routledge, 2021); and Liza Blake, "Early Modern Asexuality (and Aromanticism)," in *The Asexuality and Aromanticism Bibliography*, September 2022, https://acearobiblio.com/2022/08/22/early-modern-asexuality-and-aromanticism/.

One way to describe this set of essays is as an assemblage of shame-lessly invested, virtuosic close readings. They give beautiful, fetishistic attention to textual detail — fetishistic in the sense of Sigmund Freud's subject, in *Fetishism*, who "had exalted a certain sort of 'shine on the nose'" as the object of his erotic investment. He was actually, Freud breezily deduces, into noses themselves, which "he endowed at will with the luminous shine which was not perceptible to others."[5] The object of the fetishistic gaze, in this image, is a glancing sheen on the surface of a ubiquitous everyday object — a certain play of light with the body oils on the surface of the skin and the tilt of another's head. It enhances and marks ordinary noses, rendering them specially alluring to the fetishist. But it exists, in the first instance, *just for him*; he sees it where he needs to see it, where not just anyone can.

One way I would describe the aim of a kinky methodology, then, the task of the *fetishistic* reader or literary critic, is *making visible the "shine on the nose"* of a text: describing the precise formal, affective, erotic, ideo-logical, etc. effect one sees, so clearly that others can suddenly see it too where they could not before. These essays do that, I find, in their atten-tion to the valences of tossed-off and interstitial language: the Dom/sub affects that Gina Filo finds anew in Robert Herrick's lyrics, and Gillian Knoll brings out in John Lyly's drama; and the dynamics of bondage, restraint, and complex, shifting power roles that James Mulder sees in Christopher Marlowe's epic poetry. Fetishism in Freud's account is erotic investment displaced from its "proper" destination (for Freud's subject is the aspirationally cisheterosexual male): a woman's vagina, which, in Freud's narrative, is so primally horrifying in its difference from the penis as to divert desire into the fetish object, a fantasy substi-tute phallus. (This is told, and, somehow, often read, as an utterly *straight* story.) One of the anxieties transmitted in the concept of fetishism, par-

---

5. Sigmund Freud, "Fetishism," in *The Complete Psychological Works of Sigmund Freud*, vol. 21, trans. James Strachey (London: Hogarth Press, 1927), 152.

ticularly as it attaches to kink practices, is that the naked human body may not magnetize the totality of sexual desire — that artificial, made things, prostheses, technologies, accessories (ornamental and functional), gear, and paraphernalia might hold more erotic attraction. Fetishism enacts a challenge to heteropatriarchy (for anyone can wield these things), anthropocentrism, and the "natural," which is why I locate a kink methodology in these essays' sybaritic attention to the material things and substances in texts: Beatrice Bradley's body fluid spatter analysis, and Heather Frazier on the politics and erotics of urine.

Kink method, like queer method, makes a case for the radical pleasures, and generative social potentials, of practices — and performances of practices — deemed sinful, criminal, or pathological. Some (not all) of these essays offer such reparative readings of stigmatized phenomena, like cuckoldry in Erika Lyn Carbonara's and Nathaniel Leonard's essays, the interracial erotic pairings Kirk Quinsland analyzes in Shakespeare, or the specter of public sex Erin Kelly raises in *The Taming of the Shrew*.

The essays in this volume are wise to the limitations of a model of human "subjectivity" or "social identity" that presumes a coherent, internally motivated locus of agency, in the early modern period or indeed any other. Kink methodology contains the knowledge that erotic pleasures, preferences, and power dynamics — indeed, selves — are, perhaps more often than we allow (and not just in the Renaissance), constituted by and in *doing*, in physical practices. One of the interventions that kink method brings to the study of sexuality is this (new) materialist understanding of eroticism as constituted through the continual, dynamic enactment of material phenomena in space-time. Kink method is aware that what happens — the iterated movements, gestures, expressions, and exchanges among bodies, forces, and materials in the world — is what *makes* us, and the world.

Yet at the same time, a kink methodology interrogates what is left out by a strict historicist, archival-evidence-or-it-didn't-happen model of sexuality, as the kinky readers in this volume ebulliently demonstrate. Kink analysis in fact torpedoes homogenized or prescriptive historical notions of sexual normativity. All of these essays demonstrate, in different ways, that attempts to define kink as a departure from retroactively imagined statistical "norms" of sexuality do not hold up in early modern archives — and maybe do not hold in any time, for seemingly minoritarian kinky dynamics prove again and again to be all too constitutive of the larger erotic and aesthetic forms that make up a genre, or a culture. They all must contend with the complicated, by no means "straight"-forward, role of the phallus, recalling Eve Kosofsky Sedgwick's argument that decidedly other-than-hetero-erotic energy, transacted through form, fancy, and materials, natural and artificial, is a constitutive force shaping English literature itself.[6] After all, so much of what constitutes early modern sexuality *as represented in literary archives* can and should be — and will be, thanks to this volume — called kinky, including hyper-realized portrayals of "normative" patriarchal social hierarchies, kicked into the gear of kink (or camp). In holding together this performative, materially enacted model of subjecthood and an expansive attitude toward reading for desire across historical difference, kink method intervenes in a refreshing way in our field's critical debates about the alterity of the past, and how to study sexuality before coherent sexual identities, under very different normative and disciplinary regimes, etc. Through a kink lens, these historiographic observations look very different from, say, David Halperin's model of early modern sexuality,[7] because kink method attends to the *eros* inhering in aesthetic dynamics of power, desire, and style, which do not necessarily correspond to social categories.

Finally, perhaps most interestingly, something I would call a *kink formalism* (in conversation with Michelle Dowd and Lara Dodds's notion of

6. See Eve Kosofsky Sedgwick, *Between Men: English Literature and Male Homosocial Desire* (New York: Columbia University Press, 1985).
7. See David Halperin, *One Hundred Years of Homosexuality* (Abingdon, UK: Routledge, 1989); and Sedgwick, *Epistemology*, 46–48.

feminist formalism) emerges from these essays' attunement to the rhythms of the scene: the pace of plotting, the rhythms of a scene's blocking and stage directions.[8] A kink interpretive practice is honed on exquisite attunement to who does what, when, with what, and to whom, and to how it feels *in time*. Much of this collection is about drama, a genre whose literal scenes lend their structure to the BDSM *scene* of erotic play. But a kink reading practice also finds scene-level dynamics in the fantasy space-timescapes of poetry and frothing prose treatises. The essays here cover a wide range of scales, sizes, or scopes in terms of their formal objects of analysis, or what aspect of the text the author is examining as kink, or with a kink methodology. The fine details of bodily acts and substances come in for analysis (Bradley; Frazier), as well as specific power dynamics (Carbonara; Kelly; Leonard; Mulder). But these writers also locate kinkiness in mechanisms of literary and/or theatrical representation (Bradley; Mulder), turns in the figuration of affect (Filo; Knoll), and the overarching dramatic power dynamics of a text (Quinsland; Leonard).

Think Kink

So, can it then be said that attunement to kink makes for superior literary criticism? This is not a facetious claim: kink is an aesthetic phenomenon. It can be defined as "sex, aestheticized": a primal human drive elevated to the level of an aesthetic form. Kink shares with literary reading itself a fanatical attention to the made thing. And kink method is especially able to see how the idiosyncratic form of a text dramatizes an aesthetics of relationality — human and other-than-human, erotic and athwart of the erotic. This kinky form of attention alights on scenes of literary production — as in Beatrice Bradley's analysis of the poetics

---

8. See Lara Dodds and Michelle M. Dowd, eds., *Feminist Formalism and Early Modern Women's Writing: Readings, Conversations, Pedagogies* (Lincoln, NE: University of Nebraska Press, 2022).

of fluid on skin, or Nathaniel Leonard's provocative claim that revenge tragedy is a cuckolding-kink genre — to illuminate how texts themselves are created according to communally used and understood codes. Poetry coteries and playing companies, like kink subcultures, have their in-group vocabularies and customs, the frameworks that shape the new iterations of the form. Texts, like kinky sex "scenes," are made: made of formal poetic and generic conventions, conceits, and meta-theatrical devices. If kink is about the style, the form, the aesthetic structure of both literary texts and social rituals, and of social rituals *as figured in* literary genres, kink method might offer a new theoretical angle on the old, complicated question of just how a literary text is related to the culture that produced it. And if, as I argued at the beginning of this piece, both kinky sex and scholarly conferencing share the structure of performance, there is an oblique case to be made that writing and publishing poetry, or writing, acting in, producing, and/or printing a play are, in different ways, structurally kinky enterprises, animated by collective, convention-bound aesthetic forms and distinctly sadomasochistic pleasures/pains. I would even go so far as to suggest that literary criticism, and in some ways all of literary academia, exists in a kinky power relation, bound by envy, anxiety, identification, dependence, disavowal, exploitation, pleasure, and pain, to these arts of cultural production.

These essays' attention to the *languages* of power exchange, affective solicitation, and other kink dynamics in texts has made me hear new valences in some of our stalwart critical metaphors. In fact, this collection makes visible — to me, and, I assume, to many of its readers, for the first time — a submerged kink heritage inflecting the long-standing critical vocabulary used in politically engaged literary criticism after Michel Foucault, particularly around gender and sexuality. For instance, think about how often scholarship describes the *constraints* imposed by material conditions, patriarchy, heteronormativity, racial classification, state power, class norms, etc., and subjects' *resistance to* those constraints, their struggling against what binds them, or their *agency* in twisting (partially) free. This bondage metaphor (for that's what it is) conditions, via the ropes, cords, or chains of its vehicle, the framing questions we learn to ask about the social and ideological dynamics in a work of literature: What forms did resistance to hegemonic constraints take? How tight were the constraints, or was there play? How effective was the resistance? How were the constraints loosened and/or re-tightened in the end?

I think, not incidentally, that something has been lost from this metaphor (which is everywhere in Foucault's early work, in *Discipline and Punish* and in *The History of Sexuality*) in the course of its widespread adoption by Anglophone literary studies. As Foucault uses it, *constraint* (*contrainte*) is almost always a force acting in a dialectic with something else, usually with an incitement of some kind: constrained *to* tell, constrained *to* speak, constrained by obligations to act and by relational systems. It's a dynamic in a larger system of active and passive dynamics; it is not unilateral, or definitive. Constraint in Foucault is *generative,* not preventive: of energies, processes, discourses, and desires. Through his lifelong participation in the gay BDSM/leather scenes of Paris and San Francisco, Foucault knew the pleasure and generativity of constraint: both the literal experience of bondage and the psychic, social, and conventional constraints that constitute a sexual subculture and one's participation in it. I wonder how our field's habits around the use of *constraint* in Marxist/materialist, feminist, etc. literary criticism might have been impoverished by a "vanilla" reading of Foucault, in which the salient feature of *constraint* is that it is imposed without the desire or participation of the constrained, and the emphasis is on the agency it forecloses rather than on the discursive and aesthetic forms it bodies forth.

In this light, Foucault's *repressive hypothesis,* as well as the model of sexuality he offers in its place, can be re-claimed as a constitutively kink theory, in that it acknowledges and calls out the perverse pleasures on display in the story we love to tell ourselves, not only in what gets called the *repression* or disciplining of sex, but in the (arguably kinky) popular investment in a narrative of sexual *repression* versus *freedom*: "Why do we say, with so much passion and so much resentment against our most recent past, against our present, and against ourselves, that we are repressed? By what spiral did we come to affirm that sex is negated? What led us to show, ostentatiously, that sex is something we hide, to say it is something we silence?"[9] It bears thinking about how the "straight" or "vanilla" reception of Foucault may have conditioned not only critics' understanding of this *repressive hypothesis*, but our received understanding of the much more complex story he tells instead, with its emphasis on the pleasures and identities incited by proliferating sexual *constraints* and their discourses. Kink theory, I would follow Foucault so far as to say, posits a uniquely multivalent model of power itself, alive to the pleasures of pain and of power, in both exerting and being subject to it.

Even besides this nuanced theorization of power, the kink literary methods on display in these essays turn received critical metaphors of *freedom* versus *constraint* over and inside out. Along with psychoanalytic thinkers like Adam Philips and Eve Kosofsky Sedgwick, kink methodology points out the countless dynamics besides the push-pull of constraint versus resistance in which humans' relations to sex, gender, or social norms can be figured.[10] But kink method also opens up a universe of variety and complication *within* the critical vocabulary of bondage and constraint. There is more than one kind of constraint, and more than one kind of resistance. More than one kind of control, and more than one kind of submission to control. These terms do not self-evidently or monolithically explain anything. The very definition of aesthetics I

9. Michel Foucault, *The History of Sexuality, Volume 1: An Introduction*, trans. Robert Hurley (New York: Pantheon, 1978), 8–9.
10. Adam Philips, *Unforbidden Pleasures* (New York: Farrar, Straus and Giroux, 2015); Eve Kosofsky Sedgwick, *Touching Feeling: Affect, Pedagogy, Performativity* (Durham, N.C.: Duke University Press, 2003).

applied to kink above — innovation within constraint — understands the constraints of genre and form as *productive* of the aesthetic object.

We Have Always Been Kinky

The Introduction to this collection, as well as several of the essays, interrogate what the study of kink brings to early modern literature: what kink readings can illuminate about gender, sexual behaviors, social structures, and genres in the period. But, in this textual act of *Aftercare*, I want to devote equal care and attention to processing what these essays have shown me about kink — how inquiring into kink dynamics in early modern literature enriches our concept of what kink is and does.

1) Kink is not only a quintessentially aesthetic practice; it is in large part a specifically literary, textual phenomenon. Kink is disseminated as a set of forms through genre-bending written texts, used in scenes of auto- and alloerotic gratification and community building, in addition to their intended purposes. This collection draws on a venerable, often submerged kink genealogy of writing in queer theory: from Foucault to Gayle Rubin, Leo Bersani, and Patrick Califia (to name only the most "out," visible vanguard), and on through Amber Jamilla Musser, Christina Sharpe, and Ariane Cruz. Kink's theoretical heritage of course extends back to Freud, Richard von Krafft-Ebing, and Leopold von Sacher-Masoch. Kink's literary genealogy, which includes the Marquis de Sade, Angela Carter, Dorothy Allison, and Samuel Delany, has also been extended here to consider John Lyly (in Gillian Knoll's essay) and Robert Herrick (in Gina Filo's) on the same map, along with the canonical poets and playwrights — Shakespeare, Marlowe, Thomas Middleton, Francis Beaumont and John Fletcher — whose figuration of bodies, affects, and power dynamics these essayists ask us to see anew.

2) Both Erika Carbonara's reading of cuckoldry in *A Chaste Maid in Cheapside* and Erin Kelly's treatment of publicity and shame in *The Taming of the Shrew* show that kink is a collective phenomenon, constituted

in a community, a culture. However, a kink analytic gets especially interesting where the scene of literary production being analyzed is a solitary one (paging Gina Filo on Robert Herrick!). To paraphrase Bishop George Berkeley's question about trees in the forest with nobody by to perceive them, if a kinky impulse forms within a person's fancy and no one is there to recognize it and participate in it, does it make a kink? Can a writer belong to the kink archive if they're alone, and *not* physically doing anything kinky, or even sexual? Sedgwick would say, in no uncertain terms, absolutely: that "many people have their richest mental/emotional involvement with sexual acts that they don't do, or even don't *want* to do"[11] — and she should know; Sedgwick herself identified as a "sexual pervert" only via her elaborate sadomasochistic fantasy life.[12] Fantasies are as much a part of culture as acts; a culture fashioned from fantasies and realized in textual forms is still a culture, through which readers can recognize themselves and others. The kinky readings explored in this collection are, to me, wayward queer descendants of Sedgwick's, alive to the same "almost astrologically lush plurality"[13] of overlapping orders and levels of meaning that Sedgwick honors in psychoanalytic thought, and aware of the complex ways in which fantasy, even unconscious fantasy, can be brought into signification.

3) Kirk Quinsland's, Nathaniel Leonard's, and Erin Kelly's essays show that kink can be, in a very substantive way, about *pain*: intensities of bodily, psychic, social, and historical pain — shame, hurt, wounds, suffering — that cannot be folded into any sanitized notion of pleasure. Echoing Heather Love's intervention in *Feeling Backward: Loss and the Politics of Queer History*, this volume gives the lie to the idea that liberation necessarily follows from "sex positivity," or that trauma can be effectively rewritten by a politics of pleasure. One of the things kink method must

11. Sedgwick, *Epistemology*, 25, emphasis in the original.
12. See Eve Kosofsky Sedgwick, *A Dialogue on Love* (New York: Beacon Press, 2000).
13. Sedgwick, *Epistemology*, 23.

contend with is that, all the best practices of consent notwithstanding, kink may not be essentially "safe," because no form of living, making, or relating in this world is safe.

4) Beatrice Bradley's and Heather Frazier's essays show that kink is about materialization, in a very literal, ontological sense: how matter is materialized, and how matter functions as a sign system. Bradley's close reading of the "money shot" gives a radical new gloss to "fluid" as a critical term, commonly used to modify *identity* or *sexuality*. Here bodies themselves are fluid(s), erotic investments are fluid(s), and energy economies are fluid(s). Distinctions between individual bodies or identities are de-emphasized by kink's focus on the circulation of energy in and through matter. Kink is instead about the materialization, in and with bodies, of pleasures, power, and affective entanglements — indeed, the materialization of energy, known in physics to be consubstantial with matter itself. In fact, I would go so far as to say that kink literary analysis undoes a dualistic bright line between energy and matter, which is to say, between the intangible and the tangible.

5) Erika Carbonara's, James Mulder's, and Kirk Quinsland's engagements with role-playing — both as an activity depicted in early modern texts and as a fantasmatic practice of reading and spectatorship, through which texts are used, within a culture and across time — show that kink is constituted by imitation and replay, by a perverse return to the scene where gratification has been found in the past. Thus kink time is not one-way or linear, but recursive. Though, like all performance, kink is defined by a special ordering of time, kink temporality is specifically attentive to *ends* — not only to climax but to denouement (aftercare!), return, and repetition.

If *aftercare* is a way of integrating the intensity of a BDSM event into one's being and re-entering ordinary time as a changed self, and thereby, perhaps, in a changed world, I want to conclude by framing some of the big questions — two about our scholarly field and two about the politics of kink — that remain yet unanswered by this collection, in hopes that readers might improvise their own roles to play in this critical scene.

1) What is *sexuality* as an object of study, and how does it diverge from *kink* or from *queerness* as objects of study or analytic methods? If what I've discussed here are things that kink readings of early modern literature make newly visible about kink, are these also things that kink readings of early modern literature make visible about sexuality *tout court*? If not, why not?

2) What is distinct about literary archives? What relationships do literary works of different genres bear to the thick, heterogeneous life of a culture (much — but not all — of which leaves other kinds of archival traces)? What is different about the literary critic's gaze, methods, and act of reading when one is looking at a literary text in order to try to find out about the culture that produced it versus reading it for other reasons (e.g., to find out what's happening in a poem)? (Is there any such thing as analyzing a literary text "for its own sake"?)

3) What is the role of intentionality in scenes of social and sexual relation, and what is the relationship of intent to consent? Conscious, deliberate, articulated, and shared intention is central to kink ethical frameworks, as a precondition for participation and a basis of trust. But good intentions have been thoroughly exposed as inadequate, indeed as a cover and excuse for perpetrating harm, in the analysis of racism.[14] Literary criticism, as well, tells a story of its progress away from the *intentional fallacy*, toward analyzing what's made and done over what was intended.[15] Does intention have a special value in scenes of sexual relation as opposed to other genres of scene? Is it more important and/or more legible? Pleas of the rapist/harasser's lack of intent to harm are a commonplace of rape culture, despite how clearly it can be perceived by

14. See Ibram X. Kendi, *Stamped from the Beginning: The Definitive History of Racist Ideas in America* (New York: Bold Type Books, 2016).
15. See W.K. Wimsatt, Jr., and M.C. Beardsley, "The Intentional Fallacy," *The Sewanee Review* 54, no. 3 (July–September 1946): 468–88.

the person being harmed. (As Oliver Wendell Holmes said, "Even a dog distinguishes between being stumbled over and being kicked"[16]). How do these questions complicate the task of reading for consent — and for violation — in early modern texts, without flattening out consent's extreme historical contingency? And relatedly: How complete can consent be in a world structured by such relentless inequities?

4) And finally: Why does kink matter? The trans-historical fact is that all of these kinky ways of seeing, inclinations, predilections, and practices are marginalized because they are a threat to the delusional, violent dictates of cisheteropatriarchy. Kink queries and mocks and sends up and détournes and re-writes the violence cisheteropatriarchy levies against those it deems to be *not* patriarchal men (women, queers, and gender nonconforming people) — but also the violence that cisheteropatriarchy demands *of* straight, cis men. Kink opens a portal into forms of love, vulnerability, and collectivity that patriarchy forbids for those men. At this terrifying moment of upsurging state persecution of sexual and gender minorities by Republican lawmakers, when anti-trans, anti-gay, and anti-kink rhetorics are actively, deliberately being muddled together and folded in with paranoid rhetorics of child sexual abuse in order to license even further state and mob violence, the long historical view of kink explored by the essays in this volume is uniquely important. Critical lenses derived from marginalized desires and sexual practices — like queer theory, asexuality studies, and now kink method — help us to see both the through lines and the sea changes as the discourse of sexuality keeps morphing into new forms. *Cuck*, meaning *cuckold*, as a case in point, circulates today as a slur in the misogynistic and homophobic lexicon of *men's rights activist* culture, which holds up a version of patriarchal masculinity defined by domination of women *and* of other men —

---

16. Oliver Wendell Holmes, Jr., "Lecture 1: Early Forms of Liability," *The Common Law* (Boston, 1881; Project Gutenberg, December 2000), https://www.gutenberg.org/files/2449/2449-h/2449-h.htm.

and which increasingly serves as a gateway to recruit young men into far-right and white supremacist politics.

This collection writes toward a utopian scene, one which may live only in our imaginations, in which the power and reach of violent cisheteropatriarchy — the entire complex of misogyny, cissexism, queer phobia, whore phobia, ableism, white supremacy, classism, and colonialism — is shriveling and shrinking, with fewer and fewer people buying its false promises of entitlement and impunity in exchange for abiding by its narrow dictates. *The Kinky Renaissance* participates in the collective task, which I pray will continue after all of us contributors are dead, of peeling and chipping away at cisheteropatriarchy, piercing its facade and knocking out so many of its structural joints that, someday, where it sits, irrelevant and exposed in all its ugliness and hypocrisy, no one can imagine why anyone ever wanted anything to do with it. If I may be so bold as to invoke Octavia Butler's futurist incantation, by way of setting my — and this volume's — intention in this fight: "So be it! See to it!"[17]

---

17. Octavia Butler, notes on writing, "I shall be a bestselling writer...," 1988, commonplace book, Henry E. Huntington Library, Octavia E. Butler papers, Accession number mssOEB, https://huntington.org/sites/default/files/styles/image_gallery/public/photo-gallery/octavia-butler_4_0.jpg?itok=X8mjXBDC.

Bibliography

This selective bibliography is not exhaustive of all the sources cited in individual chapters, each of which provides full citations for their sources in the notes. Instead, we have assembled here both primary and secondary sources from the chapters that we hope will be helpful for scholars interested in pursuing future work in premodern kink studies.

Primary Sources

Banister, John. *The Historie of Man*. London, 1578.

Beaumont, Francis and John Fletcher. *The Captain*. Edited by L. A. Beaurline. In *The Dramatic Works in the Beaumont and Fletcher Canon*, vol. 1, edited by Fredson Bowers, 541–670. Cambridge, UK: Cambridge University Press, 1966.

———. *The Maid's Tragedy*. Edited by T. W. Craik. Manchester: Manchester University Press, 1988.

"The Catologue of Contented Cuckolds: Or, A Loving Society of Confessing Brethren of the Forked Order, etc. who being met together in a Tavern, declar'd each Man his Condition, resolving to be contented, and drown'd Melancholly in a Glass of Necktar. To the Tune of, Fond Boy, etc. Or, Love's a sweet Passion, etc." Little-Britain: Printed for J.C. London, 1685.

"Cuckolds all a-Row. / Or, A Summons issued out from the Master-Cuckolds and Wardens of Fumblers- / Hall; directed to all Henpeckt and Hornified Tradesmen in and about the City of London, / requiring their appearance at Cuckolds-Point. Concluding with a pleasant new Song." Printed for R. Kell, 1685–1688.

A Dialogue Between a Married Lady and a Maid. London, 1740.

Donne, John. "The Comparison." In *The Complete Poems of John Donne*, edited by Robin Robbins. New York: Routledge, 2013.

Fletcher, John. *The Tamer Tamed*. Edited by Lucy Munro. London: Methuen Drama, 2010.

————. *The Wild-Goose Chase a Comedie.* London: Printed for Humpherey Moseley, 1652. Early English Books Online. https://www.proquest.com/books/wild-goose-chase-comedie-as-hath-been-acted-with/docview/2264211006/se-2.

"A General Summons for those Belonging to the Hen-Peck'd Frigate, to Appear at Cuckolds-Point, on the 18th. of this Instant October. Licensed According to Order. Your Presence is Required, and are Hereby Lawfully Summoned (as Belonging to the Hen-Peck'd-Frigate) to Appear at Cuckolds-Point (being the Antient Place of our Rendezvous) on the 18th. of this Instant October; […] Thomas Cann't-be-Quiet Beadle [Ladies of London.]. London: Printed for J. Deacon, 1672–1702.

Gerard, John. *The herball or General historie of plantes.* London: Printed by Adam Islip Ioice Norton and Richard Whitakers, 1633. Early English Books Online. https://www.proquest.com/books/herball-generall-historie-plantes-gathered-iohn/docview/2240902621/se-2.

Harrington, John. *A Nevv Discourse of a Stale Subiect, Called the Metamorphosis of Aiax.* London: Imprinted by Richard Field, 1596. Early English Books Online. https://www.proquest.com/books/nevv-discourse-stale-subiect-called-metamorphosis/docview/2248584507/se-2.

Jonson, Ben. *Love Restored.* In *Ben Jonson: Selected Masques*, edited by Stephen Orgel, 116–27. New Haven, CT: Yale University Press, 1970.

"Kissing his Mistris." *Poems by several hands, and on several occasions collected by N[ahum] Tate.* London, 1685.

Levens, Peter. *A Right Profitable Booke for all Diseases Called, the Pathway to Health.* London: Printed by I. Roberts for Edward VVhite, 1596. Early English Books Online, http://www.proquest.com/books/right-profitable-booke-all-diseases-called/docview/2240892214/se-2.

Lyly, John. *The Woman in the Moon (The Revels Plays).* Edited by Leah Scragg. Manchester: Manchester University Press, 2006.

Marowitz, Charles. *The Shrew (Freely Adapted from William Shakespeare's "The Taming of the Shrew").* London: Calder and Boyars, 1975.

Miles, Abraham. "Mirth for Citizens: Or, A Comedy for the Country." Printed for P. Brooksby, c. 1672–1696. English Broadside Ballad Archive. http://ebba.ds.lib.ucdavis.edu/ballad/37229/xml.

"Poor Anthony's Complaint / And Lamentation against his miseries of / marriage, meeting with a scolding wife." Printed for J. Conyers at the

Black Raven in Fetter-lane, c. 1662–1692. English Broadside Ballad Archive. https://ebba.english.ucsb.edu/ballad/31889/xml.

Rowley, William and Thomas Middleton. *The Changeling.* Edited and annotated by Douglas Bruster. In *Thomas Middleton: The Collected Works,* edited by Gary Taylor and John Lavagnino, 1632–78. Oxford, UK: Oxford University Press, 2007.

Shakespeare, William. *Macbeth.* In *The Norton Shakespeare,* edited by Stephen Greenblatt, Walter Cohen, Jean E. Howard, and Katharine Eisaman Maus, 2564–2618. New York: W. W. Norton & Company, 1997.

———. *The Taming of the Shrew.* Edited by Barbara Hodgdon. London: Arden Shakespeare, 2010.

———. *The Taming of the Shrew: Texts and Contexts.* Edited by Frances E. Dolan. New York: Bedford, 1996.

———. *Titus Andronicus.* Edited by Jonathan Bates. New York: Bloomsbury Publishing, 1995.

———. "Venus and Adonis." In *Shakespeare's Poems,* edited by Katherine Duncan-Jones and H. R. Woodhouse, 125–229. New York: Bloomsbury Publishing, 2007.

Stanley, Thomas. "The Enjoyment." *Poems by Thomas Stanley, Esquire.* London, 1651.

The Taming of a Shrew. Edited by Stephen Roy Miller. Cambridge, UK: Cambridge University Press, 1998.

Tasso, Torquato. *Gerusalemme Liberata.* Milan: Ulrico Hoepli, 1898.

Taylor, John. *Bull, Beare, and Horse, Cut, Curtaile, and Longtaile. VVith Tales, and Tales of Buls, Clenches, and Flashes ....* London: Printed by M. Parsons, for Henry Gosson, 1638. Early English Books Online. https://www.proquest.com/books/bull-beare-horse-cut-curtaile-longtaile-vvith/docview/2240892079/se-2.

T. R. *Hey for Horn Fair, the General Market of England, Or, Room for Cuckolds being a Merry Progress of Nine several Sorts of Cuckolds here Discovered ...: Full of Mirth and Merry Discourse, Newly Presented from Horn Fair to all the Merry Good Fellows in England : To which is Added, the Marriage of Jockie and Jenny* [Hey for Horn Fair. Room for cuckolds. Marriage of Jockie and Jenny.]. London: Printed for F. Coles, T. Vere, and J. Wright, 1674.

The Welsh-Mens Glory, Or, the Famous Victories of the Antient Britans Obtain'd upon St. David's Day. London: Printed by Thomas Dawks, his Majesties

British printer, at the west-end of T', 1684. Early English Books Online. https://www.proquest.com/books/welsh-mens-glory-famous-victories-antient-britans/docview/2240899958/se-2.

Secondary Sources

"Ace Week 101: Aces and Sex or Kink." The Ace and Aro Advocacy Project. October 28, 2021. https://www.taaap.org/2021/10/28/ace-week-21-aces-sex-kink.

Akhimie, Patricia. *Shakespeare and the Cultivation of Difference: Race and Conduct in the Early Modern World.* Abingdon, UK: Routledge, 2018.

Alfar, Cristina Leon. "Staging the Feminine Performance of Desire: Masochism in *The Maid's Tragedy.*" *Papers on Language and Literature* 31, no. 3 (1995): 313–33.

Amin, Kadji. *Disturbing Attachments: Genet, Modern Pederasty, and Queer History.* Durham, NC: Duke University Press, 2017.

Anderson, Judith. *Reading the Allegorical Intertext: Chaucer, Spenser, Shakespeare, Milton.* New York: Fordham University Press, 2008.

Angel, Katherine. *Tomorrow Sex Will Be Good Again: Women and Desire in the Age of Consent.* London: Verso Books, 2021.

Arvas, Abdulhamit. "Leander in the Ottoman Mediterranean: The Homoerotics of Abduction in the Global Renaissance." *English Literary Renaissance* 51, no. 1 (2020): 31–62. https://doi.org/10.1086/711601.

Bailey, Amanda. "Occupy Macbeth: Masculinity and Political Masochism in *Macbeth.*" In *Violent Masculinities: Male Aggression in Early Modern Texts and Culture*, edited by Jennifer Feather and Catherine E. Thomas, 191–212. New York: Palgrave Macmillan, 2013.

Baker, Moira P. "'The Uncanny Stranger on Display': The Female Body in Sixteenth- and Seventeenth-Century Love Poetry." *South Atlantic Review* 56, no. 2 (1991): 7–25.

Barret, J. K. *Untold Futures: Time and Literary Culture in Renaissance England.* Ithaca, NY: Cornell University Press, 2017.

Bates, Catherine. *Masculinity, Gender, and Identity in the English Renaissance Lyric.* Cambridge, UK: Cambridge University Press, 2007.

Bauer, Robin. *Queer BDSM Intimacies: Critical Consent and Pushing Boundaries.* London: Palgrave Macmillan, 2014.

Bergeron, David. "Fletcher's *The Woman's Prize*, Transgression, and *Querelle des Femmes*." *Medieval and Renaissance Drama in England* 8 (1996): 146–64. http://www.jstor.org/stable/24322255.

Beringer, Alison L. *The Sight of Semiramis: Medieval and Early Modern Narratives of the Babylonian Queen*. Tempe, AZ: ACMRS Press, 2016.

Berlant, Lauren and Lee Edelman. *Sex, or the Unbearable*. Durham: Duke University Press, 2014.

Berlant, Lauren and Michael Warner. "Sex in Public." *Critical Inquiry* 24, no. 2 (1998): 547–66. https://doi.org/10.1086/448884.

Blake, Liza. "Early Modern Asexuality (and Aromanticism)." *The Asexuality and Aromanticism Bibliography*. September 2022. https://acearobiblio.com/2022/08/22/early-modern-asexuality-and-aromanticism/.

Boose, Lynda. "Scolding Bridles and Bridling Scolds: Taming the Woman's Unruly Member." *Shakespeare Quarterly* 42, no. 1 (1991): 179–213. https://doi.org/10.2307/2870547.

Bourdieu, Pierre. *Distinction: A Social Critique of the Judgement of Taste*. Translated by Richard Nice. Cambridge, MA: Harvard University Press, 1984.

Braden, Gordon. "Hero and Leander in Bed (and the Morning After)." *English Literary Renaissance* 45, no. 2 (2015): 205–30. https://doi.org/10.1111/1475-6757.12046.

Bray, Alan. *The Friend*. Chicago: University of Chicago Press, 2003.

———. *Homosexuality in Renaissance England*. London: Gay Men's Press, 1982.

Bredbeck, Gregory. *Sodomy and Interpretation: From Marlowe to Milton*. Ithaca, NY: Cornell University Press, 1991.

Britton, Dennis Austin. *Becoming Christian: Race, Reformation, and Early Modern English Romance*. New York: Fordham University Press, 2014.

Bromley, James. *Clothing and Queer Style in Early Modern English Drama*. Oxford: Oxford University Press, 2021.

———. *Intimacy and Sexuality in the Age of Shakespeare*. Cambridge, UK: Cambridge University Press, 2012.

Brown, Georgia. *Redefining Elizabethan Literature*. Cambridge, UK: Cambridge University Press, 2004.

Brown, Pamela Allen. *Better a Shrew Than a Sheep: Women, Drama, and the Culture of Jest in Early Modern England*. Ithaca, NY: Cornell University Press, 2003. https://doi.org/10.7591/9781501722363.

Bruster, Douglas. "The Horn of Plenty: Cuckoldry and Capital in the Drama of the Age of Shakespeare." *Studies in English Literature, 1500–1900* 30, no. 2 (1990): 195–215. https://doi.org/10.2307/450514.

Bullard, Angela D. "Tempering the Intemperate in Spenser's Bower of Bliss." *Spenser Studies* 31–32 (2018): 167–87. https://doi.org/10.1086/695575.

Cahill, Patricia. "The Play of Skin in *The Changeling*." *postmedieval: a journal of medieval cultural studies* 3, no. 4 (2012): 391–406. https://doi.org/10.1057/pmed.2012.26.

Califia, Patrick. "Public Sex." 1982. Reprint in *Public Sex: The Culture of Radical Sex*. Pittsburgh PA: Cleis Press, 1994.

———. *Speaking Sex to Power: The Politics of Queer Sex*. Jersey City, NJ: Cleis Press, 2001.

Campana, Joseph. *The Pain of Reformation: Spenser, Vulnerability, and the Ethics of Masculinity*. New York: Fordham University Press, 2012.

Carlström, Charlotta. "Spiritual Experiences and Altered States of Consciousness: Parallels between BDSM and Christianity." *Sociological Forum* 33, no. 4 (2018): 749–66. https://doi.org/10.1177/1363460720964035.

Cefalu, Paul. "The Burdens of Mind Reading in Shakespeare's *Othello*: A Cognitive and Psychoanalytic Approach to Iago's Theory of Mind." *Shakespeare Quarterly* 64, no. 3 (2013): 265–94. https://www.jstor.org/stable/24778472.

Chang, Jerry Yung-Ching. "The Pornoethnography of *Boys in the Sand*: Fetishisms of Race and Class in the 1970s Gay Fire Island Pines." *Women's Studies Quarterly* 43, no. 3 (2015): 101–15. https://www.jstor.org/stable/43958553.

Chapman, Matthieu. *Anti-Black Racism in Early Modern English Drama: The Other "Other."* Abingdon, UK: Routledge, 2016.

Cheng, Anne Anlin. *Second Skin: Josephine Baker & the Modern Surface*. Oxford: Oxford University Press, 2010.

———. "Shine: On Race, Glamour, and the Modern." *PMLA* 126, no. 4 (2011): 1022–41. https://doi.org/10.1632/pmla.2011.126.4.1022.

Chess, Simone. *Male-to-Female Crossdressing in Early Modern English Literature: Gender, Performance, and Queer Relations*. Abingdon, UK: Routledge, 2019.

Chess, Simone, Colby Gordon, and Will Fisher, eds. "Early Modern Trans Studies." Special issue, *Journal for Early Modern Cultural Studies* 19, no. 4 (2019).

Christina, Greta. "The Ethics of Public Sex." *Greta Christina's Blog.* October 9, 2009. https://gretachristina.typepad.com/greta_christinas_weblog/2009/10/ethics-of-public-sex-1.html.

Clare, Janet. "'She's Turned Fury': Women Transmogrified in Revenge Plays." In *Revenge and Gender in Classical, Medieval and Renaissance Literature*, edited by Lesel Dawson and Fiona McHardy, 221–36. Edinburgh: Edinburgh University Press, 2018.

Clark, Sandra. "The Economics of Marriage in the Broadside Ballad." *Journal of Popular Culture* 36, no. 1 (2002): 119–33. https://doi.org/10.1111/1540-5931.00034.

Clarke, Mary Cowden. "Katherine and Bianca: The Shrew, and the Demure." In *The Girlhood of Shakespeare's Heroines in a Series of Tales*, 95–184. New York: A.C. Armstrong, 1881.

Cole, Samantha. "'The Money Shot': How Porn Made Cum So Valuable." *Vice.* September 30, 2020. https://www.vice.com/en/article/bv8q45/history-of-the-money-shot-cum-fetish.

Cooney, Helen. "Guyon and His Palmer: Spenser's Emblem of Temperance." *The Review of English Studies* 51, no. 202 (May 2000): 169–92. https://doi.org/10.1093/res/51.202.169.

Corcoran, Kellye. "Cuckoldry as Performance, 1675–1715." *Studies in English Literature, 1500–1900* 52, no. 3 (2012): 543–59. https://doi.org/10.1353/sel.2012.0029.

Cowart, Leigh. *Hurts So Good: The Science and Culture of Pain on Purpose.* New York: Public Affairs, 2019.

Craig, Elaine. "Laws of Desire: The Political Morality of Public Sex." *McGill Law Journal* 54, no. 2 (2009), 355–85. https://doi.org/10.7202/038658ar.

Craven, Alice Mikal. "Representing Semiramis in Shakespeare and Calderón." *Shakespeare* 4, no. 2 (2008): 157–69. https://doi.org/10.1080/17450910802083443.

Crocker, Holly. "The Tamer as *Shrewd* in John Fletcher's *The Woman's Prize: Or, The Tamer Tamed.*" *Studies in English Literature, 1500–1900* 51, no. 2 (2011): 409–26. https://www.jstor.org/stable/23028082.

Cruz, Ariane. *The Color of Kink: Black Women, BDSM, and Pornography*. Durham, NC: Duke University Press, 2014.

Daniel, Drew. "'Let me have judgment, and the Jew his will': Melancholy Epistemology and Masochistic Fantasy in *The Merchant of Venice*." *Shakespeare Quarterly* 61, no. 2 (2010): 206–34. https://doi.org/10.1353/shq.0.0144.

Daniell, David. "The Good Marriage of Katherine and Petruchio." *Shakespeare Survey* 37 (1984): 23–32. https://doi.org/10.1017/ccol0521267013.003.

Darcy, Robert F. "'Under my hands … a double duty': Printing and Pressing Marlowe's *Hero and Leander*." *Journal for Early Modern Cultural Studies* 2, no. 2 (2002): 26–56. https://doi.org/10.1353/jem.2002.0015.

Davis, Imani. "Kink." *Poem-a-Day*. Academy of American Poets. February 3, 2023. https://poets.org/poem/kink?mc_cid=031c76dab8&mc_eid=307c62b1f7.

Dean, Tim. "Afterword: The Raw and the Fucked." In *Raw: PrEP, Pedagogy, and the Politics of Barebacking*, edited by Ricky Varghese, 285–304. London: Zed Books Ltd, 2019.

———. *Unlimited Intimacy: Reflections on the Subculture of Barebacking*. Chicago: University of Chicago Press, 2009.

Deleuze, Gilles. *Coldness and Cruelty*. In *Masochism: "Coldness and Cruelty" and "Venus in Furs,"* by Gilles Deleuze and Leopold von Sacher-Masoch, translated by Jean McNeil, 9–138. New York: Zone Books, 1989.

Desai, Adhaar Noor. "Scientific Misrule: Francis Bacon at Gray's Inn." *Philological Quarterly* 98, nos. 1–2 (2019): 119–36.

DiClaudio, Dennis. *The Deviant's Pocket Guide to Outlandish Sexual Desires Barely Contained in Your Subconscious*. Washington: Quarto Publishing Group USA Inc., 2019.

DiGangi, Mario. *The Homoerotics of Early Modern Drama*. Cambridge, UK: Cambridge University Press, 1997.

———. *Sexual Types: Embodiment, Agency, and Dramatic Character from Shakespeare to Shirley*. Philadelphia: University of Pennsylvania Press, 2011.

Dodds, Lara and Michelle M. Dowd, eds. *Feminist Formalism and Early Modern Women's Writing: Readings, Conversations, Pedagogies*. Lincoln, NE: University of Nebraska Press, 2022.

Dolan, Frances E. *Marriage and Violence: The Early Modern Legacy*. Philadelphia, PA: University of Pennsylvania Press, 2008. https://doi.org/10.9783/9780812201772.

Dugan, Holly. *The Ephemeral History of Perfume.* Baltimore: Johns Hopkins University Press, 2011.

Duncan-Jones, Katherine. "Much Ado with Red and White: The Earliest Readers of Shakespeare's *Venus and Adonis* (1593)." *The Review of English Studies* 44, no. 176 (1993): 479–501. https://www.jstor.org/stable/517333.

Dyer, Richard. *White: Essays on Race and Culture.* New York: Routledge, 1997.

Edelman, Lee. "Unbecoming: Pornography and the Queer Event." In *Post/Porn/Politics: Queer-Feminist Perspective on the Politics of Porn Performance and Sex Work as Cultural Production,* edited by Tim Stüttgen, 195–211. Berlin: b_books, 2009.

Eisendrath, Rachel. *Poetry in a World of Things: Aesthetics and Empiricism in Renaissance Ekphrasis.* Chicago: University of Chicago Press, 2018.

Felski, Rita. "Redescriptions of Female Masochism." *The Minnesota Review,* nos. 63–64 (2005): 127–39.

Fennell, Julie. "'It's all about the journey': Skepticism and Spirituality in the BDSM Subculture." *Sociological Forum* 33, no. 4 (2018): 1045–67. https://doi.org/10.1111/socf.12460.

Findlay, Alison. *A Feminist Perspective on Renaissance Drama.* Oxford: Blackwell Publishers, 1999.

Fischel, Joseph. *Screw Consent: Sex and Harm in the Age of Consent.* Berkeley, CA: University of California Press, 2019.

Fisher, Will. "The Erotics of Chin Chucking in Seventeenth-Century England." In *Sex Before Sex: Figuring the Act in Early Modern England,* edited by James M. Bromley and Will Stockton, 141–69. Minneapolis: University of Minnesota Press, 2013.

———. "'Stray[ing] lower where the pleasant fountains lie': Cunnilingus in *Venus and Adonis* and in English Culture, c. 1600–1700." In *The Oxford Handbook of Shakespeare and Embodiment: Gender, Sexuality, and Race,* edited by Valerie Traub, 333–46. Oxford: Oxford University Press, 2016.

———. "'Wantoning with the Thighs': The Socialization of Thigh Sex in England, 1590–1730." *Journal of the History of Sexuality* 24, no. 1 (2015): 1–24. https://doi.org/10.7560/JHS24101.

Fitzpatrick, Joan. "Foreign Appetites and Alterity: Is There an Irish Context for *Titus Andronicus?*" *Connotations* 11, nos. 2–3 (2001–2002): 127–45.

Foucault, Michel. *The History of Sexuality, Volume 1: An Introduction.* Translated by Robert Hurley. New York: Pantheon, 1978.

Freccero, Carla. *Queer/Early/Modern*. Durham, NC: Duke University Press, 2006.

Freeman, Elizabeth. *Time Binds: Queer Temporalities, Queer Histories*. Durham, NC: Duke University Press, 2010.

Freud, Sigmund. *The Standard Edition of the Complete Psychological Works*. Vol. 18. Translated by James Strachey. London: Hogarth Press & Institute of Psychoanalysis, 1953–74.

Gamble, Joseph. "Practicing Sex." *Journal for Early Modern Cultural Studies* 19, no. 1 (2019): 85–116. https://doi.org/10.1353/jem.2019.0013.

———. *Sex Lives: Intimate Infrastructures in Early Modernity*. Philadelphia: University of Pennsylvania Press, 2023.

Garcia, Christien. "Merely Barebacking." In *Raw: PrEP, Pedagogy, and the Politics of Barebacking*, edited by Ricky Varghese, 263–84. London: Zed Books Ltd, 2019.

Glickman, Charlie. "Consent and Public Disgrace." *Charlie Glickman PhD* (blog). March 20, 2011. https://charlieglickman.com/consent-and-public-disgrace/.

———. "The Nuances of Consent: More Thoughts about Public Disgrace." *Charlie Glickman PhD* (blog). March 29, 2011. http://new.charlieglickman.com/the-nuances-of-consent-more-thoughts-about-public-disgrace/.

Goldberg, Jonathan. *Sodometries: Renaissance Texts, Modern Sexualities*. Palo Alto, CA: Stanford University Press, 1992.

Goldberg, Jonathan, ed. *Queering the Renaissance*. Durham, NC: Duke University Press, 1994.

Gordon, Colby. "A Woman's Prick: Trans Technogenesis in Sonnet 20." In *Shakespeare/Sex: Contemporary Readings in Gender and Sexuality*, edited by Jennifer Drouin, 269–89. London: Bloomsbury, 2020.

Gowing, Laura. *Common Bodies: Women, Touch, and Power in Seventeenth-Century England*. New Haven: Yale University Press, 2003. https://doi.org/10.2307/j.ctv1pzk6gh.

Graham, Katherine M. "'[Nor] Bear I in this Breast / So Much Cold Spirit to be Called a Woman': The Queerness of Female Revenge in *The Maid's Tragedy*." *Early Theatre* 21, no. 1 (2018): 107–26.

Green, Stuart P. *Criminalizing Sex: A Unified Liberal Theory*. Oxford: Oxford University Press, 2020. https://doi.org/10.1093/oso/9780197507483.001.0001.

Grier, Miles. "Are Shakespeare's Plays Racially Progressive? The Answer Is in Our Hands." In *The Cambridge Companion to Shakespeare and Race*, edited by Ayanna Thompson, 237–53. Cambridge, UK: Cambridge University Press, 2021.

Grimmett, Roxanne. "'By Heaven *and* Hell': Re-evaluating Representations of Women and the Angel/Whore Dichotomy in Renaissance Revenge Tragedy." *Journal of International Women's Studies* 6, no. 3 (2005): 31–39.

Guy-Bray, Stephen. *Shakespeare and Queer Representation*. Abingdon, UK: Routledge, 2021.

———. "Spenser's Filthy Matter." *The Explicator* 62, no. 4 (2004): 194–95. https://doi.org/10.1080/00144940409597218.

Haber, Judith. *Desire and Dramatic Form in Early Modern England*. Cambridge, UK: Cambridge University Press, 2009.

Hall, Kim F. "'These bastard signs of fair': Literary Whiteness in Shakespeare's Sonnets." In *Post-Colonial Shakespeares*, edited by Ania Loomba and Martin Orkin, 64–83. London: Routledge, 2003.

———. *Things of Darkness: Economies of Race and Gender in Early Modern England*. Ithaca, NY: Cornell University Press, 1996.

Halperin, David. *One Hundred Years of Homosexuality*. Abingdon, UK: Routledge, 1989.

Hammill, Graham. *Sexuality and Form: Caravaggio, Marlowe, and Bacon*. Chicago: University of Chicago Press, 2000.

Hammonds, Evelynn. "Black (W)holes and the Geometry of Black Female Sexuality." *differences* 6, no. 2–3 (1994): 126–45. https://doi.org/10.1215/10407391-6-2-3-126.

Hammons, Pamela S. *Gender, Sexuality, and Material Objects in English Renaissance Verse*. Abingdon, UK: Routledge: 2010.

Hanna, Cheryl. "Sex Is Not a Sport: Consent and Violence in Criminal Law." *Boston College Law Review* 42, no. 2 (2001): 239–90. https://lira.bc.edu/work/ns/c1235e1f-b53d-42d9-8be9-4460f3769000.

Hardy, Janet W. and Dossie Easton. *The Ethical Slut: A Practical Guide to Polyamory, Open Relationships, and Other Freedoms in Sex and Love*. 3rd ed. Emeryville, CA: Ten Speed Press, 2017.

Harries, Brian J. "The Fall of Mediterranean Rome in *Titus Andronicus*." *Mediterranean Studies* 26, no. 2 (2018): 194–212. https://doi.org/10.5325/mediterraneanstu.26.2.0194.

Heisel, Andrew. "'I Don't Know Whether to Kiss You or Spank You': A Half Century of Fear of an Unspanked Woman." *Jezebel*. April 12, 2016. https://jezebel.com/i-dont-know-whether-to-kiss-you-or-spank-you-a-half-ce-1769140132.

Helfer, Rebecca. *Spenser's Ruins and the Art of Recollection*. Toronto: University of Toronto Press, 2012.

Hendricks, Margo. "Race and Nation." In *The Cambridge Guide to the Worlds of Shakespeare*, edited by Bruce Smith and Katherine Rowe, 663–668. Cambridge, UK: Cambridge University Press, 2016.

Herrick, Robert. *The Poetical Works of Robert Herrick*. Edited by L. C. Martin. Oxford: Clarendon Press, 1956.

Herrup, Cynthia. *A House in Gross Disorder: Sex, Law, and the 2nd Earl of Castlehaven*. Oxford: Oxford University Press, 2001.

Hill, Thomas. *The Gardeners Labyrinth Containing a Discourse of the Gardeners Life*. London: by Henry Bynneman, 1577. Early English Books Online, https://www.proquest.com/books/gardeners-labyrinth-containing-discourse-life/docview/2248559510/se-2.

Holland, Sharon. *The Erotic Life of Racism*. Durham, NC: Duke University Press, 2012.

Hunt, Lynn. "Introduction." In *The Invention of Pornography: Obscenity and the Origins of Modernity, 1500–1800*, edited by Lynn Hunt, 9–46. New York: Zone Books, 1993.

Hyman, Wendy Beth. "Seizing Flowers in Spenser's Bower and Garden." *English Literary Renaissance* 37, no. 2 (Spring 2007): 193–214. https://doi.org/10.1111/j.1475-6757.2007.00101.x.

Iyengar, Sujata. *Shades of Difference: Mythologies of Skin Color in Early Modern England*. Philadelphia: University of Pennsylvania Press, 2004.

Jacobson, Miriam. *Barbarous Antiquity: Reorienting the Past in the Poetry of Early Modern England*. Philadelphia: University of Pennsylvania Press, 2014.

Johnson, Viola. "The Love that Dare Not Speak Its Name: Playing With and Against Racial Stereotypes." *Black Leather ... in Color* (1994): 8–9.

Kadue, Katie. "Flower Girls and Garbage Women: Misogyny and Cliché in Ronsard and Herrick." *Modern Philology* 118, no. 3 (2021): 319–39. https://doi.org/10.1086/712403.

Kahn, Coppélia. "The Taming of the Shrew: Shakespeare's Mirror of Marriage." *Modern Language Studies* 5, no. 1 (1975): 88–102. https://doi.org/10.2307/3194204.

Keenan, Jillian. *Sex with Shakespeare: Here's Much to Do with Pain, but More with Love*. New York: William Morrow, 2016.

Kendi, Ibram X. *Stamped from the Beginning: The Definitive History of Racist Ideas in America*. New York: Bold Type Books, 2016.

Kerrigan, John. *Revenge Tragedy: Aeschylus to Armageddon*. Oxford: Clarendon Press, 2001.

Kesson, Andy. "'It is a pity you are not a woman': John Lyly and the Creation of Woman." *Shakespeare Bulletin* vol. 33, no. 1 (2005): 33–47. https://doi.org/10.1353/shb.2015.0001.

———. "*The Woman in the Moon* Onstage." *Before Shakespeare* (blog). August 19, 2017. https://beforeshakespeare.com/2017/08/19/the-woman-in-the-moon-onstage/.

———. "The Women in the Moons." *Before Shakespeare* (blog). March 10, 2018. https://beforeshakespeare.com/2018/03/10/women-in-the-moons/.

Kesson, Andy and Emma Frankland. "'Perhaps John Lyly Was a Trans Woman?': An Interview about Performing *Galatea*'s Queer, Transgender Stories." *The Journal for Early Modern Cultural Studies* 19, no. 1 (2019): 284–98. https://doi.org/10.1353/jem.2019.0048.

Knoll, Gillian. "Binding the Void: The Erotics of Place in *Antony and Cleopatra*." *Criticism: A Quarterly for Literature and the Arts* 58, no. 2 (2016): 281–304. https://doi.org/10.13110/criticism.58.2.0281.

———. "*Coitus Magneticus*: Erotic Attraction in *A Midsummer Night's Dream*." *Modern Philology* 117, no. 3 (2020): 301–22. https://doi.org/10.1086/707082.

———. *Conceiving Desire in Lyly and Shakespeare: Metaphor, Cognition, and Eros* Edinburgh: Edinburgh University Press, 2020.

Kostihová, Marcela. "Discerning (Dis)taste: Delineating Sexual Mores in Shakespeare's *Venus and Adonis*." In *Disgust in Early Modern English Literature*, edited by Natalie K. Eschenbaum and Barbara Correll, 69–81. New York: Routledge, 2016.

Kunat, John. "'I have done thy mother': Racial and Sexual Geographies in *Titus Andronicus*." In *Titus Andronicus: The State of the Play*, edited by Farah Karim-Cooper, 89–110. London: Bloomsbury, 2019.

Kuzner, James. "*All's Well That Ends Well* and the Art of Love." *Shakespeare Quarterly* 68, no. 3 (2017): 215–40. https://www.jstor.org/stable/4855 9740.

Landrum, David. "Robert Herrick and the Ambiguities of Gender." *Texas Studies in Literature and Language* 49, no. 2 (2007): 181–297.

Langley, Eric F. "Anatomizing the Early-Modern Eye: A Literary Case-Study." *Renaissance Studies* 20, no. 3 (June 2006): 340–55. https://doi.org/10.1111/j.1477-4658.2006.00161.x.

———. "'Lascivious Dialect': Decadent Rhetoric and the Early-Modern Pornographer." In *Decadences: Morality and Aesthetics in British Literature*, edited by Paul Fox, 231–55. Stuttgart: ibidem Press, 2014.

Largier, Niklaus. *In Praise of the Whip: A Cultural History of Arousal*. Princeton, NJ: Princeton University Press, 2007.

Leonard, John. "Marlowe's Doric Music: Lust and Aggression in *Hero and Leander*." *English Literary Renaissance* 30, no. 1 (2000): 55–76. https://doi.org/10.1111/j.1475-6757.2000.tb01164.x.

Levine, Caroline. *Forms: Whole, Rhythm, Hierarchy, Network*. Princeton, NJ: Princeton University Press, 2015.

Little, Arthur L., Jr. "Critical White Studies." In *The Cambridge Companion to Shakespeare and Race*, edited by Ayanna Thompson, 267–77. Cambridge, UK: Cambridge University Press, 2021.

———. "Re-Historicizing Race, White Melancholia, and the Shakespearean Property." *Shakespeare Quarterly* 67, no. 1 (2016): 84–103. https://doi:10.1353/shq.2016.0018.

MacKendrick, Karmen. *Counterpleasures*. New York: New York University Press, 1999.

MacKinnon, Catharine A. "OnlyFans Is Not a Safe Platform for 'Sex Work.' It's a Pimp." *New York Times*. September 6, 2021. https://www.nytimes.com/2021/09/06/opinion/onlyfans-sex-work-safety.html.

Marcus, Leah. "The Shakespearean Editor as Shrew-Tamer." *English Literary Renaissance* 22, no. 2 (1992): 177–200. https://doi.org/10.1111/j.1475-6757.1992.tb01037.x.

Marlowe, Christopher. *Hero and Leander*. In *English Sixteenth-Century Verse: An Anthology*, edited by Richard S. Sylvester, 498–525. New York: W. W. Norton, 1984.

Marshall, Cynthia. *The Shattering of the Self: Violence, Subjectivity, and Early Modern Texts.* Baltimore: Johns Hopkins University Press, 2002.

Marsh, Christopher. "A Woodcut and Its Wanderings in Seventeenth-Century England." *Huntington Library Quarterly* 79, no. 2 (2016): 245–62. https://doi.org/10.1353/hlq.2016.0010.

Martinez, Katherine. "The Overwhelming Whiteness of BDSM: A Critical Discourse Analysis of Racialization in BDSM." *Sexualities* 24, no. 5–6 (2021): 733–48. https://doi.org/10.1177/1363460720932389.

Masten, Jeffrey. *Queer Philologies: Sex, Language, and Affect in Shakespeare's Time.* Philadelphia: University of Pennsylvania Press, 2016.

———. *Textual Intercourse: Collaboration, Authorship, and Sexualities in Renaissance Drama.* Cambridge, UK: Cambridge University Press, 1997.

McEachern, Claire. "Why Do Cuckolds Have Horns?" *Huntington Library Quarterly* 71, no. 4 (2008): 607–31. https://doi.org/10.1525/hlq.2008.71.4.607.

McIntosh, Hugh. "The Social Masochism of Shakespeare's Sonnets." *SEL: Studies in English Literature, 1500–1900* 50, no. 1 (2010): 109–25. https://doi.org/10.1353/sel.0.0083.

Menon, Madhavi. "Spurning Teleology in *Venus and Adonis.*" *GLQ: A Journal of Lesbian and Gay Studies* 11, no. 4 (2005): 491–519.

Mikesell, Margaret. "'Love Wrought These Miracles': Marriage and Genre in *The Taming of the Shrew.*" *Renaissance Drama* 20 (1989): 141–67. https://doi.org/10.1086/rd.20.41917252.

Moore, Lisa Jean. *Sperm Counts: Overcome by Man's Most Precious Fluid.* New York: New York University Press, 2007.

Moschovakis, Nicholas R. "'Irreligious Piety' and Christian History: Persecution as Pagan Anachronism in *Titus Andronicus.*" *Shakespeare Quarterly* 53 (2002): 460–86. https://www.jstor.org/stable/3844237.

Moulton, Ian Frederick. *Before Pornography: Erotic Writing in Early Modern England.* Oxford: Oxford University Press, 2000.

Musser, Amber Jamilla. *Sensational Flesh: Race, Power, and Masochism.* New York: New York University Press, 2014.

———. "Sweat, Display, and Blackness: The Promises of Liquidity." *Feminist Media Histories* 7, no. 2 (2021): 92–109. https://doi.org/10.1525/fmh.2021.7.2.92.

Nagel, Joane. "Ethnicity and Sexuality," *Annual Review of Sociology* 26 (2000): 107–33. https://doi.org/10.1146/annurev.soc.26.1.107.

Ndiaye, Noémie. "Aaron's Roots: Spaniards, Englishmen, and Blackamoors in *Titus Andronicus*." *Early Theatre* 19, no. 2 (2016): 59–80. https://www.jstor.org/stable/90018447.

Newmahr, Staci. *Playing on the Edge: Sadomasochism, Risk, and Intimacy*. Bloomington: Indiana University Press, 2011.

Nocentelli, Carmen. *Empires of Love: Europe, Asia, and the Making of Early Modern Identity*. Philadelphia: University of Pennsylvania Press, 2013.

Normandin, Shawn. "The Wife of Bath's Urinary Imagination." *Exemplaria* 20, no. 3 (2008): 244–63. https://doi.org/10.1179/175330708X334538.

North, Anna. "Movies, Censorship, and the 'Myth' of Female Ejaculation." *Jezebel*. October 8, 2009. https://jezebel.com/movies-censorship-and-the-myth-of-female-ejaculatio-5377327.

———. "When Prejudice Is Sexy: Inside the Kinky World of Race Play." *Jezebel*. March 14, 2012. https://jezebel.com/when-prejudice-is-sexy-inside-the-kinky-world-of-race-5868600.

Olivier, Jacques. *A Discourse of Women, Shewing their Imperfections*. London: Printed for Henry Brome, 1662. Early English Books Online. https://www.proquest.com/books/discourse-women-shewing-their-imperfections/docview/2240926442/se-2.

Orlin, Lena Cowen. *Private Matters and Public Culture in Post-Reformation England*. Ithaca, NY: Cornell University Press, 1994. https://doi.org/10.7591/9781501737381.

Panek, Jennifer. "'A Wittall Cannot Be a Cookold': Reading the Contented Cuckold in Early Modern English Drama and Culture." *Journal for Early Modern Cultural Studies* 1, no. 2 (2001): 66–92. https://doi.org/10.1353/jem.2001.0020.

Paris, Jamie. "Bad Blood, Black Desires: On the Fragility of Whiteness in Middleton and Rowley's *The Changeling*." *Early Theatre* 24, no. 1 (2021): 113–37. https://doi.org/10.12745/et.24.1.3803.

Parker, Patricia. *Literary Fat Ladies: Rhetoric, Gender, Property*. New York: Methuen, 1987.

Parten, Anne. "Falstaff's Horns: Masculine Inadequacy and Feminine Mirth in *The Merry Wives of Windsor*." *Studies in Philology* 82, no. 2 (1985): 184–99. https://www.jstor.org/stable/4174203.

Partridge, Eric. *Shakespeare's Bawdy.* Milton Park, UK: Taylor & Francis, 2005.

Paster, Gail Kern. *The Body Embarrassed: Drama and the Disciplines of Shame in Early Modern England.* Ithaca, NY: Cornell University Press, 1993.

————. *Humoring the Body: Emotions and the Shakespearean Stage.* Chicago: University of Chicago Press, 2004.

————. "The Pith and Marrow of Our Attribute: Dialogue of Skin and Skull in *Hamlet* and Holbein's *The Ambassadors.*" *Textual Practice* 23, no. 2 (2009): 247–65.

Pequigney, Joseph. *Such Is My Love: A Study of Shakespeare's Sonnets.* Chicago: University of Chicago Press, 1985.

Pollard, Tanya. *Greek Tragic Women on Shakespearean Stages.* Oxford: Clarendon Press, 2017.

Price, Bronwen. "The Fractured Body—Censorship and Desire in Herrick's Poetry." *Literature and History* 2, no. 1 (1993): 23–41. https://doi.org/10. 1177/030619739300200102.

Raber, Karen, Joseph Campana, Vin Nardizzi, and Laurie Shannon. "Queer Natures: Bodies, Sexualities, Environments." Plenary panel session at the Shakespeare Association of America, Atlanta, GA, April 7, 2017. https://www.youtube.com/watch?v=YVgx9-6wTOE.

Ramachandran, Ayesha. "Clarion in the Bower of Bliss: Poetry and Politics in Spenser's 'Muiopotmos.'" *Spenser Studies* 20 (2005): 77–106. https:// doi.org/10.1086/SPSv20p77.

Rambuss, Richard. *Closet Devotions.* Durham, NC: Duke University Press, 1998.

————. "What It Feels Like for a Boy: Shakespeare's *Venus and Adonis.*" In *A Companion to Shakespeare's Works,* vol. 4, edited by Richard Dutton and Jean E. Howard, 240–58. Malden: Blackwell Publishing, 2003.

Roberts, Jeanne Addison. "Horses and Hermaphrodites: Metamorphoses in *The Taming of the Shrew.*" *Shakespeare Quarterly* 34, no. 2 (1983): 159–71. https://doi.org/10.2307/2869831.

Robinson, Kyla. "Speaking the Unspeakable: The Curious Case of Race Play in the American BDSM Community." Unpublished preprint (2018). https://doi.org/10.13140/RG.2.2.21727.97443.

Royster, Francesca T. "White-limed Walls: Whiteness and Gothic Extremism in Shakespeare's *Titus Andronicus.*" *Shakespeare Quarterly* 51, no. 4 (Winter 2000): 432–55. https://doi.org/10.2307/2902338.

Rubin, Gayle. *Deviations: A Gayle Rubin Reader.* Durham, NC: Duke University Press, 2011.

Rubright, Marjorie. "Transgender Capacity in Thomas Dekker and Thomas Middleton's *The Roaring Girl (1611).*" *Journal for Early Modern Cultural Studies* 19, no. 4 (2019): 45–74. https://doi:10.1353/jem.2019.0037.

Sacher-Masoch, Leopold von. *Venus in Furs.* In *Masochism: "Coldness and Cruelty" and "Venus in Furs,"* by Gilles Deleuze and Leopold von Sacher-Masoch, translated by Jean McNeil, 143–293. New York: Zone Books, 1989.

Samudzi, Zoé. "What 'Interracial' Cuckold Porn Reveals about White Male Insecurity." *Vice.com.* July 31, 2018. https://www.vice.com/en/article/594yxd/interracial-cuckold-porn-white-male-insecurity-race.

Sanchez, Melissa E. *Erotic Subjects: The Sexuality of Politics in Early Modern English Literature.* Oxford: Oxford University Press, 2011.

———. *Queer Faith: Reading Promiscuity and Race in the Secular Love Tradition.* New York: New York University Press, 2019.

———. *Shakespeare and Queer Theory.* New York: Bloomsbury Publishing, 2019.

———. "'Use Me but as Your Spaniel': Feminism, Queer Theory, and Early Modern Sexualities." *PMLA* 127, no. 3 (2012): 493–511. https://doi.org/10.1632/pmla.2012.127.3.493.

Saunders, Ben. *Desiring Donne: Poetry, Sexuality, Interpretation.* Cambridge, MA: Harvard University Press, 2006.

Savage, Dan. "Savage Love." *Chicago Reade.* April 9, 2009. https://chicagoreader.com/columns-opinion/savage-love-22/.

Schafer, Elizabeth. Introduction to *The Taming of the Shrew: Shakespeare in Production,* by William Shakespeare, 1–76. Edited by Elizabeth Schafer. Cambridge, UK: Cambridge University Press, 2002. https://doi.org/10.1017/9781316564028.

Schanfield, Lillian. "'Tickled with Desire': A View of Eroticism in Herrick's Poetry." *Literature and Psychology* 39, no. 1 (1993): 63–83.

Schoenfeldt, Michael. "The Art of Disgust: Civility and the Social Body in *Hesperides*." *George Herbert Journal* 14, nos. 1–2 (1990/1991): 127–54. https://doi.org/10.1353/ghj.1990.0011.

———. *Bodies and Selves in Early Modern England: Physiology and Inwardness in Spenser, Shakespeare, Herbert, and Milton*. Cambridge, UK: Cambridge University Press, 1999.

Schotanus, Susanne. "Racism or Race Play: A Conceptual Investigation of the Race Play Debates." *Zapruder World: An International Journal for the History of Social Conflict* 4 (2017). https://doi.org/10.21431/Z3001F.

Schubert, Karsten. "A New Era of Queer Politics? PrEP, Foucauldian Sexual Liberation, and the Overcoming of Homonormativity." *Body Politics* 12, no. 8 (2021): 1–41. https://dx.doi.org/10.2139/ssrn.3901719.

Schwarz, Kathryn. *Tough Love: Amazonian Encounters in the English Renaissance*. Durham, NC: Duke University Press, 2000.

Scott, Catherine. *Thinking Kink: The Collision of BDSM, Feminism and Popular Culture*. Jefferson, NC: McFarland & Company, 2015.

———. "Thinking Kink: The Right to Play With Race." *Bitch Media*. August 8, 2012. https://www.bitchmedia.org/post/thinking-kink-the-right-to-play-with-race-feminist-magazine-bdsm-sex.

Sedgwick, Eve Kosofsky. *A Dialogue on Love*. New York: Beacon Press, 2000.

———. *Epistemology of the Closet*. Berkeley: University of California Press, 1990.

———. "Paranoid Reading and Reparative Reading: Or, You're So Paranoid, You Probably Think This Introduction Is about You." In *Novel Gazing: Queer Readings in Fiction*, edited by Eve Kosofsky Sedgwick, 1–40. Durham, NC: Duke University Press, 1997.

———. *Touching Feeling: Affect, Pedagogy, Performativity*. Durham: Duke University Press, 2003.

Shannon, Laurie. "Nature's Bias: Renaissance Homonormativity and Elizabethan Comic Likeness." *Modern Philology* 98, no. 2 (2000): 183–210. https://doi.org/10.1086/492960.

———. *Sovereign Amity: Figures of Friendship in Shakespearean Contexts*. Chicago: University of Chicago Press, 2001.

Shapiro, Michael. "Framing the Taming: Metatheatrical Awareness of Female Impersonation in *The Taming of the Shrew*." *Yearbook of English Studies* 23 (1993): 143–66. https://doi.org/10.2307/3507978.

Shaw, George Bernard. *Shaw on Shakespeare.* Edited by Edwin Wilson. London: Cassell, 1962.

Shor, Eran and Golshan Golriz. "Gender, Race, and Aggression in Mainstream Pornography." *Archives of Sexual Behavior* 48 (2019): 739–51. https://doi.org/10.1007/s10508-018-1304-6.

Silvestrini, Molly. "'It's not something I can shake': The Effect of Racial Stereotypes, Beauty Standards, and Sexual Racism on Interracial Attraction." *Sexuality and Culture* 24 (2020): 305–25. https://doi.org/10.1007/s12119-019-09644-0.

Simmons, Patricia. "Manliness and the Visual Semiotics of Bodily Fluids in Early Modern Culture." *Journal of Medieval and Early Modern Culture* 39, no. 2 (2009): 331–73. https://doi.org/10.1215/10829636-2008-025.

Simula, Brandy L. "'A Different Economy of Bodies and Pleasures'?: Differentiating and Evaluating Sex and Sexual BDSM Experiences." *Journal of Homosexuality* 66, no. 2 (2019): 209–37. https://doi.org/10.1080/0091836 9.2017.1398017.

Smith, Bruce. *Homosexual Desire in Renaissance England: A Cultural Poetics.* Chicago: University of Chicago Press, 1991.

Smith, Ian. "Barbarian Errors: Performing Race in Early Modern England." *Shakespeare Quarterly* 49, no. 2 (1998): 168–86. https://doi.org/10.2307/2902299.

Smith, Jesus G. and Aurolyn Luykx. "Race Play in BDSM Porn: The Eroticization of Oppression." *Porn Studies* 4, no. 4 (2017): 433–46. https://doi.org/10.1080/23268743.2016.1252158.

Snorton, C. Riley. *Black on Both Sides: A Racial History of Trans Identity.* Minneapolis: University of Minnesota Press, 2017.

Snow, Aurora. "Why Porn's 'Interracial' Label Is Racist." *The Daily Beast.* April 14, 2017. https://www.thedailybeast.com/why-porns-interracial-label-is-racist.

Spenser, Edmund. *The Faerie Queene.* Edited by A. C. Hamilton. Harlow: Pearson Education Limited, 2006.

Srinivasan, Amia. *The Right to Sex: Feminism in the Twenty-First Century.* New York: Farrar, Straus and Giroux, 2021.

Starks, Lisa S. "Immortal Longings: The Erotics of Death in *Antony and Cleopatra.*" In *Antony and Cleopatra: New Critical Essays*, edited by Sara Munson Deats, 243–58. Abingdon, UK: Routledge, 2005.

Sterling Brown, David. "Remixing the Family: Blackness and Domesticity in Shakespeare's *Titus Andronicus*." In *Titus Andronicus: The State of the Play*, edited by Farah Karim-Cooper, 111–33. London: Bloomsbury, 2019.

Stockton, Will. *Members of His Body: Shakespeare, Paul, and a Theology of Non-monogamy*. New York: Fordham University Press, 2017.

Strahilevitz, Lior. "Consent, Aesthetics, and the Boundaries of Sexual Privacy after Lawrence v. Texas." *DePaul Law Review* 54 (2005): 671–700. https://chicagounbound.uchicago.edu/cgi/viewcontent.cgi?article=253 5&context=journal_articles.

Sun, Chyng, Matthew B. Ezzell, and Olivia Kendall. "Naked Aggression: The Meaning and Practice of Ejaculation on a Woman's Face." *Violence Against Women* 23, no. 14 (2017): 1710–29. https://doi.org/10.1177/1077801216666723.

Thauvette, Chantelle. "Defining Early Modern Pornography: The Case of *Venus and Adonis*." *Journal for Early Modern Cultural Studies* 12, no. 1 (Winter 2012): 26–48. https://www.jstor.org/stable/23242178.

Thompson, Ayanna. *Performing Race and Torture on the Early Modern Stage*. Abingdon, UK: Routledge, 2008.

Toulalan, Sarah. *Imagining Sex: Pornography and Bodies in Seventeenth-Century England*. Oxford: Oxford University Press, 2007.

Traub, Valerie. *Desire and Anxiety: Circulations of Sexuality in Shakespearean Drama*. Abingdon, UK: Routledge, 1992.

———. *The Renaissance of Lesbianism in Early Modern England*. Cambridge, UK: Cambridge University Press, 2002.

———. "Racializing Subjectivity in the 17th-Century Erotic Narrative." Phyllis Rackin Lecture, University of Pennsylvania, March 1, 2023.

———. *Thinking Sex with the Early Moderns*. Philadelphia: University of Pennsylvania Press, 2016.

Tuck, Greg. "Mainstreaming the Money Shot: Reflections on the Representation of Ejaculation in Contemporary American Cinema." *Paragraph* 26, nos. 1–2 (March/July 2003): 263–79. https://doi.org/10.3366/para.2003.26.1-2.263.

Tupper, Peter. *A Lover's Pinch: A Cultural History of Sadomasochism*. Lanham, MD: Rowman and Littlefield, 2018.

Turner, Victor. *From Ritual to Theatre: The Human Seriousness of Play*. New York: PAJ Publications, 1982.

Vaccaro, Christopher, ed. *Painful Pleasures: Sadomasochism in Medieval Cultures.* Manchester: Manchester University Press, 2022.

Varghese, Ricky. "Introduction: The Mourning After." In *Raw: PrEP, Pedagogy, and the Politics of Barebacking,* edited by Ricky Varghese, 1–20. London: Zed Books Ltd, 2019.

Varnado, Christine. "'Invisible Sex!': What Looks Like the Act in Early Modern Drama?" In *Sex Before Sex: Figuring the Act in Early Modern England,* edited by James M. Bromley and Will Stockton, 25–52. Minneapolis: University of Minnesota Press, 2014.

———. *Shapes of Fancy: Reading for Queer Desire in Early Modern Literature.* Minneapolis: University of Minnesota Press, 2020.

Vickers, Nancy. "Diana Described: Scattered Woman and Scattered Rhyme." *Critical Inquiry* 8, no. 2 (1981): 265–79. https://doi.org/10.1086/448154.

Wainwright, Anna. "'Tied Up in Chains of Adamant': Recovering Race in Tasso's Armida Before, and After, Acrasia." *Spenser Studies* 35 (2021): 181–212. https://doi.org/10.1086/711936.

Weigman, Robyn and Elizabeth A. Wilson. "Introduction: Antinormativity's Queer Conventions." *differences* 26, no. 1 (2015): 1–25. https://doi.org/10.1215/10407391-2880582.

Weiss, Margot. *Techniques of Pleasure: BDSM and the Circuits of Sexuality.* Durham, NC: Duke University Press, 2011.

Williams, D. J., Jeremy N. Thomas, Emily E. Prior, and M. Candace Christensen. "From 'SSC' and 'RACK' to the '4Cs': Introducing a New Framework for Negotiating BDSM Participation." *Electronic Journal of Human Sexuality* 14 (2014). http://www.ejhs.org/volume17/BDSM.html.

Williams, Linda. "Film Bodies: Gender, Genre, and Excess." *Film Quarterly* 44, no. 4 (Summer 1991): 2–13.

———. *Hard Core: Power, Pleasure, and the "Frenzy of the Visible."* Berkeley, CA: University of California Press, 1989.

Williams, Mollena. "Consent, Control, Compassion, and Why I Am Fucking Tired of Explaining Why 'Race Play' Is Different From Racism." *The Perverted Negress* (blog). December 18, 2015. http://www.mollena.com/2015/12/race-play-vs-racism/.

———. *The Toybag Guide to Playing with Taboo.* Emeryville, CA: Greenery Press, 2010.

Wiseman, Jay. *SM 101.* Emeryville, CA: Greenery Press, 1996.

Contributors

Beatrice Bradley is Assistant Professor of English and Faculty Affiliate in Women's and Gender Studies at Muhlenberg College. Her research and teaching bring together early modern literature, critical theory, and histories of medicine to rethink the materiality and psychology of embodiment. She is currently working on her first book project, tentatively titled *The Erotics of Sweat: Residues of Embodiment in the Early Modern World*. Recent essays have appeared or are forthcoming in *English Literary Renaissance*, *Milton Studies*, and *Shakespeare Studies*.

Erika Carbonara is a PhD candidate with a focus on early modern queerness at Wayne State University in Detroit, Michigan. She is currently working on her dissertation, tentatively titled, "'It Is a Bawdy Planet': Conceptualizing Early Modern Kink Identities and Practices," in which she interrogates portrayals of communities as essential to kinky identities. In addition to early modern kink and queerness, her other scholarly interests include early modern ephemera, pre-modern sleep habits, and Nathan Field's *Amends for Ladies*.

Gina Filo received her PhD from the University of Oregon in 2020 and is now an Assistant Professor of English at Southeastern Louisiana University. Her work explores the intersections of gender, sexuality, embodiment, selfhood, and poetics in early modern English literature.

Heather Frazier graduated with her Ph.D. in English Literature from The Ohio State University in 2021. Her dissertation, "The Erotics of Excrement in Early Modern English Drama," addresses how early modern English plays pair sexual and excremental language to upend and reinforce traditional power structures. She has also published the peer-reviewed article, "'Hath not thy rose a canker?': Monstrous Generation and Comic Subversion in *King Henry VI, Part 1.*"

Joseph Gamble is Assistant Professor of English at the University of Toledo and the author of *Sex Lives: Intimate Infrastructures in Early Modernity* (University of Pennsylvania Press 2023).

Erin E. Kelly is an Associate Professor of English at the University of Victoria in British Columbia, Canada. She has served as associate editor of the journal *Early Theatre* since 2011. Recent projects include chapters, articles, and introductions on Wilson's *Three Ladies of London*, Middleton's *The Revenger's Tragedy*, and the history of scholarly peer review as well as on Shakespeare's *Taming of the Shrew*.

Gillian Knoll is Associate Professor of English at Western Kentucky University and author of *Conceiving Desire in Lyly and Shakespeare: Metaphor, Cognition, and Eros* (Edinburgh University Press, 2020).

Nathaniel C. Leonard, currently serves as an Associate Professor of English and Chair of the English Department at Westminster College in Fulton, Missouri. His research primarily focuses on the complex relationship between metatheatricality, the restaging of culture, and dramatic genre in early modern English drama. Leonard's work has also been published in *The Journal for Early Modern Cultural Studies, Studies in English Literature*, and *Shakespeare Bulletin*.

James Mulder is Lecturer of English and Media Studies and Co-Coordinator of the Gender and Sexuality Studies Program at Bentley University in Waltham, MA. His research focuses on trans and gender studies as well as early modern poetry and drama. His work has appeared in *SEL: Studies in English Literature 1500-1900* and *The Journal of Popular Culture*.

Kirk Quinsland is an Advanced Lecturer in English at Fordham University. His writing focuses on queer theory and drama, and he is ostensibly working on a book to be titled *Negative Space: Homophobia and the Early Modern Stage*.

Christine Varnado is an associate professor of English and Global Gender & Sexuality Studies at the University at Buffalo-SUNY. She is the author of *The Shapes of Fancy: Reading for Queer Desire in Early Modern Literature* (Minnesota, 2020), as well as essays on invisible sex, getting used and liking it, the weather in *Macbeth*, whiteness in *The Merchant of Venice* and the 1924 silent film *The Thief of Bagdad*, and the prefix *post-*. Her current book project is on *Macbeth*, abortion, and the queerness of reproduction, birth, and death.

Acknowledgments

Gillian Knoll and Joseph Gamble

This project began in a conversation in January of 2020 when Gillian approached Joey with an idea for a Shakespeare Association of America seminar that would encourage participants to leverage the conceptual affordances of contemporary kink cultures in order to better understand early modern sexuality. The conversation that began that day has continued non-stop since then, picking up a wide variety of interlocutors as it went. This volume represents the culmination of the first phase of that conversation and, we hope, the beginning of a much broader discussion in the field at large.

We (Gillian and Joey) would like to thank the many people who have been a part of this conversation over the past few years. First, a profound thanks to each and every one of our contributors. We are so proud of the work that you have all produced, and so grateful to have been able to play a part in bringing it to the world. We would also like to thank all of the participants in our original SAA seminar who brought such brilliant work and camaraderie to the (virtual) table even in the midst of the height of the pandemic. We would particularly like to thank Will Fisher and Simone Chess whose work and leadership have been great inspirations to us, and who have absolutely paved the way for this collection.

Jillian Keenan's *Sex with Shakespeare* was also a real inspiration, and we hope that if you are reading this you will seek out her book, too. Our sincere thanks to Mario DiGangi for his assiduous care in shepherding the essays in this volume. And for all of their hard editorial labor, we thank Geoff Way, Roy Rukkila, and the entire ACMRS team (including Amy Guenther, who so expertly edited copy).

Joey would also like to personally thank Gillian for sparking this whole project with her characteristic brilliance, generosity, and effervescence. She has seemingly effortlessly created and sustained (for years!) a scene in which one can imagine new ways of encountering the past, and it has been thrilling and humbling to have had a front row seat.

Gillian would like to thank Joey first and foremost for saying yes — to this project, to working together, and to the many "should we" and "could we" questions that arose as this volume took shape. Without Joey's buoyant and inspiring yes, this book certainly would not exist, nor would its dazzling introduction (written mostly by Joey). Gillian is especially grateful for the friendship that blossomed through this collaboration. It has been a singular privilege and a pleasure to think, read, and write alongside you, dear friend.